CHANGING HUMAN BEHAVIOR

This project
was supported by
Friends Medical Science Research Center, Inc.
Catonsville, Maryland

CHANGING HUMAN BEHAVIOR
CURRENT THERAPIES AND
FUTURE DIRECTIONS

Edited by

O. Lee McCabe, Ph.D.

Friends Medical Science Research Center, Inc.
Catonsville, Maryland
and
Department of Psychology
Loyola College
Baltimore, Maryland

Grune & Stratton
A Subsidiary of Harcourt Brace Jovanovich, Publishers
New York   San Francisco   London

Library of Congress Cataloging in Publication Data
Main entry under title:

Changing human behavior

    Includes bibliographical references and index.
    1. Psychotherapy. I. McCabe, Lee, 1939-
DNLM: 1. Behavior therapy. WM420 C458]
RC480.C47   616.8'91   77-22073
ISBN 0-8089-1015-9

Grune & Stratton, Inc.
111 Fifth Avenue
New York, New York 10003

Distributed in the United Kingdom by
Academic Press, Inc. (London) Ltd.
24/28 Oval Road, London NW1

Library of Congress Catalog Number 77-22073
International Standard Book Number 0-8089-1015-9

Printed in the United States of America

To the memory of
my mother and father
and to
Gail and Michael Lee

CONTENTS

PREFACE

Unquestionably, these are times of enormous challenge for the helping professions. Pathogenic influences that have always been with us are now arising in the context of unprecedented societal ferment. The mass media relentlessly highlight the various threats to the integrity of man's psyche and society: crime, drug abuse, alcoholism, unemployment, ethnic strife, inflation, overpopulation, pollution, etc. It is reasonable to expect the future to bring with it more obstacles to man's internal development and equilibrium. Accordingly, the art and science of dealing with the inevitable problems of achieving adjustment and self-actualization under such circumstances is the theme of the present volume.

Although the historical roots of psychotherapy are grounded in person-to-person transactions, from these roots have sprung a diverse flora of theories, tactics, and strategies of treatment such that the beginning student as well as the experienced professional often feels overwhelmed by the sheer variety of viewpoints. This bewildering diversity of therapeutic approaches is largely an expression of the complexity of psychiatric disorders with which clinicians are faced. However, the problem of methodological plurality is compounded by the paradox that, despite the nonapplicability of a single therapeutic strategy to all patients and problems, a stubborn form of provincialism continues to pervade many approaches. Early in the development of a theory or technique such isolationism may facilitate the achievement of identity, if not survival; however, imperviousness to outside influences ultimately precludes development and growth. Despite an increasing recognition of the need to move away from monolithic schools of thought, the contemporary literature on psychotherapeutic techniques remains a collection of parochial conceptualizations of the nature of behavior and behavior change.

Although contemporary psychiatric therapies seem to be begging for an integrated theory to unify them, searching for therapeutic synthesis is, in the words of Joel Kovel, "like hunting a unicorn." In the absence of synthesis, there is a pressing need for interdisciplinary communication and ideological cross fertilization. Continued progress demands periodic scrutiny of current trends and recent innovations not only within the traditional psychotherapeutic establishment, but also outside of this establishment and in other sectors of the medical and behavioral sciences. The individual viewpoints comprising the present volume were combined in this spirit of uniting diverse approaches in view of the mutual challenge they share in improving the quality of human functioning. The theme of the book presumes that the best way to prevent the torpor besetting closed models of therapy is to encourage those working in diverse but related disciplines to outline recent developments and to extrapolate from current trends the shape of the future—for to predict and forecast is to create, and ultimately determine, what the future will be.

It has been said that nothing is as powerful as an idea. Accordingly, each contributor was chosen on the basis of the reputation which the force of his ideas has generated. Since the dynamic nature of the field suggested the need for the authors to submit original manuscripts, only two of the papers contained herein have appeared previously in the professional literature—those by Eugene Gendlin and Nathan Kline. Dr. Gendlin's work, which addresses client-centered experiential therapy, is a future-oriented paper that has retained its timeliness and relevance. Dr. Kline has taken a previously published classic and updated it in accordance with the present theme; students of the burgeoning new field of psychopharmacology should find the paper instructive and provocative. The other 12 papers were prepared specifically at the request of the Editor.

The book is organized into four major sections. These sections present behavior change strategies based on "The Human Relationship," "Behavior Analysis and Biofeedback," "Neurosurgical and Pharmacological Intervention," and "Consciousness, Self Awareness, and Human Potentials." Each of the four major sections is preceded by a brief prologue to the area that the papers address. These brief overviews are intended to set the tone for the works in that section by suggesting unifying conceptual frameworks or by outlining emergent issues or controversies surrounding the content of the papers.

As with most such efforts, this volume is the product of the contributions of many people. The original project was supported by the scientific and administrative staffs of Friends Medical Science Research Center, Inc. Special gratitude is offered to Richard Meacham of the Friends' organization for his encouragement and aid at crucial stages in the implementation of the venture. I am indebted to Drs. Thomas E. Hanlon and Charles Savage for their valuable suggestions, to Ms. Edwina Wilkinson for her proofreading skills, to Hazel Bohmer and Diane DeNicio for their typing talents, and to Dorothy Sullivan for her untiring efforts as editorial assistant.

O. Lee McCabe

CONTRIBUTORS

Perry Black, M.D., C.M.
Associate Professor of Neurological Surgery;
Associate Professor of Psychiatry
The Johns Hopkins University School of Medicine
Baltimore, Maryland

Joseph V. Brady, Ph.D.
Professor of Behavioral Biology
The Johns Hopkins University School of Medicine
Baltimore, Maryland

Eugene B. Brody, M.D.
Editor-in-Chief
Journal of Nervous and Mental Disease
Professor of Psychiatry and Human Behavior
University of Maryland School of Medicine
Baltimore, Maryland

Joel Elkes, M.D.
Distinguished Service Professor
The Johns Hopkins University
Baltimore, Maryland

Charles B. Ferster, Ph.D.
Professor
Department of Psychology
The American University
Washington, D.C.

Roland Fischer, Ph.D.
    Research Coordinator
    Maryland Psychiatric Research Center
    Department of Psychiatry, School of Medicine
    University of Maryland
    Baltimore, Maryland

Cyril M. Franks, Ph.D.
    Professor and Director
    The Psychological Clinic
    Rutgers University
    New Brunswick, New Jersey

Eugene T. Gendlin, Ph.D.
    Richmond College
    Staten Island, New York

Alyce M. Green, B.A.
    Co-Director Voluntary Controls Program
    Research Department
    The Menninger Foundation
    Topeka, Kansas

Elmer E. Green, Ph.D.
    Director, Voluntary Controls Program
    Research Department
    The Menninger Foundation
    Topeka, Kansas

Thomas E. Hanlon, Ph.D.
    Chief, Socio-Environmental Research
    Maryland Psychiatric Research Center
    Department of Psychiatry, School of Medicine
    University of Maryland
    Baltimore, Maryland

Gerald G. Jampolsky, M.D.
    Director
    Center for Attitudinal Healing
    Tiburon, California

Nathan S. Kline, M.D.
    Director
    Rockland Research Institute
    New York Department of Mental Hygiene
    Orangeburg, New York

O. Lee McCabe, Ph.D.
Chief, Behavioral Research
Friends Medical Science Research Center, Inc.
Catonsville, Maryland
Department of Psychology
Loyola College
Baltimore, Maryland

John C. Rhead, Ph.D.
Clinical Research Psychologist
Maryland Psychiatric Research Center
Department of Psychiatry, School of Medicine
University of Maryland
Baltimore, Maryland

Charles Savage, M.D.
Chief of Psychiatry
Veterans Administration Hospital
Baltimore, Maryland

William H. Sweet, M.D., D.Sc.
Professor of Neurosurgery
Harvard Medical School
Cambridge, Massachusetts

Charles T. Tart, Ph.D.
Associate Professor
Department of Psychology
University of California, Davis
Davis, California

Elliot S. Valenstein, Ph.D.
Professor
Neuroscience Laboratory Building
The University of Michigan
Ann Arbor, Michigan

Otto Allen Will, Jr., M.D.
Medical Director
Austen Riggs Center, Inc.
Stockbridge, Massachusetts

Irvin D. Yalom, M.D.
Professor of Psychiatry
Stanford University Medical Center
Stanford, California

PART ONE

The Human Relationship

Prologue

Psychotherapy may be regarded as a skill that can be acquired by people with a variety of professional backgrounds. It can be conceived as a technique to be administered to a patient or client in the same way that any other treatment is administered. Such a technique may presumably be learned and used by anyone with the requisite intelligence, knowledge, background, and interests. This view places the psychotherapeutic process in the category of "external" maneuvers, applied by suitably skilled technicians in the same manner as drugs or surgery. The patient "complies" with the procedure as he might comply with limited dietary intake and a regular medication schedule in the case of diabetes. His private, intimate, or personal involvement, however, is not required. He is, in fact, in the medical tradition, a "patient" who awaits the outcome rather than an active participant in the process.

There is significant disagreement with this view among a variety of psychotherapists, including analysts. Many, especially those trained in the Freudian school, do emphasize the importance of precise, even "surgical" interpretations, based on an understanding of the patient's psychology couched in psychodynamic terms. In the past 15 or 20 years, however, there has been increasing acceptance of the view that even those analysts who attempt to preserve meticulously the "analytic incognito" (essential to maximize transference development) cast a long shadow over the couch. Others, particularly those stemming from the Sullivanian tradition, have made the person of the therapist a central concern. Some therapists, it appears, do better with certain kinds of patient problems and personalities than others, and the difference is less in their training than in a kind of fit between the characters of the helper and the help-seeker. The life experience of the therapist can become an issue under these circumstances. As Rainer Maria Rilke noted in *Letters to a Young Poet,* the person who helps another is often able to do so because he has surmounted significant troubles in his own life. In our own department, for years, when selecting new residents we tended to distrust people with placid surfaces and unrippled life histories, occasionally referring to them—however unjustly—as having a "normal character disorder."

I do not deprecate technical knowledge and I prefer the professional psychotherapist whose scholarship and dedication is reflected in the achievement of doctoral level education. Nor am I entirely comfortable with the current tendency to attach the term "therapy" to the broad range of humanly useful, creative, or tension-reducing experiences, e.g., dancing or painting. However, I do believe that the nature and effectiveness of any psychotherapeutic process is related to the person of the therapist and the way in which his personal characteristics influence his interaction with the patient. Effective psychotherapy requires an involvement with humanity that can only come from the recognition of one's own. This awareness converts the interaction between helper and seeker from one between subject and object to one between two human beings.* The therapist, in Sonneman's phrase, no longer strives to "turn the other into an object within (his private world), a shadow of (his) being." The goal, instead, becomes the achievement of a moment of contact, of communication. This

*Brody, E. Existence, action and context in psychotherapy with schizophrenic patients. A commentary on Mullahy's presentation of Sullivan's theory of schizophrenia. *International Journal of Psychiatry,* 1967, *4* (6), 525–529.

moment provides a point in time when existence is shared with the heretofore isolated help-seeker. The seeker does not encounter a willful being in the person of a therapist, but rather one with an openness of inner horizon that permits the sharing of his world.

EUGENE B. BRODY, M.D.
Editor-in-Chief
Journal of Nervous and Mental Disease
Professor of Psychiatry and Human Behavior
University of Maryland School of Medicine
Baltimore, Maryland

1. INTERPERSONAL PSYCHOTHERAPY

The Future of the Therapeutic Relationship as an Agent of Change

Otto Allen Will, Jr., M.D.

Anyone who addresses his remarks to a period designated as the "future" is likely to succumb (knowingly or not) to assorted temptations, and in so doing reveal himself as lacking in knowledge, as pretentious, or as simply foolish. For example, a prediction may be based upon what *seems* to have been and what seems to be in the present, without an awareness of many relevant events that are unknown or go unrecognized. We are well advised to direct our attention to the occurrence of events in patterns. As used here the word "pattern" means "a reliable sample of traits, acts, or other observable features characterizing an individual,"[1] a group, or a social or cultural situation. Sullivan defined pattern as "the envelope of insignificant particular differences."[9] [p104] We are concerned with groupings of selected acts of human beings that are observable and identifiably recurrent; numerous variations from one person to another we may (at least for the time being) arbitrarily ignore as "insignificant," seemingly limitless, and inexplicable. Thus "pattern" signifies overall characteristics of behavior—"the envelope" of activities that in terms of a particular approach, or study, of a problem are held to be significant in comprehending that problem. On the basis of the consistency of certain

5

patterns we attempt to predict the probability of their repetition and continuance, to identify influences likely to modify or extinguish them, and to project their courses into the future, which (in our culture) is an extension of the past and the present on a linear scale.

In the social field of the psychotherapist, one must study oneself mainly as perceived in transactions with other people—professionally, particularly with patients. To study oneself in a truly objective manner is not possible; the therapist, being participant as well as observer, cannot (and should not) divorce himself from the field of observation. There is another factor that may bedevil the earnest professional. As he seeks to be objective, precise, and even reductionistic, he is confronted not only by his own ignorance, but by the notion (unpalatable as it may be to him) that there seems to be a factor of chance and unpredictability operating in our universe and in ourselves.

To a great extent uncertainty is a major constituent in the matrix of our lives. We may have some feeling of assurance in making forecasts of what may happen in large groups of human beings—the mob, the youth, the elderly, the hungry, the "psychotic," and so on—and even then it is advisable to be cautious and to consider hedging our bets. It may be useful on occasion to describe the collective and characteristic behaviors of "schizophrenics;" however, the psychotherapist does not meet with a "schizophrenic," but with a human being, who has, despite his apparent (or actual) similarities to others so designated (and perhaps also defined as "sick," "perverse," "good," or "evil"), a uniqueness of his own. To some extent—within the limitations of his biological endowment, experience, culture, and social position—he can select among options and thus exert his "will;" he is not entirely a creature of his past and his genetic structure, or a victim of his present and his future, although he may, for the most part, experience himself as meaningless and helpless in the web of circumstances that seem to compose his existence.

There are many hazards in prophecy. In daring a look into the future, the psychotherapist may rashly put caution aside and presume the role of expert in areas in which he is not knowledgeable or experienced. It is well to be modest in suggesting that the occurrences of tomorrow may be a direct or simple extension of what we know as the present; it is more difficult—and at times perilous—to attempt predictions of a distant future, as they may reflect not only accumulations of at least seemingly dependable data, but also personal bias, cherished fantasies, hopes, and despair. It may be heady stuff for the clinician to think of himself as a sage, but he must then remind himself (or be told by others) that he is first a clinician whose range of professional expertness is limited.

Despite such qualifications and stringencies, we are properly required to learn from our pasts, observe what goes on in the here and now, recognize the possible unpredictable influences of ignorance and chance, and engage in the act of foresight—or divination. We must beware that we do not create a prospect out of our own hubris, disillusionments, anger, or despair. If that which appears to be coming is not in keeping with what we have known or might wish to be, we could act to make the most dire forecasts come true. If we cannot now envisage a "better" future, we could renounce all futures, finding dissolution easier to accept than change, and putting into action a racial "death wish" whereby much, if not all, of what we are and have created is destroyed.

PSYCHIATRY

The term "psychiatry" as generally used refers to a branch of medicine, a medical specialty. In this particular sense of the word the practitioner is concerned primarily with problems of symptomatology, etiology, pathology, physiology, diagnosis, prognosis, and treatment as these are related to "mental diseases." In many instances there are uncertainties, lack of knowledge, and disagreements about several (or even all) of these factors. As the search for greater clarity and certainty continues and various theories and treatments are proposed, used, abandoned, or clung to, there is currently no compelling evidence that the complex ways of man's living can be reduced to simple formulae or "explained" in terms of unitary causes.

The psychotherapist is confronted with many situations and behavioral variants that do not readily fit into the classical medical model of disorder.[5] He may look upon the problems with which he and his patient must deal as inadequate, destructive, inappropriate, unduly complicated, or overly simplified forms of behavior, exhibited in interpersonal situations and arising (to an imprecisely determined extent) from experiences in a multitude of interpersonal fields. Recognizing that man is bound to biological limitations, individual differences, and imposed physical and cultural advantages and handicaps of great variability, a psychiatrist may (but by no means always or necessarily) consider the "sick" behavior as having been formed largely in response to social, cultural, and existential influences and as having purposes and goals. From this point of view, psychiatry is concerned with a broad range of human activities. This not to say that the psychiatrist (or psychotherapist) is an "expert" in all aspects of human behavior; he is not. However, he can at least be aware of the broader implications of his theories and practices. The following quotation is relevant at this juncture. Speaking of the contributions to psychiatry of William Alanson White, Sullivan said:

> There was effected in Dr. White's vision the first synthesis of the two great trends of psychiatric meaning—the medical discipline concerned with human ills, and the other great body of observational techniques, formulations, hypotheses, and experiments which are included in all those efforts to understand social situations and deal with social problems as they have appeared in the history of man.[8]

PSYCHOTHERAPY

Common to all definitions of psychotherapy is the concept of change. The procedure—individual, group, or other variant—is designed to modify behavior that has been defined as personally or socially painful, troublesome, undesirable, or unacceptable. Often there is no general agreement about this definition; society, family members, a patient, and a therapist may differ in their views of what constitutes sickness and health, failure and success, progress and retrogression, the desirable and undesirable, and so on. In any case, we should recognize that the psychotherapeutic encounter—as all other well-intentioned interventions in the lives of human beings—can be harmful as well as beneficial. The therapist must bear the burden of responsibility; he is no neutral observer of some passing scene.

No psychotherapeutic approach is simply "individual." Other people are always more or less directly and influentially involved—family members, friends, enemies, employers, associates in a hospital team—in addition to memories of the past and expectations of the future. Psychotherapy is involved with problems of symbolism, meaning, learning, and alteration. The therapist's task is to aid a patient to gain further knowledge of behavior (his own and that of others); increased understanding of its possible origins, forms, functions, and goals; its advantages and disadvantages; the options or choices that are available; and the restrictions ("real" or otherwise) and costs of taking, modifying, curtailing, or abandoning certain actions. The therapist does not devise, plan, or attempt to enforce a way of life for his patient; he cannot tell another person (in this instance his patient) how life should be led; he can attempt to discover some of the reasons for the adoption and continuance of a particular course of living and to clarify the prices that must be paid for whatever one does. The therapist is not an expert in finding ways to bring about contentment, happiness, success, marital and other pleasures, and so on. Whatever expertness he has lies in his ability to observe and make some sense of happenings in the complex social fields in which he and his patient are in varying ways and degrees both participants and observers. His major professional task is to recognize and deal with multiple expressions of anxiety in interpersonal situations.

THE "FUTURE" IN MORE GENERAL AND LONG-RANGE TERMS

We cannot speak of psychiatry and psychotherapy without reference to the society and the culture in which they are practiced. To a great extent the beliefs and values of a social group define, permit, and limit the theories and activities of the therapist, who therefore mirrors his culture in his practices. To a lesser extent the therapist may influence his society, commenting on its values, its directions, its nature, and approving of it or opposing it, while he is himself a member of it; should he vary too widely from its accepted norms he will be lonely, estranged, and perhaps ridiculed, ostracized, and even destroyed. In speaking of the future of psychotherapy, attention must be turned to the speculations that have been advanced regarding the possible future of societies and mankind.

In a sense, man lives in a single universe of self-perception, although we may say that at times he seems to live in the past, again in the present, and yet again in the future. Despite their apparent distinction in our view of time, these periods merge, one into the other, forming in their conjunction a unity of personal existence.

Man is solicitous of his being, as he is aware of his ignorance of his personal beginnings and outcomes, his need for recognition of his presence and purposefulness, his temporality, and his aloneness. There are questions about the life of a human being that frequently may be unrecognized in any clear fashion or go unspoken; I think, however, that their total absence from awareness is unlikely. Among these questions are the following: "Is there hope for me? Is there importance or meaning in what I do? Shall I be forgiven for what I conceive of—or 'know'—to be evil"? "Is blind, unfeeling, and empty death to be my end? Are there consequences to give structure to my existence? Shall I somehow live on, be born again, reappear in other form, or disappear to unimaginable nothingness?" In recognition of man's interdependence with his fellows on Earth, the question must be: "Is there hope for mankind?" As stated here the question is in temporal terms.

To this query the economist and philosopher Robert Heilbroner responds:

> The outlook for man, I believe, is painful, difficult, perhaps desperate, and the hope that can be held out for his future prospect seems to be very slim indeed. Thus, to anticipate the conclusions of our inquiry, the answer to whether we can conceive of the future other than as a continuation of the darkness, cruelty, and disorder of the past seems to me to be, no; and to the question of whether worse impends, yes.[3]

Heilbroner says that for the continuing survival of the human race, the structure of the world—in its physical, cultural, political, and social organizations—must be changed radically. As a result of the changes that he considers to be necessary, our simple physical existence would be altered grossly; a social universe would be created that would lead to the present world (at least from the point of view of westernized industrialized countries) being not only out of date, but unfamiliar if not totally unrecognizable.

In speaking of the acceleration of social evolution brought about to a great extent through the development of industrial technology, the anthropologist L. Eiseley says:

> So fast does this change progress that a growing child strives to master the institutional customs of a society which, compared to the pace of past history, compresses centuries of change into his lifetime. I myself, like others of my generation, was born in an age which has already perished. At my death I will look my last upon a nation which, save for some linguistic continuity, will seem increasingly alien and remote. It will be as though I peered upon my youth through misty centuries. I will not be merely old; I will be a genuine fossil embedded in onrushing man-made time before my actual death.[1]

The factors that now exist and seem to push man with increasing force and urgency into changing his ways and his course, to contemplate and finally face up to his own annihilation, have been noted and commented upon by many observers; there is evidence that such portents can no longer be denied, ignored, or somehow "explained away." Among these signs are the following major developments:

1. *Population.* There has been an extraordinary acceleration in the increase of the world population. Should current increases not be curtailed

markedly, the present world population of approximately 3.6 billion could reach something like 41 billion within the next 100 years. Some of the results of such rapid growth would be mass starvation, the pillaging of natural resources, unemployment, social disorder, and wars. Dr. Philip Handler, President of the National Academy of Sciences, recently spoke "On the State of Man" as follows:

> Cruel as it may sound, if the developed nations do not intend the colossal all-out effort commensurate with this task [a massive program of aid and development for "underprivileged" and needy countries] then it may be wiser to let nature take its course as Aristotle described it: "From time to time it is necessary that pestilence, famine and war prune the luxuriant growth of the human race."[2]

2. *War.* The proliferation and increasingly wide distribution of nuclear weapons poses the threat of their use as blackmail by impoverished nations, with the possible creation of "wars of redistribution," goods being obtained by force rather than through trade. Except in terms of magnitude, this method is not new and has long been in practice.

3. *Environmental deterioration.* The world's environmental resources, as currently known, are inadequate to meet the demands likely to be placed on them. If industrial activity is increased for the exploitation of these resources beyond their present usage, the resulting increases of energy and heat will predictably give rise to significant climactic changes, in themselves threatening to human and other life on this planet. A limitation and a reduction in industrial growth to accommodate to these dangers (and reduce or eliminate their threats) would require alterations in living styles unacceptable to many societies—particularly the "more privileged."

4. *Science and technology.* Advances in this area have made the above "problems" of modern living possible. Again I refer to Heilbroner:

> . . . [T]he dangers we have discussed do not descend, as it were, from the heavens, menacing humanity with the implacable fate that would be the consequence of the sudden arrival of a new Ice Age or the announcement of the impending extinction of the sun. . . . On the contrary. . . all the dangers we have examined—population growth, war, environmental damage, scientific technology—are *social* problems, originating in human behavior and capable of amelioration by alteration of that behavior.[3]

The suggestion is made (by Heilbroner for one) that these dangers are not likely to be dealt with successfully by the voluntary cooperation of societies, nation-states, or men in general; the sacrifices required to meet the demands for change will appear to be too great, the problems will seem too distant to require immediate action, and denial and rationalization will be too ready a refuge. The setting of limits to actual and potential destructive social and technological developments may require the establishment of strictly controlled, austere, and authoritarian societies, in which our own current concepts of individuality and freedom would probably not be possible or tolerated. I personally wish to deny the probability—or possibility—of such prospects being realized. I shrink from what I experience as the personal threat of such changes, but I cannot label such an outlook nonsense or turn away from considering it. Despair, however, is no adequate reply—biological or social.

This prospect, these dangers, these apprehensions are not new; the crowding of the earth with people, the recognition of the limitation of natural resources that once seemed to be limitless, the refinement and increase in power of the instruments for killing, the growing awareness that the techniques of "science" are not in themselves sufficient to "save mankind," and the great facilitation of communication devices that may make the world our neighborhood and also harden us to what we see so repetitively, both near and impersonally far away—all of these factors make matters once speculative assume a reality that cannot lightly be pushed aside. In 1948 Sullivan wrote:

> I say to you with the utmost seriousness of which I am capable that this is no time to excuse yourself from paying the debt you and yours owe the social order with some such facile verbalism as "nothing will come of it; it can't be done." Begin, and let it be said of you, if there is any more history, that you labored nobly in the measure of man in the twentieth century of the scientific, Western World. [7]

In 1974, some years later, Heilbroner wrote in a somewhat similar vein:

> I do not intend to condone, much less to urge, an attitude of passive resignation, or a delegation of the human prospect to the realm of things we choose not to think about. Avoiding evil remains, as it always will, an enemy that can be defeated; and the fact that the collective destiny of man portends unavoidable travail is no reason, and cannot be tolerated as an excuse, for doing nothing. This general admonition applies in particular to the intellectual elements of Western nations whose privileged role as sentries for society takes on a special importance in the face of things as we now see them. It is their task not only to prepare their fellow citizens for the sacrifices that will be required of them but to take the lead in seeking to redefine the legitimate boundaries of power and the permissible sanctuaries of freedom, for a future in which the exercise of power must inevitably increase, and many present areas of freedom, especially in economic life, be curtailed. [3]

Lastly, for the moment, I refer to a report to the Club of Rome entitled "Mankind at the Turning Point," by Mihajlo Mesarovic and Eduard Pestel. The authors say that industrial countries must stop "further overdevelopment" and limit their use of resources now seen to be finite. Such limitation will not be readily accepted in a world in which many of us have been taught the ethic of creating more and expanding, rather than conserving and doing with less. The following statement by these authors must at least be heard, if not accepted and acted upon:

Unless this lesson is learned in time, there will be a thousand desperadoes terrorizing those who are now rich, and eventually nuclear blackmail and terror will paralyze further orderly development.[6]

THE "POPULARITY" OF PSYCHOTHERAPY

During the years that I have spent in the general field of psychiatry, the medical specialty itself, and the more limited (or in some ways broader) practice known as psychotherapy, the latter field has not been professionally (or publicly) popular, nor accepted as being fully respectable. The psychiatrist, in the strictest use of the term, may retain his identity as a physician and as a member of what we called in times past a subspecialty—perhaps of internal medicine. The psychotherapist has no such clear identity; he is often (rightly or not) suspect—a "shrink," a kin of the witch doctor, a practitioner of the "talking way," with its mixture of magic and the conventions of "how to live that everybody knows."

The psychotherapist must confront, if not find a lasting peace with, the common objections to and hazards of his occupation:

1. Whatever his experience and training, the psychotherapist is not fully "expert" in the sense that a mechanical engineer can be expert. The interpersonal field is too uncertain, unknown, and unpredictable to be defined with great precision. We do seek for greater certainty, but this is no place for the person who must depend on exactitude for his own satisfaction or security.

2. Therapy is often prolonged, being a matter of learning, growth, and the formation of a human relationship through which are encouraged an increase in trust, clarity of communication, and self-respect. This is not a process whereby a disease is "removed" from a patient; in many ways it is similar to education, particular attention being given to the personality traits that constrict awareness and interfere with interest, concentration, creativity, and the acquisition of new ideas and skills.

3. There is no guarantee of "success" in this work; success itself is difficult to define, not being equated necessarily with conventional concepts of achievement, contentment, or happiness. That is, the patient must in some way "fit in" to his society and yet find a life style of his own. In this task the therapist acts as a facilitator.

4. The patient will not necessarily like his therapist, congratulate him, or recognize that much has been accomplished in treatment—even in those instances in which "obvious" growth has taken place. The therapist cannot seek to use his patient as a source of praise, condolence, gratitude, or other emotional support. In many ways the therapist's job is similar to that of the parent and the teacher; he fosters attachment, dependency, curiosity, and understanding in the service of a personal freedom; when he is successful the patient leaves, separation being the sometimes painful—yet happy—reward of parent, educator, and therapist. The therapist may expect to be blamed for setbacks and disappointments and to go unnoticed if all goes well enough. That is, I think, as it should be, but at times one may hunger for more tangible appreciation. In such cases it is well to be reminded that this is how one earns one's living.

5. There are other methods of treatment that are less personal and painful, require less time, and may be said to be more simply effective—such as the use of chemotherapy, electroshock, large doses of vitamins, manipulation of cerebral functioning by means of surgical operations and electrode transplants in the brain, behavioral conditioning techniques, various group activities ("confrontations," "marathons"), and so on. The therapist is unendingly reminded of these other ways of modifying human behavior, and he may feel out of date in the face of a continually developing multitude of "treatments" and their often stridently enthusiastic adherents and proponents.

6. The psychotherapeutic process is not easily measured, tested, or evaluated. It does not, and probably should not, lend itself to the linear, cause-and-effect, control group methods of study. Thus the therapist may feel that he is amateurish, inferior, and foolishly and blindly romantic in a society that places great value on objectivity and science.

7. Psychotherapy is expensive in terms of time, money, and the personal distress that commonly accompanies insight and change. A therapist may feel guilty when he measures the small number of patients that he deals with against the needs of the many.

8. At times the therapist may gravely doubt himself. He may be troubled by the thought that his work is a kind of pseudoprofessional nonsense, a web of illusions that will be harshly dispelled if human

behaviors are found to have causes that can be dealt with through the use of diet, drugs, milieu changes, genetic manipulations, surgical interventions, etc.

9. The personal involvement with troubled people is not always a soothing occupation. The therapist will himself experience anger, hurt, guilt, shame, boredom, depression, and discouragement. He will be required to consider carefully his own motivations—alone, through personal therapy, and throughout his life by consultation with able and trusted colleagues. Over the years the attitudes and confidences to which he is exposed may come to be experienced as a heavy burden.

10. The practice of psychotherapy can foster a lonely existence, intensely marked by the quality of uncertainty that is the essence of all human existence. The therapist may find himself becoming isolated as the years pass by; he may be looked upon as somehow "invulnerable" to the ordinary emotional vicissitudes, temptations, and risks of life, and find then that there is no one to whom he can turn and reveal without fear or shame his own doubts and frailties.

CURRENT TRENDS

The future of psychotherapy—as we now know the procedure—does not appear to me to be promising. I refer particularly to the treatment method that relies heavily on the development and understanding of the human relationship as a means of personality change, as evidenced in a focus on the one-to-one encounter and ancillary contacts with members of a hospital team, a family, and formal or informal social groups—in or out of a psychiatric institution. I do not include here the wide range of activities that are primarily psychologically oriented—sociotherapy, various "milieus," family treatment, "encounter" and other groups, etc. Among the reasons that lead me to entertain a point of view that is personally distressing are the following:

1. The often painful nature of a process in which emphasis is placed on the exploration of the personalities of those involved, with the inevitable exposure and evaluation of motives, accomplishments, failures, and life's uncertainties;
2. The cost in terms of time, money, and energy;
3. The difficulty of "proving" the efficacy of the procedure in an objective, "scientific" fashion—that is, the therapist is asked to

demonstrate that the human relationship can be a major factor, not only in contributing to human distress labeled psychiatric, but also in alleviating such disorders;

4. The common ambivalence about entrusting one's self to a human relationship—professional or otherwise;

5. The social pressures to get things done quickly, cheaply, efficiently, and painlessly, without public exposure of the more extreme forms of human distress that are more or less hidden within all of us—and to provide some kind of psychiatric services to "everybody" in a semblance of egalitarianism;

6. The current trend to select treatment programs in conformity with demands that often would not desirably control the choice of therapy of any nature—for example, finances, exemplified in part by insurance programs that limit the length of treatment and thus more or less directly influence diagnosis and choice of professional intervention; and

7. The possibility that social, economic, and political requirements may lead to the development of more controlled, authoritarian governments in which there may be further restrictions of emphasis on the importance of the individual and a curtailment of much of what we have come to value and honor as "freedom."

CONTROL AND ETHICS

The psychotherapist has professional responsibilities in three areas that are not easily or satisfactorily combined:

1. He is bound to use his skills to aid in reducing his patients' distress, facilitate their personal growth, and further the use of their actual and potential abilities.

2. He is required to aid his patients in finding ways to express themselves as unique individuals, while, at the same time they effect some form of compromise with culture and society that is neither blind subservience nor mindless rebellion.

3. He must learn as best he can from his work, and make his observations known to his society—speaking the truth as he judges it to be, for its more public use (if for use at all), for better or for worse.

It seems to me that much of the psychiatrist's work, both in the past and in the present, has been concerned with problems of control.

Frequently there is little or no clarity about what is to be controlled, the reasons for exerting control, the forms of control, the personal and civil rights involved, the simple human propriety of what is done, and for whose benefit (if any) control is being exercised. In brief, that which we do has motives and consequences and cannot be separated from questions of ethics and morality. As psychotherapists we cannot be neutral; we must, at least, be clear as to our values. Often we shall not be able to reconcile to our satisfaction the seemingly (and actual) compelling needs of our patients, our society, and ourselves. Of necessity such conflicts must be recognized; should they not seem to exist I think that it is likely that some aspect of the situation is being ignored or denied. I find no great comfort in this idea, but if there is a design for life there is, for me, no evidence that it is one of certainty, peace, and predictability.

IN CONCLUSION

I expect that the human relationship known as psychotherapy will continue in one form or another. What we now do may be modified greatly by increases in knowledge of human behavior in social and physical terms. For man's survival I think that rapidly developed information about his assets, liabilities, and limitations must be made available to all of us. The psychotherapeutic process is a major road leading to such information; it is a remarkable and unique instrument of research and, for that reason alone, should not be abandoned or weakened in efforts to find get-rich-quick methods of investigation and treatment. I speak, now personally, having spent many years in efforts to be of use "psychotherapeutically" to those who have "tried everything." I say, quite simply, that it is too easy to abandon those who declare themselves to be—or are seen to be—"hopeless." There are not miracles in the work in which we are usually engaged, but I continue to have confidence in the human relationship as a major agent of healing.

Psychotherapy is a procedure concerned with personal growth, learning and human values. It is one of the few interpersonal situations today in which privacy exists, and serious concern for the welfare of another human being can be expressed unashamedly. The problems with which it deals are not simply those of "pathology," but are matters characteristic of all human living—attachment, dependency, anxiety, fear, self-esteem, the image of one's body and self, loss, and separation—to name a few.

Psychotherapy is also concerned—primarily, in my view—with symbolism, those reflections and representations of experiences and perception that are transmitted through learning and social–cultural processes and that are freely created, rather than being an expression of some assumed or actual biological connection between symbol and object or event. On this subject I refer to Von Bertalanffy, who said:

Apart from satisfaction of biological needs man shares with animals, he lives in a universe not of things but of symbols.[10]

Similarly, Kaplan has noted:

During the past fifty years it has become increasingly recognized that symbolic activity is among the most characteristic features of human existence and that the whole development of human culture is based upon man's capacity for transforming simple sensory material into symbolic vehicles—carriers of the finest intellectual and emotional distinctions. So important is symbolic activity in human life that one of the outstanding contemporary philosophers (Cassirer) has urged: "Instead of defining man as an *animal rationale,* we should define him as an *animal symbolicum.* By so doing we can designate his specific difference . . ."[4]

In relation to this subject I again return to Sullivan:

. . . [A]ll human behavior so purely and unquestionably manifests the organization of experience into what are in effect signs—whether signals or symbols—that an attempt to discriminate intelligibly in human behavior between what is symbolic and what is nonsymbolic is far more misleading than it is helpful. Therefore, without denying that there may be purely nonsymbolic performances in human beings, I would say that for the purposes of psychiatric theory I am concerned exclusively with covert and overt symbolic activity—that is, with activity influenced by the organization into signs of previous experience of satisfaction, or in terms of avoiding or minimizing anxiety.[9] [p186]

As psychotherapists we deal with events that involve both understanding and control. Thus we speak of drives, instincts, hungers, needs, aggression, sex, and so on. Man has also, if I comprehend (and not merely prehend the matters at hand), a necessity to symbolize—to create a symbolic structure of his being and his universe. Such creativity may constitute his greatest (or most apparent) strength; it could also constitute his fatal weakness. Should man become so enamored of his own creations that he could envisage no alternatives to them, or tolerate no changes in them, he might lure himself into following what he has designated as the "right" or the "truth" without regard for other possibilities—and thus move blindly along a path to his own destruction.

The psychotherapist is largely involved with this world of symbols. He gives his attention to the untangling of those constructions that have led or contributed to the aberrations of behavior called neurotic, psychotic, or even "normal," and that may serve not only to enrich and perpetuate life, but also to denigrate and destroy it. Psychotherapy, from this point of view, is an encounter among symbolic structures, the covert and distorted aspects of which are usually predominant; it is concerned with the politics of symbols and their alleged and actual meanings, and cannot safely be abandoned if knowledge of ourselves is not only desirable but necessary.

Psychotherapy is a form of the human relationship, designed to encourage the human being's need for attachment and dependency, for knowledge, for growth, for separation, and for freedom (define the last as you will). I do not think that it will—whatever its form or its description—fade away.

REFERENCES

1. Eiseley, L. *The invisible pyramid*. New York: Charles Scribner's Sons, 1970, p. 22.
2. Handler, P. On the state of man, cited by A. Lewis, Pruning by famine. *The Berkshire Eagle,* November 6, 1974, p. 27.
3. Heilbroner, R. L. *An inquiry into the human prospect.* New York: W. W. Norton, 1974, p. 22.
4. Kaplan, B. An approach to the problem of symbolic representation: Nonverbal and verbal. *Journal of Communications,* 1961, *11,* 52–62.
5. Kety, S. From rationalization to reason. *American Journal of Psychiatry,* September 1974, *131,* 957–963.
6. Mesarovic, M., & Pestel, E. Mankind at the turning point, cited by A. Lewis, To hear a bell toll. *The Berkshire Eagle,* November 15, 1974, p. 19.
7. Sullivan, H. S. Towards a psychiatry of peoples. *Psychiatry,* 1948, *11,* 105–116.
8. Sullivan, H. S. *Conceptions of modern psychiatry.* New York: W. W. Norton, 1953, p. 10.
9. Sullivan, H. S. *Interpersonal theory of psychiatry.* New York: W. W. Norton, 1953.
10. Von Bertalanffy, L. *Robots, men and minds.* New York: George Braziller, 1967, p. 22.
11. *Webster's seventh new collegiate dictionary.* Springfield, Mass.: G. & C. Merriam, 1972.

2. PSYCHOANALYSIS

Psychodynamics and Psychoanalysis: Future Prospects

Charles Savage, M.D.

When I agreed to write a paper on the future prospects of psychoanalysis, I did so as a mark of respect for Dr. Lee McCabe, the editor of this work, and for psychoanalysis, friends of more than one and three decades, respectively. Nevertheless, my instantaneous reaction was that I had acted out of rashness. "For fools rush in where angels fear to tread," as Alexander Pope has stated. However, sober reflection reminded me that over the past two decades many presidential addresses delivered to the American Psychoanalytic Association were devoted to the "Future of Psychoanalysis." Thus, it is reassuring to know that in attempting such a treatise I am following in the path of the angels and that many of the criticisms in this work have been anticipated by leading theoreticians of psychoanalysis and stem from the mainstream of organized psychoanalysis. Honest self-criticism is a healthy sign; yet, all around us there are signs of disease. Hardly a meeting passes without some dire warning from the Nestors in our midst. Even our youth, from whom we expect some shred of optimism, are equally gloomy; thus, "the prospects of Psychoanalytic Practice are increasingly grim"—this from the National

Council of Psychoanalytic Candidates.[14] Views equally dour have been expressed about psychoanalytic theory and education as well as practice.

The situation was well summed up by Astley and Royden in their Presidential Address of December 20, 1970:

1. The milieu, in which the university on the one hand, and psychoanalysis on the other, would like to steer a steady course has nowadays become a seething multidimensional flux, and we are—with all of mankind—like naval apprentices struggling to round the Horn at night in an equinoctial gale;

2. there is no guarantee of smoother seas ahead, and little indeed of hope that the period ten years hence will provide any greater serenity;

3. as psychoanalysts we are at best viewed today by the majority of our fellow voyagers as either irresponsible and irrelevant, or unimportant, at worst, because we have unfixed the underworld, as responsible for much of the woe that besets humanity;

4. being human and frightened, we analysts disagree among ourselves, are suspicious of one another's personal views and group persuasions, and opt diversely for various courses or for attempting to heave-to and claim a spurious placidity;

5. to change the metaphor utterly but not the situation in Arnold's phrase:
    ". . . we are here as on a darkling plain
    Swept with confused alarms of struggle and flight,
    Where ignorant armies clash by night."[1]

In the same address, Astley gave an ominous example which, while intended to reflect on the poverty of our educational system, nevertheless has much wider applications: In the course of supervision one day, Astley remarked, *Flectere si nequeo superos, Acheronta movebo.* You will doubtless recognize this quotation as the superscription to Freud's classic, *The Interpretation of Dreams.* The candidate recognized it only belatedly (after it was pointed out to him) and even then had not the slightest idea what it meant. My own translation would be, "If I cannot bend the heavens, then I can at least move the deep." Astley was a little more pungent in his rendition, "If I can't get anything out of those people up there, at least I can raise hell!"

AN ISLAND OF FREEDOM

I found this story sad and shocking. First, that candidates are so poorly educated; second, that they are so short on curiosity; and third, that psychoanalysts have forgotten how to raise hell. If we analysts can recapture our erudition, our curiosity, and our ability to raise hell, then to the question, "Does psychoanalysis have a future?" I would answer a resounding "Yes!" It seems to me that this is the one area of human intercourse that has the strength and integrity to resist the encroachment of the State on our lives. It has been the one island of human privacy and dignity left to us. I think it no accident that it was the invasion of a psychoanalyst's office that helped bring down the Nixon Administration. Solzhenitsyn pointed out that this could never have happened in Russia. There the government would merely have needed only to ask the psychiatrist what was going on. The fondest wishes of the secret police would have been fulfilled.

While we may be proud of our island of freedom, its firmness as a bastion should not be assumed. As Ecclesiastes reminds us, "There is no discharge in that war." The rights to privacy and confidentiality we once took for granted are now protected by government guidelines. These guidelines also contain provisions for the introduction of police spies and informants.[11]

The issue of third party payments, Peer Review, and Professional Standards Review Organization formations casts an ominous shadow.[3] Once data given the carrier is computerized and fed into a data bank, how then can this information ever be confidential when it is at least accessible to other carriers? Not only does this system endanger confidentiality, it threatens to control the very practices of psychoanalysis.

Pressure for this move toward closer control derives largely from the realization of the skyrocketing costs of health care and the increasing use of health insurance, prepayment or some form of third-party payment. Psychiatry in general, and intensive psychotherapy and psychoanalysis in particular, are under special pressure engendered out of fear that these forms of care are too expensive and could "break the insurance bank." Psychoanalysis will be under enormous pressure to furnish convincing evidence that the frequency and duration of psychoanalytic treatment produces results substantially different from these produced by other treatment methods.[4]

However, I am not sanguine that even if such evidence were forthcoming it would convince government planners in high policy positions who also write books on *The Death of Psychiatry*.[20] Since in that book psychoanalysis is not mentioned in the Index or the Table of Contents, and since psychoanalytic psychotherapies merit a scant two pages in the chapter on "Systems of 'Psychotherapy' as Toothpaste," we analysts would be ingenuous to assume that the author would be receptive to evidence, or that such major decisions are made on the basis of evidence.

More likely, major decisions will be made either on the basis of prevailing political philosophy or simplistic cost–effectiveness rules of thumb, and there will remain an insufficient economic base to support both psychoanalysis and community-based programs. The solution that psychoanalysts become an effective pressure group is not an attractive one. Neither is dying. Clearly, the fate of psychoanalysis is tied to the future of society as a whole.

PROBLEMS WITHIN PSYCHOANALYSIS

We will leave that clouded crystal ball and look at the problems within psychoanalysis itself. Many are related to the syncretic functions of psychoanalysis as science, education, and therapy—uneasy syncretism. The state of psychoanalysis as science has long been troublesome. Over a decade ago, in his Presidential Address entitled "The Identity Crisis in Psychoanalysis,"[9] Gitelson declared that the time had come for psychoanalysis to assert itself as an independent science, divorcing itself from psychotherapy, psychiatry, and the mental hygiene clinic. However, Gitelson's recommendation of longer training analyses seems irrelevant to the development of psychoanalysis as an independent science.

Colby,[6] in the same year, reviewed the whole state of psychotherapy and found it chaos. He examined existing therapeutic paradigms—psychoanalysis, existentialism, learning theory—and found them all wanting. He called for the scrapping of old paradigms. However, to paraphrase Thomas Carlyle in *Heroes and Hero Worship,* the times may call loudly for the emergence of a new paradigm and none may emerge. One may argue whether "the new psychotherapies and encounters of the seventies"[5] demonstrate progress or are fads. The nude marathon and sexual surrogate therapy, radical though they may be ethically, are paradigmatically nothing new and may be seen as technical modifications. Even the revisionist schools of psychoanalysis are seen by Rangell [16] as fitting comfortably within the framework of orthodox psychoanalysis. He feels that their development would have been more profitable within that confine.

Gitelson's ambitious goal of psychoanalysis as an independent science raises many problems. Can it meet the canons of science at all? Burnham[4] has raised grave doubts that it can. Burnham's views, briefly summarized, are as follows: Psychoanalytic theories are too loosely defined to be verified by customary scientific methods. The evidence supporting psychoanalytic theories is private, leaving no opportunity to adduce counterevidence or alternative evidence. Corollary data (as opposed to that drawn from the couch) is dubious, being drawn from myths, folklore, and the arts. There are insufficient safeguards against the suggestion of evidence through interpretation. Alternative interpretations may be equally plausible. (See also Glover,[10] who criticizes Melanie Klein on just these grounds.) Finally, Burnham argues that psychoanalytic theory building relies too heavily on analogic, metaphoric thinking with escalating reifications. We shall return to this point later.

PSYCHOANALYSIS—ART AND SCIENCE

Faced with these difficulties we may wonder with Colby whether it is better to view psychoanalysis as a fine art, as that of making fine wines, and borrow from other sciences as wine making borrows from microbiology and biochemistry. We are faced with the fact that not only are there intrinsic limitations in trying to build scientific theory on data obtained from the couch, but now this traditional method of the individual case study has been pushed as far as it can and no longer meets our requirements for theory building.

Loewald has stressed that psychoanalysis *is* an art, but he notes that this is not a universally held sentiment:

Most of us, whether engaged solely in psychoanalytic practice or engaged also in psychoanalytic research and theory building, stress the scientific aspects and potentialities of our discipline. Freud did so, and he rejected the suggestion that there might be something nonscientific or unscientific, something resembling art, about psychoanalysis. In the recent past there has been much emphasis on psychoanalysis as a basic science, or as the foundation for, or as a part of, a general psychology. It has been claimed that this constitutes the lasting value of psychoanalysis and doubts have been expressed even within the ranks of psychoanalysts themselves with regard to its viability as a form of psychotherapy. I, myself, have no doubt about its therapeutic value and potentialities, although I do question whether we can expect general or ready recognition of its therapeutic worth and effects—given the anti-individualistic tendencies and simplistic behavior modification trends in our culture.[13]

Loewald concludes with the assertion that art and science are not in opposition and that he is not speaking in an "anti-scientific spirit." He says: "Science's dignity is not so readily offended today by the suggestion that both art and science make use of creative imagination."[13] Whether scientists and analysts will be offended by his remarks remains to be seen.

Part of the problem is that Freud so thoroughly exploited the couch scientifically that he left little room for subsequent strip miners. Eissler wrote:

> It is breathtaking to review what Freud extracted during the course of four decades, from the free associations of eight subjects who lay on a couch for 50 minutes per day. The input–output quotient was here truly enormous. This question, however, remains: Did Freud extract from his patients' associations all the knowledge that is to be gained from the psychoanalytic situation?[7]

To his own question, Eissler answers "yes," although he admits of qualifications. The breathtaking quality of Freud's achievement is also attested to by Rieff.[17]

"By January 1914, when Freud sat down to write his *History,* a great part of the psychoanalytic canon had already been established, all by the hand of one man—Freud himself. It is as if Paul had composed the entire New Testament; or more aptly, as if Moses had compiled the entire Pentateuch." Thus, the clinical case approach that yielded results almost exponentially in Freud's hands had reached its asymptote. In a like manner, we must recognize a similar dead end in theory building itself.

This is far too formidable a problem to tackle briefly. The interested reader is referred to the works of Home,[12] Schafer,[18] and in particular to the masterful survey and summary of the problem by Wallerstein,[21] from whom I have borrowed extensively. They state, in short, that our theory is not a theory at all but a metaphor which must be abjured. Metapsychology has been weighed in the balance and found wanting. Wallerstein reflects Home's assertion that psychoanalysis is essentially an "individual and artistic enterprise." He summarizes Schafer's view of our theory as metaphor and calls it misleading if proposed as part of science:

> In this progression not only do such constructs as psychic energy and drive theory, force and instinct disappear, but literally so do all of metapsychological (i.e., general psychological) conceptualizing via such terms as structure, space, locus, superficial and deep, psychoanalysis as a depth psychology, levels and layers, underlying factors and causes, hierarchic organizations (as of impulse and defense), mental process or mechanism, regulatory structures, functions and relationships. All this is eschewed as metaphor. . . .[21]

With this view of it as metaphor, our theory—structural, topographic, and dynamic—seems to fade away like the Cheshire Cat in *Alice in Wonderland,* leaving only the grin.

EDUCATION

The attempts by psychoanalysis to solve its educational problems are legion. They range from the nihilistic suggestion of Bernfeld[2] to the detailed innovations of Pollock et al.[15] Bernfeld[2] recommended dismantling the entire educational superstructure and returning to the good old days of tutorials arguing that—as has been argued for public schools in general—things could hardly be any worse and might conceivably be better. However, we may consider that both psychoanalytic institutes and public schools are here to stay; as Churchill noted, you cannot persuade a man to give up his skin by force of argument. A proposal somewhat in the opposite direction was to develop the institutes on the university model, granting degrees in psychoanalysis. This system would broaden the base of psychoanalysis considerably by accepting those with a Masters degree in another discipline. Though this alternative was proposed strictly as an experimental program, it did not find wide acceptance. Presumably, we are not about to give up the medical model of mental illness, nor the M.D. degree requirement for psychoanalysts, even though our salvation depends upon it.

CONCLUSION

The history of Western Man is the history of the constant tension between reason and unreason, between romanticism and rationalism. Too much romanticism can lead to Naziism; too much rationalism to Stalinism. A continuing dialogue, a via media, is the only guarantee against excesses. Freud was both the supreme rationalist and romanticist combined. He used the techniques of psychoanalysis to discover how thin is the layer of civilization, how shallow are the pretenses of the eighteenth and nineteenth centuries, how rich and fiery is the seething cauldron that underlies man's activities. Metapsychology has papered this all over, but if we can follow Wallerstein[21] in his prediction of the death of metapsychology, we may look forward to a rebirth of psychoanalysis. Then, the doors of perception will be cleared, and the student on opening Freud will experience what Keats described *On First Looking into Chapman's Homer:*

> Yet did I never breathe its pure serene
> Till I heard Chapman speak out loud and bold.
>
> Then felt I like some watcher of the skies
> When a new planet swims into his ken;

> Or like stout Cortez when with eagle eyes
> He stared at the Pacific—and with all his men
> Look'd at each other with a wild surmise—
> Silent, upon a peak in Darien.

POSTLUDE

In his *Essays of Three Decades,* Thomas Mann wrote of "Freud and the Future" as follows:

May we hope that this may be the fundamental temper of that more blithely objective and peaceful world which the science of the unconscious may be called to usher in?

Its mingling of the pioneer with the physicianly spirit justifies such a hope. Freud once called his theory of dreams "a bit of scientific new-found land won from superstition and mysticism." The word "won" expresses the colonizing spirit and significance of his work. "Where id was, shall be ego," he epigrammatically says. And he calls analysis a cultural labor comparable to the draining of the Zuider Zee. Almost in the end the traits of the venerable man merge into the lineaments of the grey-haired Faust, whose spirit urges him

> to shut the imperious sea from the shore away,
> Set narrower bounds to the broad water's waste.
> Then open I to many millions space
> Where they may live, not safe-secure, but free
> And active. And such a busy swarming I would see
> Standing amid free folk on a free soil.

The free folk are the people of a future freed from fear and hate, and ripe for peace.*

Today Mann's vision of the future seems roseate, perhaps utopian, as does mine, now, in retrospect. Mann foresaw a new beginning in terms of freedom from the shackles of ignorance. I foresaw a new beginning in terms of our freedom from the shackles of ignorance. I foresaw a new beginning in terms of our freedom from the carapace of metapsychology. Let no one doubt that the death of metapsychology is at hand; only see Gill and Holzman's treatise on the subject.[8] It is the most brilliant and devastating critique since Minucius Felix. It defies summary. It supersedes all previous work on metapsychology. No thoughtful student of human behavior can disperse with it. Only invincible ignorance can resist it.

*Translated by H. T. Lowe-Porter from *Essays of Three Decades*. New York: Knopf, 1947.

Yet it is not easy to live without metapsychology, as though a broken compass is better than none at all.

Schafer[19] offers us a lodestone. He says: "It is time to stop using the mixed physiochemical and biological language of Freudian metapsychology. This is the language of force, energy, cathexis, mechanism, and sublimation combined with the language of function, structure, drive, object, and adaptation." Yet learning a new language, i.e., "action language" is not easy and interferes with our clinical task; but then, so did metapsychology. How then can we deploy our new freedom? We lost the opportunity offered by Gitelson to establish ourselves as a separate discipline independent of psychiatry. Now we are subject to government guidelines established by antipsychoanalytic psychiatrists. We lost the opportunity offered by Pollock et al. to establish a university of psychoanalysis.

If we cling blindly to metapsychology, we may let still another opportunity for a rebirth of psychoanalysis slip by.

REFERENCES

1. Astley, M., & Royden, C. Psychoanalysis: The future. *Journal of the American Psychoanalytic Association,* 1974, *22,* 83–96.
2. Bernfeld, S. On psychoanalytic training. *Psychoanalytic Quarterly,* 1962, *31,* 453–482.
3. Burnham, D. Peer review and PSRO formations. *Journal of the American Psychoanaltyic Association,* 1974, *22,* 448–449.
4. Burnham, J. C. Psychoanalysis and American medicine 1894–1918: Medicine, science and culture. *Psychological Issues,* 1967, *20,* 250.
5. Charny, I. The new psychotherapies and encounters of the seventies: Progress or fads? *Reflections,* 1975, *10,* 1–16.
6. Colby, K. Psychotherapeutic processes. *Annual Review of Psychology,* 1964, *15,* 347–370.
7. Eissler, K. R. Irreverent remarks about the present and the future of psychoanalysis. *International Journal of Psychoanalysis,* 1969, *50,* 461–471.
8. Gill, M., & Holzman, P. S. Psychology versus metapsychology. *Psychological Issues,* 1967, *9,* 36.
9. Gitelson, M. On the identity crisis in American psychoanalysis. *Journal of the American Psychoanalytic Association,* 1964, *12,* 451–476.
10. Glover, E. The therapeutic effect of an inexact interpretation. *International Journal of Psychoanalysis,* 1931, *12,* 397–411.
11. HEW, Department of Confidentiality of Alcohol and Drug Abuse Patient Records. *Federal Register,* 1975, *40,* 27802–27821.
12. Home, J. J. The concept of mind. *International Journal of Psychoanalysis,* 1966, *47,* 43–49.

13. Loewald, H. W. Psychoanalysis as an art and the fantasy character of the psychoanalytic situation. *Journal of American Psychoanalytic Association,* 1975, *23,* 277–299.

14. National Council of Psychoanalytic Candidates and Clinical Associates. (Undated letter.) Statement to the Executive Council of the American Psychoanalytic Association.

15. Pollock, G., Burnham, D., Kafka, J., & Savage, C. *Training in psychoanalytic research.* Panel discussion—The Washington Psychoanalytic Society, February 8, 1973.

16. Rangell, L. Psychoanalysis and the process of change: An essay on the past, present and future. *International Journal of Psychoanalysis,* 1975, *53,* 87–99.

17. Rieff, P. *The triumph of the therapeutic uses of faith after Freud.* New York: Harper & Row, 1966.

18. Schafer, R. Internationalization: Process or fantasy? *The Psychoanalytic Study of the Child,* 1972, *27,* 411–438.

19. Schafer, R. *New language for psychoanalysis.* New Haven: Yale University Press, 1976.

20. Torrey, E. F. *The death of psychiatry.* Radnor, Pa.: Chilton, 1974.

21. Wallerstein, R. Psychoanalysis as a science—Its present status and future tasks. Presented at the scientific meeting of the San Francisco Psychoanalytic Institute and Society, September 1974.

3. CLIENT-CENTERED THERAPY

Experiential Psychotherapy: A Short Summary (and Some Long Predictions)

Eugene T. Gendlin, Ph.D.

A little more than a decade ago client-centered therapy was embattled in emphasizing that helpful change happens only through the client's own steps of concrete feeling. It was client-centered therapy which emphasized that an individual isn't changed by concepts, by being told what's wrong, by being argued with, or by agreeing with a correct explanation. The word "client" was intended to define psychotherapy along the lines of a legal rather than a medical model. The doctor can treat the patient even without the patient's knowing what the steps of treatment are, and certainly without the patient's being in charge of the treatment. The lawyer, on the contrary, must operate entirely as an adjunct to a process of which the client always remains in charge. It would be absurd for the lawyer to sue, or not to sue, in the client's name but on the lawyer's responsibility. The same idea was then doubly encoded into the name of the orientation by terming it "client-centered," which emphasizes what the very word "client" already emphasizes.

This article was previously published in *New Directions in Client-Centered Therapy,* Edited by J. T. Hart and T. M. Tomlinson (Houghton Mifflin, 1970). It appears here with the kind permission of the author and the publisher.

Nevertheless, this approach was very confusing at the time. It seemed to be based on a preference for democracy, as if the therapist were saying, "As an expert I know a lot, of course, but I will deny that I know anything since it is more in accord with my values that you make up your own mind and arrive at conclusions by yourself." This attitude seemed silly to many people, and although it was certainly never phrased that way, client-centered therapy struck many people as an inappropriate application of democratic ideals.

In my early writings I tried to articulate the underlying principles that were really at stake. It was not because we preferred the client's own process that we insisted on responding only to him and not with our own ideas and diagnoses. Rather, in order for something more than our own ideas to happen, the work *had* to be with the client's own process, his own felt meanings and steps of resolution. But wasn't this always known by all therapists of any view? Yes, in general it was known, but specifically, from moment to moment in the therapy interview, it was *not* known how to respond to an individual so that this process would occur in him. Thus psychoanalysis held that interpretation was the key element, and the patient was often sent home to do the experiential work alone as "homework." Similarly, the usefulness of transference was explained in general as the need for the patient to relive (not merely rethink) his problems, but the time in therapy was spent "interpreting the transference," to show him that he was repeating old patterns. It was a mystery how the patient ever came to change. "Working through" was called the most essential part of treatment, but no exact instructions for therapists were available for anything but interpretation. In general, of course, everyone agreed to the need for an emotional process if any real change was to occur; but in specific terms, there was systematic knowledge only of how the patient *was*. There were very sophisticated ways of talking about all different types of maladjustment—and even a few ways of talking about adjustment. However, there were no ways of talking about the steps therapists and patients should take during interviews to help the patient move toward greater health.

THE BASIC PRINCIPLE

Client-centered therapy emphasized "reflection of feeling," which was generally taken to mean repeating what the client says. Client-centered therapy was thus itself half in the old mold. Somehow, mysteriously, by saying what the client said, something new will occur, the client will soon say something new, and then we can respond to that. By featuring responsivity at every small, specific, momentary step, the client-centered method did in practice what could only later be formulated in theory. The therapist carried forward not only what the client verbally stated, but also the client's experiential process. One can *feel* a change or an impact when another person responds exactly to one's felt meaning. "Respond" can mean understand, but it can also mean "point to" or even "want to know about," as long as it is exactly this felt meaning you now have, in saying that which you just said. Elsewhere have I dealt with the theoretical explanation of why such responding "carries forward" the individual's experiential process so that he changes.[6] Here I want only to show that *this responsivity to specific felt meaning at each step engenders, carries forward, and changes the individual's ongoing experiential process.* This is the underlying principle that is implicit in client-centered therapy and its early quaint rules for therapist responding. Note that this principle is interactive, it is what T does that has experiential effects in C. It isn't a matter of things T says—often he says nothing new. It is a matter of T being another person, or another person responding exactly to what C feels—that is what changes C.

The interactive character of this responding is all the clearer when what T says verbally is already known to C, and what C says—at least initially—is also already known to C. To what is change due? Only to the fact that saying something to T is different than just saying it to oneself, and hearing oneself responded to by T is a new and different experience than just knowing about something in oneself.

However, the "feeling" to which T responds was thought to be an emotion, such as anger, or gladness, or fear. While such terms are often used, mostly "the feeling" isn't really an emotion; rather, it is similar to "feeling worried that such-and-such would happen, and wishing it wouldn't because . . . ." In other words, feelings are always already processes of interaction, of living in situations, of struggling but not quite succeeding in living situations.

Thus client-centered therapy has had to be reformulated. Feelings are really "felt meanings," implicitly complex experiencings of situations, of processes that are stopped or constricted. Responses by a therapist, point by point, moment by moment, to the individuals' concrete bodily felt meaning "carry forward" the process, i.e., allow present experiencing to move beyond hangups.

In retrospect we can now look at the old client-centered rules and understand their underlying reason, which was to engender and maximize this experiential process, staying with it, focusing on it, grappling with it, carrying it forward. Every meaning, every hunch, and every diagnostic possibility can be referred back to it. "Is that what you feel? Was that your point in saying what you said?" A response that is not directed at the client's experience is merely getting off the track, a digression, and interesting generalization perhaps, or a good categorization, but not helpful in the real work of therapy.

Experiential felt meanings are "preconceptual," not exactly this or that concept but an organic texture of bodily felt living. Therefore, verbalized ideas are "exactly it" only if there is a concretely felt effect in saying them. Only if what we say and think makes an experiential shift is anything changed.

As we look at the old client-centered rules and examine the reasoning behind them, we can now see many other ways to serve this purpose. In general, we have reversed most of the rules we used to obey—and still we serve the same basic principle in doing so. We are able to make this change because we can now formulate the principle: not to distract or digress from the experiential process of the client's concretely felt meanings, but to point to them, help him wrestle with them, carry them forward by our personal and exact responses to them or inquiries concerning them—that is the principle.

OLD RULES—NEW MEANINGS

We used to have the rule: *"Don't interpret."* (Most of our rules said "don't." In obeying these "don'ts" we implicitly acted in ways that we can formulate and define only now.) Why not interpret? Because it will get the client off his experiential track (we can now say). Interpretation will shift his attention away from his concrete mass of confused and preconceptual felt meaning and into generalizations, intellectualizations, and concepts that are interesting in themselves but apply to him only indirectly. Rather than getting him in touch with himself, interpretations encourage him to know himself through knowing a general idea that fits him. An interpretation tells him what category he is in, and thus he deals with general categories rather than with himself.

However, once we have formulated this experiential principle underlying the rule "don't interpret," we can interpret. We can use any and every promising diagnostic notion that strikes us as therapists. It won't be generalized but will point specifically to a short step that can be taken from where the client is. Diagnostic interpretive ideas *might* help the client discover an avenue of experiential "give," of movement in his directly felt referent, an "opening up" or "unfolding." I emphasize "might" because it may not. To use interpretive ideas in responding experientially means precisely to use them in reference to the concretely felt meaning the client now has or *can* now have. We know that a response was useless if what we said produced no felt shift, no "Aha," no experiential corroboration in him, no series of steps that he now goes through. It is important, in that case, to bring the client quickly back into his experiential flow, where he was a moment before. If the client says, "Yes, that *must* be true, ah, I guess," I might say something like, "That seems true to you, but it doesn't really get at this. You were just saying . . . ." I thereby bring him back to where I distracted him. In this way, moments later, I may say something based on totally different theories, or memories of other patients, or psychopathological categories. It would be foolish for me to try to decide then which was right, this response or the one before. Interpretations used experientially, used in reference to experiencing, aren't used as factual statements, and it doesn't work to ask which is right or if they are both wrong. Rather, an interpretation either opens up experiential corroboration so that the client goes through a whole series of steps ("and another thing is, and yes, that also fits with . . . and furthermore . . ."), or we gain nothing with it, however much the client may agree that it *must* be so.

If I have a certain diagnostic notion, I have in some way derived my impressions from the client's behavior. Usually I try to remember his behavior specifically and then retranslate my diagnostic notion into what it was in that which he said or did that gave me that impression; if I have forgotten, I wait until I sense it again. I find a very short step from what he is now saying that he might take in the direction of my notion. If I am right, a sequence of experiential steps will begin there; if I am wrong, I will have gotten him off the track only very minimally. It is like tapping along the wall looking for a hollow sound. The rightness of where you hear the sound is shown by where loose bricks can be pulled out, where a hidden stairway reveals itself, where one can *go* down that stairway . . . many steps. By the time we are down the stairs, it is a silly question whether indeed that first hollow sound was or wasn't hollow. However right we may be in general, we can't go down a stairway that we insist *must* be behind some brick that doesn't give.

All our old client-centered rules become more exact "do" rules: by applying the principle of responding to specific felt meanings, "don'ts" become "do's."

For example, consider: *"Don't answer the client's questions."* Why did we hold that rule? Because if we answer we don't find out why he asks, and we don't continue on his track; we don't explore that whole mass of felt concern that is only hinted at obliquely in his question. Nowadays, however, I first honestly answer just about any question—and then very soon thereafter I say, "Why do you ask?" Answering often gives me a chance to show what I think about the client, which usually is very close to his own experience but still in my words, with my way of seeing things.

We used to tell therapists: *"Don't express your own opinion."* Now if I am asked for it, I almost always do express my opinion, rather briefly, but showing exactly the sequence of thoughts I go through. Then I say, "But it isn't likely that would fit you, because you're a different person, and besides, you probably thought of that already anyway and it doesn't work." I thereby return him to his own track. (Of course he might have many feelings about the fact that I have the opinion I have, but we can explore these too, if he expresses or lets me sense these reactions in him. His reactions will again be his own process, and we will try to respond to each other honestly in reference to his process and his concretely felt steps.)

In effect, we previously urged therapists: *"If you're puzzled about something, don't mention it."* We wanted to pursue what the client was puzzled about, not the therapist's questions, associations, and ideas about it. We still avoid distracting questions, but now we think that expressing our puzzlement about his felt expressions will lead to clarification. The client will have the added solidity of having laid out the steps clearly; he may even discover something new; and he experiences the fact that his therapist really follows every step or else says that he doesn't. It makes that which often is at first a complex, compressed maze of autistic meaning into a clear interpersonal chain of meanings that are given interactive solidity, point by point.

We used to say: *"If you didn't respond rightly to something a minute ago, the moment has passed. Don't bring it up now. You have to wait till the client brings it up again."* All our effort was to maximize and not derail the client's process. Now I can say: "Just a minute, I am still mulling over what you said a while ago, and I . . . ." I can even say: "This reminds me, all week I've been thinking about what you said last week, and I said XYZ. That wasn't right, really you must have meant . . . ." The client should know that I think all week about what he says, if I do. The principle is to respond to his experiential process. Our rules achieved that indirectly by *not* doing other things; in this example, by not deciding when and what will be talked about.

We used to teach: *"If you have strong liking and appreciation for the client, don't mention it." "If there is something you think he ought to talk about, forget it." "If he is silent, you must remain silent too, indefinitely."*

A look at how we learned to work with silent schizophrenics shows how far we have come. There, too, we had to grasp the underlying principle. Then we learned how to use ourselves to serve that principle, to respond to a silent patient's experiential process.

You will notice that I have been asserting what the therapist ought to do as expressed in one principle: maximize the client's experiential process, using your own to do so. This principle can be stated specifically in terms of the three "conditions" that described it in more old-fashioned language. *Empathy* seemed to be restating the client's verbal content, although really it always meant pointing sensitively to his felt meaning to help him focus on it and carry it further. *Congruence* seemed to mean saying what we as therapists thought. Really it meant responding from our own ongoing experiential process, showing the steps of thought and feeling we go through, responding not stiltedly or artificially, but out of our felt being. As verbal content, congruence seems contradictory to empathy (in empathy we tell only about the client, while in congruence we tell about ourselves). As experiential processes, empathy and congruence are exactly the same thing, the direct expression of what we are now going through with the client in response to him. Finally, *unconditional positive regard* as content contradicts the other two conditions. "If you don't like him now, then you aren't unconditional, and if you say so, you're not empathic, but if you keep still about it, you're incongruent." However, unconditional regard really meant appreciating the client as a person regardless of not liking what he is up against in himself (responding to him in his always positive struggle against whatever he is trapped in). It includes our expressions of dismay and even anger, but always in the context of both of us knowing we are seeking to meet each other warmly and honestly as people, exactly at the point at which we each are.

Thus the therapist's erstwhile rather formal role has changed into the therapist using himself, using his own actual ongoing experiential process. This is the real meaning of the therapist's conditions, rather than their contradictory literal meanings.

The basic principle we see more clearly today is that the client-centered response, which I now call *the experiential response,* is the honest untrammeled pointing at the client's *felt meaning.*

The forecast will be expressed in eight predictions.

FORECASTS

Prediction One: *There will be a universal "experiential" method of psychotherapy using all useful procedures in reference to the individual's own process.*

As recently as 1910, medicine had a number of different orientations. There was no single approach until enough was known to comprise a recognized body of knowledge that everyone practiced and into which new discoveries could be integrated. Psychotherapy in the next decade will also move beyond the stage of different sects or orientations. With a wide variety of research, we are showing that successful change in psychotherapy occurs when the patient engages in an experiential process. Successful clients work in a way that can be recognized in the research studies of their verbalizations. We are now at the stage where we can tell from a few samples of tape-recorded interview behavior whether or not the ongoing therapy is of the sort that eventuates in success. This prognostication is undoubtedly possible in all orientations, regardless of what concepts or therapist styles are used.

Although research has not yet examined all the other orientations, the transition from specific rules (our client-centered "don'ts") to experiential ("do") rules is just as possible in every other orientation and is now occurring in many of them. In all orientations the experiential method is implicated—but not yet recognized—as making the difference between success and failure. For example, consider the Jungian "directed daydream" during which the analyst interprets the archetypal structures that arise. Jung was concerned with dreams as symbols of "transformation," since they function to produce an experiential shift the patient can feel, which then makes his subsequent imagery different and makes him different. However, too often the analyst and patient remain fascinated with the imagery as such, with its archetypal universal meaning, and there is no emphasis on the necessary zigzag between feeling and imagery to determine whether and when a felt difference has occurred. That fascination sometimes produces intriguing books about psychotic imagery without the patients improving and without attending to the way one can use imagery to produce the necessary experiential shifts. Similarly, Albert Ellis has renamed his "Rational Therapy." He now calls it "Rational–Emotive Therapy" because, again, not all the rational arguments and attacks on "irrationality" count; what counts is whether and when they produce an "emotional" shift. The emotional is the essential element.

Consider again psychoanalytic interpretation. Everything depends upon whether therapist and patient spend the hour arguing (or, for that matter agreeing) on their interpretative generalizations and analyses, which can be endless, or whether they swiftly rummage through the variety of possible interpretations to arrive at one that produces what Fenichel calls a "dynamic shift."[2] Psychoanalysis can become and is in fact becoming experiential, moving constantly back and forth between its rich interpretive repertoire and the patient's direct experiential process in shifts that alone can guide the analyst. Role playing, changed environments, body relaxation, and body armor interpretation all have the same potential to provide means for obtaining an experiential shift. They can be guided step by step in a direction the patient feels as freeing, or they can be used rather blindly, guided by a therapist's guesses, values, and diagnoses. Whether one begins inside (as we do) with words and then refers to bodily feeling by focusing one's attention on it, or begins outside, by role playing, bodily gestures, or deconditioning, in each approach one seeks to create a shift that will be felt and will lead to a difference in feeling and action.

This discussion seems to say only that the experiential method provides the essential focus, guide, and moment-by-moment aim. The procedures of the orientations all seem different from one another. What will become of the different procedures? I believe we will learn to use them all when they can be helpful. Already, most therapists no longer use only the procedure they were taught—client-centered therapists do not merely reflect feelings; many analysts discard the couch. In the past, a new and total method of therapy originated every time someone found one useful thing to do. It was customary then to insist that the new method could be universally applied, or to argue that it could do nothing at all. I am impressed with the power of Lindsley's Skinnerian method of "pinpointing the behavior" to be changed, counting it when it occurs, and changing what usually happens as a consequence. However, although I am very far from perfect or perfectly satisfied with myself, I find few nontrivial behaviors to count and change. Different methods work for different problems at different junctures. (I would not say for different people, because we don't know that as yet.) Clearly, a cat phobia or any other isolatable behavior that the patient feels is undesirable is more amenable to deconditioning than a general malaise with life in which no one or several specific behaviors stand out.

All these "methods" are really tools, procedures, or useful ideas one can try. The basic method that cuts across them all is that any procedure, word, or deed must be used in a continual zigzag that moves toward the experiential sense of the individual, and from it again with a new start if there has been a change, or toward a new attempt at something else if this one hasn't effected an experiential shift. Thus I think in the future we will all learn all the useful tools we can, and we will subordinate no human beings to these tools, but will attempt to accomplish the reverse.

Prediction Two: *Psychotherapy, or rather what we have learned from it, will be applied to the society as a whole, in social programs.*

The whole trend of current thinking has shifted to the view that human beings are interactional creatures and that the nature of psychological ills is inherently interactive. It isn't that something is wrong with an individual's psychic machinery; there are no loose screws inside. We don't know how and need not know how to replace worn out units inside him. He isn't a machine, a self-contained box, but rather an ongoing interaction process.

Thus our definitions of psychopathology have shifted from the Freudian typology of individuals to new concepts about an individual's interactions. The new concepts aren't well worked out yet. Psychotherapy has been understood to be an interaction of patient and therapist as two genuine people who must respond to each other from, and to, each other's experiential processes. Furthermore, much of psychopathology has been recognized as a matter of family relationships (Mowrer, Bowen, Bateson,

Jackson, Haley), and the patient can be thought of as "the individual in whom the family's illness manifests itself."[1] It has also been recognized that social classes (minorities, economic classes, etc.) have their peculiar sorts of psychopathology, i.e., that the community is the locus of psychopathology. This realization has led to an entirely new view of psychopathology, expressed for instance in the often cited fact that "these days we get very few classical hysterias. . . ." If psychopathology is a form of illness of the human psyche, why isn't hysteria around anymore? Has the mosquito that breeds the hysteria germ been wiped out?

Today we recognize that psychological ills are a function of culture, environment, community practices, and typical situations. As society changes, so do the ills of its members. A few wealthy persons might be able to afford individual psychotherapy, but today's social planners are rightly impatient with this mode of treatment because it is incapable of reaching the mass of people who need it. Instead, social programs are coming more and more to the fore. I include here poverty programs, Vista, the Job Corps, community development, community mental health programs, rural planning, and so on.

The troubled person is all one; he doesn't have one set of psychological and another set of situational problems, especially if he is poor. The majority of patients in state hospitals are not there as a result of psychological problems as such, but because they can't be sent home. The masses of troubled people need help with their total situations, not just with some separate psychological part. At any rate, we can't supply them with enough "doctors" to deal with just that part. Furthermore, while they remain in an institution they cannot get fully well, and when they go home to the original sickmaking situation which hasn't changed, they get sick again, and return. A few years ago, if we arrived at this realization, we would say: "To get this one patient well you'd have to change the whole system. . . ." We meant, sadly, that of course you couldn't. Now, we are setting about to do just that.

The current flood of social programs and community programs, however, will fail unless they include the sort of therapeutic conditions and individual process we have been discovering in successful cases of therapy. Social programs must build into themselves some intimate, close, sensitive human interaction. They must give each individual an individual. Of course, these can't be professionals, nor even subprofessionals. There will never be enough of them. Instead, we must devise ways in which ordinary people can provide the therapeutic processes for one another.

Prediction Three: *Hospital patterns of*
providing therapeutic interactions will be
devised.

In our research on psychotherapy with schizophrenics in Wisconsin
we soon saw that an individual physician or psychologist, going out to the
hospital twice a week, could carry very few patients. Even these few, being
schizophrenic, lower class, threatened, and unused to therapy and
emotional talk, refused to see therapists. We found a way to scare them
less, and we could work with very many more by providing therapists who
were "available" on the ward.[3] These therapists were willing to speak to
any patient who came, sometimes sitting quietly next to a silent patient,
sometimes over many months exchanging only glances and understood
signs of greeting with patients, or allowing fearful patients to approach a
relationship and back off again, without thereby wasting months of
therapist time. This "ward availability" pattern is also used by student
volunteers (a group known as VISA) at the University of Chicago when
they visit Chicago State Hospital. Among the gigantic regular hospital staff
with its variety of professionals, none are there just to be available for
patients to talk to. It would not cost much to provide some such personnel,
especially if they need not be college-trained people. I am therefore sure
that more and more we will leave behind the whole pattern of the office
situation in which two or three times weekly we are shut in with one
individual for 50 minutes. We will find patterns in which a few available
persons can offer intimate, sensitive, understanding relationships in many
contexts.

I spoke of the structure of hospitals, but "availables" can be in
schools, community organizations, and in any social program whatever.

Prediction Four: *Everyone will routinely learn*
in school the skills of experiential focusing,
listening, and relating.

We are close to the time when every school system will teach skills of
personal problem solving and helpful interacting to everyone, much as
today we teach every child calisthenics and personal hygiene. Of course,
some will go on to become very able at these skills (like athletes), but even
those not especially talented will be taught a minimal amount.

Our research recently has shown that successful clients engage in a type of interview behavior that shows experiential focusing right from the start (a finding that Kirtner was the first to discover in 1957).[8] Eventual failure clients, though they may stay in psychotherapy for years, can be recognized from the start as those who do not focus on their felt meanings. They don't seem to know how. We have not been teaching people to focus in this way because we thought only therapy could show them how; but it has become apparent that therapy doesn't even begin if they don't know how. Thus we must teach this skill. Since it is a matter of focusing attention on preconceptual felt meanings, it doesn't require complex concepts and can probably be taught quite early in school.

Eventually we will teach everyone the experiential zigzag of focusing on felt meaning and verbalizing from that. We will teach everyone how to listen to another person and attend to, ask about, attempt to help them articulate their felt meaning. We will teach certain very specific skills of interaction; for example, the sort of honest self-expression that creates a close relationship because it doesn't blame the other person—one in which an individual begins honest expressions by starting with his own shortcomings and upsetting weaknesses first. Finally, to complete this envisioned teaching program, we will teach everyone how to recognize when he is in over his depth with someone, when he is being weirdly twisted around and is unable to feel whole, sound, and in touch with himself in the relationship, i.e., how to recognize the time to bring a third person into the relationship for help. Thus professionals will be needed more than ever when this society-wide teaching comes about, since more people will need more of such "supervision" or "consultation," which will then be known by some routine term.

In this way we will give psychotherapy back to people, for it cannot indefinitely remain the property of a professional group, but must be translated into society-wide applicability.

The training developed thus far is not being given routinely to everyone. We are at the half-way point, namely, training nonprofessionals who function in professional roles.

For example, in trying to bring together the community population and the isolated hospital patients, I devised a plan (now being put into action by the State of Illinois) for the training of "interveners." The name comes not from the word "intervention," but from the need to fill the gap with "intervenes" between hospital and community. These people will be nonprofessionals, and if the desire of the Office of Manpower and Training is followed, they will be selected from the population presently called "unemployables." They will be trained to work with patients in the hospital and will spend two days a week there. They will also be trained as community workers and will spend three days a week in a given neighborhood—its schools, churches, jails, social agencies, community organizations, and local hospital wards. They will help reconnect the patient to the community, and they will be able to discuss this return with patients in advance and "try them out" in the community before they are quite recovered, so that they can recover. Interveners will be able to take patients back to the hospital where they need not become lost indefinitely—for the interveners can realistically promise to bring the patients out again. Like many other current modes of training nonprofessionals, this project will create a new and useful, quasi-professional, job-defined role. I also consider training hospital volunteers a vital step along this road. I have been training such volunteers not to pass out doughnuts and coffee or to play cards, but instead to interact helpfully and sensitively with patients.

Prediction Five: *There will be a new social institution–An individual relationship for everyone.*

Hospital patients are only one subgroup of the population that needs close relationships. This need exists in every other segment of our population as well. This is true of the women who now come as volunteers, but it is also true of the women who stay home with their children all day, every day. It is true of the students who are forever discussing the anomie of the large university and of the high school students who take so enthusiastically to any personally relevant activity whether group or individualized. It is the case with old people, and the same need is found in churches and factories. There is no reason to think of the hospitalized patients as the only group in need of intimate relationships. The picture makes much more sense if it is enlarged. Finally, the need for preventive measures to avoid the creation of psychotics and neurotics leads ot the same conclusion, namely, the teaching of, and the providing of, routinely available close relationships so that everyone can learn to experience and express himself openly and know how to receive others who do so.

Therefore we have at last taken the plunge: in one study we are instructing pairs of ordinary individuals. They draw numbers to determine who is *T* and who is *C*. The instructions* then ask the one person to choose a personal problem of real importance in his life. We say: We would rather you chose a really important problem even though you might not feel free to tell everything about it, than one you could say everything about but which isn't so important. In the next twenty minutes we will ask that you try to understand the problem better and to help yourself with it. We will ask the other person to help you in doing so. If you don't find what he does helpful, and you wish he would respond differently, please tell him.

After 20 minutes we give the Focusing Manual (and plan to give additional quite specific instructions) to such experimental-subject therapists and patients. Then we ask them to continue another 20 minutes. We are not ready to report findings from this research as yet, but we can already see a promising and safe method in this use of ordinary persons as therapists; we are developing research to measure the behaviors of both the "patients" and "therapists."

I consider the necessary skills quite numerous and specific and am in the process of devising specific words for specific procedures of focusing, listening, and interacting. I don't think that psychotherapy is merely a general and constant attitude, nor does it depend upon the sort of person you happen to be. A full-blown experiential vocabulary for instruction in

---

*The exact instructions were as follows: We want *C* to choose some personal problem that is bothering you now, but which you also feel you could explore profitably with your partner during this afternoon's session. We don't expect you to reveal everything about yourself, but it would be better for you to choose a real problem that's important to you and not say everything about it, than to choose an unimportant problem that you feel very comfortable saying everything about.

We want *T* to respond as you wish to your partner, keeping in mind that the purpose of your discussion is to try to help him with the problem he chooses to explore with you.

Keep on what's crucial to *C;* if you (to *T*) feel you're off on a tangent that isn't interesting to you, or if your partner is asking you questions and you would rather talk at that moment about another part of the problem, say that. Talk about what's important to you, what you feel at any moment is getting to the heart of your problem. If you find that the problem you have chosen to talk about is part of a bigger problem, then follow that where it takes you. The role we are setting up for you is not one in which you are both to hold in your real feelings until later; say what you are feeling now. If you are feeling something and wonder whether it will fit in with your role here to say it, go ahead and say it. This means anything about yourself, your partner, or your role here. You might want to say to your partner, "I don't like the way you are directing the questions" or "What is all this nonsense anyway?" We're not prescribing here the direction your discussion should take—you'll probably want to say different things—but we are encouraging you to say whatever feels important for you to say at any moment.

this skill is now being devised and will undoubtedly develop further as many ordinary people engage in psychotherapy with each other.

The day is fast waning when one must plead "sick" to get a sensitive and impartial listener and willing interactor. Consider how foolish it has really been that we have given this attention only to people who were under sufficient pressure to plead "sick" and incapable of helping themselves (which in our society is judged to be a very bad thing). In fact, there is abundant evidence that everyone needs someone, that humans are interaction processes in their very nature.

We know, for example, from the Manhattan study, that up to 80 percent of the people in our society show measurable psychological disturbances of the sort requiring psychotherapy. Does this finding mean everyone is sick? Or does it mean that this state is the human condition, and that our society lacks institutions that offer the sort of interhuman process needed by people? I believe it shows the latter. In the future the individual engaging in the sort of experiential process defined here won't be called a "patient" or a "client," but a person. There will be social patterns such that everyone will routinely have some other individual with whom he is the therapist and one with whom he is the patient. For example, Goodman's pattern of older high school students working with younger boys can easily be made routine in all school systems. It can become a "social institution," that is, a regular social pattern, offered routinely. Many other patterns are conceivable. To get and keep such a relationship, one would only have to want it.

Prediction Six: *A second new social institution—Everyone will belong to a group.*

For a long time we haven't had anything on the group level that corresponds even to "friendship." To be in a group, one has to plead sick (therapy) or one has to have (or pretend to have) an interest in photography, adult education, or politics. Often groups want to continue to meet, though their reason for being is over (after the election, for example) and no socially understood pattern exists for continuing a group simply because there is a human need to belong to a group; but such a pattern is developing. We already have psychotherapy groups, T groups, development groups, sensitivity groups, church groups, political groups, encounter groups, marathon groups, management skills groups, brainstorming groups, all quite similar. Soon it will become understood that everyone needs to be in a group.

While these groups have different names, and in some cases deal with very different contents (e.g., religious doubts in a church group, politics in a Students for a Democratic Society group), a certain vital group process occurs in all of them: the newcomer finds himself listened to, responded to; he discovers that he makes sense, can articulate feelings and reach out to others; he finds he is accepted, understood, appreciated, responded to closely. He discovers that there is room for him as a person and not just as a maker of canned, appropriate statements or as a player of prescribed roles. His previously almost dumb and silent self becomes intensely alive; being in this group is intense and it is growth producing. He "breaks through," finds himself not just as a player of roles, but also speaks from himself as an experiencing, feeling, human being. He finds he can work with both roles and felt aliveness. His life outside the group naturally profits enormously from this breakthrough as he becomes less constricted and roll-defined in other situations and experiences them more in terms of an interplay between his real feelings and the prescribed words and roles. Typically, this is only the first stage of development in what then often becomes a less desirable group for him.

For a time after his breakthrough, he helps others to "break through," but does not really need to do this anymore for himself. During this period he attends partly because it is rewarding to aid others in the breaking-through process, but partly because even after breaking through one needs a group. However, the constantly new members keep such a mixed group at the breakthrough stage, and the veteran members all reluctantly drop out after getting tired of trying to pretend that they are always breaking through all over again. (This phenomena can also be observed in political and other sorts of groups, since the basic experiential process is always the same.)

In the future we will provide people with a quiet closed group in which they can move in depth, tell how things are, share life, so to speak, perhaps say little at times, perhaps do major therapeutic work when needed, but always with the sense of belonging, the anchoring which such a group provides. Then, in addition, those who want to can serve a vital function in the other type of group that is open to newcomers, where a few veterans who know how to relate intimately can swiftly bring a whole group of new people to the breakthrough point.

Such groups—and such individual relationships—will focus on the experiential process. In most settings an individual must be a certain way to be appropriate; he must talk about a certain topic, or he must behave in a certain way, share certain attitudes, speak about himself in a certain way.

Friendship, marriage, work, church—these settings define certain narrow bands of behavior as appropriate, and nothing else will do. In the groups I think are coming, anything someone does will be appropriate if it "means something to him," i.e., has an experiential reference for him.

Of course, discussions in such groups will go beyond abstractions. One will more often ask, "Why do you hold that view?" than, "Is this view tenable? What general assumptions is it based on?" The *experiential* reasons and bases of the concern may turn out to be very different, not relevant except personally, and very far from what one might have expected on abstract grounds alone. Anyone with any views might be welcomed into such a group, and people would thereby learn what sort of personal processes go into other people's having the views they do (which, currently, we can't imagine).

Prediction Seven: *Modes of human thinking and discussion will become much more widely creative and much more specific compared to current abstractionism in thought and science.*

Before the nineteenth century people held that the order of nature had an underlying rational mathematical system, and that man, too, was subject to it (Vico, Spinoza). The nineteenth century discovered a whole raft of different irrational aspects in man, and rationalism was pushed back to a few last-ditch areas. Some held that by comparing different societies, both ancient and primitive, one would arrive at a lowest common denominator of human nature that would be lawful (Comte). Some held that only the laws of economics and economic change were amenable to rational scientific analysis and could then indirectly explain everything else (Marx). Some held that the laws of psychology would provide a rational scheme, which would then explain everything else (Freud). In the twentieth century none of these attempts at a reductive science of man have been shown to work.

All rational schemes are too thin and abstract, too simple and artificial to represent human processes. We are more complicated than our schemes. We make schemes—and a lot else besides! Schemes are tools, as are words, therapeutic procedures, and social roles. The tool doesn't become the thing; one must still look at the thing one works on to guide the tool.

The experiential method is based on philosophy:[4, 5] Philosophy examines the basic types of concepts that are current, the ways of slicing up what we perceive and observe. Current philosophy, coming from the history of thought I just described, centers on the fact that schemes, models, systems, are not enough. The human activities of living, acting, and speaking in human situations are the bigger context within which any scheme, system, model, or concept must be evaluated.

How can we evaluate the explicit, the precise, the logically formed against the "bigger context" that is implicit, preconceptual, lived and acted, but not logically formed in just one way?

In psychotherapy we do this by checking every step of verbalization (the client's and the therapist's) against the client's felt sense, his experiential, bodily felt meaning. Thus we move back and forth between explicit, precise verbalizations and preconceptual, imprecise, yet governing experiencing. In society we will seek to establish this zigzag method between the explicit social role expectations and the individual's experiential feel of his self. Current thinking is more and more turning to this recognition that the formed, the precise, the defined, must be held against what is experiential and implicit because, while less precise, it is lived, actual, existential activity.

From linguistic analysis in Oxford to mysticism in San Francisco, the underlying theme is to refuse to deduce from the model, from the formed, but instead to use the formed in the context of the wider process of living that always transcends this or that form.

Of course, without precision and form we can say nothing and do little. Without form the felt and lived would be nonsensical. Experiencing is by no means lacking in form. On the contrary, it is more formed, more organized than any one scheme. Implicitly it contains history and evolution, many organic and conceptual distinctions and perceptions. Physical, animal, cultural, and individual organizations are always implicit in any living and acting. Anything actual is much *more* organized than any one system or model can tell. Therefore, when one holds precise verbalizations against the bigger context of acting and experiencing, one holds them not against something unorganized, but something organized in so many interrelated ways as to defy being represented.

The experiential method moves beyond representation. No set of words, concepts, or models can be equal to what is being experienced, lived, or done in a situation. Instead, sets of words must be seen within living and acting.

In going back and forth between felt experiencing and precise words or roles we don't discard words or social roles. We only make it possible to use these creatively, to be always more concerned with our *use* of them than with the words themselves. We are more concerned with what we are doing with them, what someone is trying to do with them, than with what can be deduced.

We will take our next set of words and our next action, not directly from what follows from some words or socially predefined roles, but from our own implicitly meaningful experiencing, which we always have as we say or do anything.

This approach is another way of talking about creativity, which has long been said to depend upon an individual who does not deduce from the given way things are set up. Only by using himself, his own live felt sense of being in a particular situation, can he sense what is wrong and devise new ways, from which new possibilities will follow that weren't visible in the way things first appeared.

This means that what we use is not only what the words (the role, the command) say, but what was supposed to be done with them, what was being attempted in using them in the context in which they were used. It means that words aren't being viewed for what they represent (what they are a picture of), but as tools in a wider process of acting and living in situations. This wider process is experienced by an individual only in a bodily, active, live felt sense. To use symbols not only in themselves, but also in whatever role they have in the wider context of living is to use them nonrepresentationally. It adds to their precise meaning the possibilities of creative change, of new definitions and moves.

The new definitions and new moves we want aren't just any new ones. We don't want them just because they are new. (An endless number of possible new nonsense could be devised.) What we want are new definitions and new moves that will follow from, and deal with, the situations we are in and—since situations are defined by what we seek to do in them—our whole experiential sense of living and acting.

In this wider "nonrepresentational" method of using words and roles we ask not what a given set of words and roles is, but what one does with it.

Actually, what one does or tries to do, what an individual is getting at or pointing out, is always much more specific than any of the verbalizations and schemes we have. Any human phenomenon worth studying is much more specific than the old line theories can as yet specifically locate, let alone represent. Thus, the method moves beyond theories and procedures as such and concentrates on how they are used. In so concentrating we encourage ourselves (and others) to discriminate and work not only on the specific facet of observation we wish to attend to, but also on creating the new terms, procedures, and definitions necessary to enable others to locate the same facet.

In science this philosophy puts the emphasis on the *creation* of variables. Not that we would forego our good scientific methods of verification. We will continue to use the scientific ways of publicly checking anything we think is true. However, we need to point out that our scientific method is highly developed only in the matter of *checking* conclusions and hypotheses. Where does one get hypotheses? If you think some thing A and some other thing B are connected, we have excellent methods of finding out if you're right or not. We have excellent methods of checking this in a way that doesn't depend on your own impressions. We have methods for making it possible for others to check this, to "replicate" publicly what you found. However, perhaps A and B are not the most interesting or important things to study. Perhaps R and S are also connected, and if we knew this we would be able to see and do many useful things; but no one has isolated R and S, no one has fashioned concepts for them, no one notices them as such, no one has discriminated something like R and S. We have no scientific method for first coming up with interesting items like that, interesting "variables" for scientific research. Today this process is still unscientific. Every scientist is expected somehow to come up with variables, perhaps in his sleep, in the shower, or as a result of whatever naturalistic observations he conducts.

Prediction Eight: *There will come about a science of man that includes the man who is the scientist and that defines specific and significant aspects of interactive living.*

I have already said that, in my opinion, the chief advance needed in the science of man is the discrimination and definition of much more specific variables than the general and ambiguous ones we use today.

Furthermore, as with all symbols, scientific terms must be seen in terms of what they do, not merely what they say. Scientific terms must come to be "operational," that is, they must be tied to specific procedures, and we must study the results of these procedures. If we place this model of operational science into the context of life, we can see that current science is a mere stick figure of what we need. We want to specify the very specific meaningful "operations" we engage in with other people, and we want to specify the results that are obtained. Client-oriented research has provided some of the first meaningful research of this sort: it defines certain ways of approaching and acting toward someone, and it defines the sort of process that then occurs in him. Of course, we seek much greater specificity—we seek a whole vocabulary of specific terms with which to study how we are and what we do with each other.

I am predicting a science not of individual differences, but of different specific manners of approaching and relating with each other. To dramatize this point, let me cite here our discovery that, for psychotherapy purposes, schizophrenic people differ from neurotics but are very much the same as normal people! That is, normal people require some of the same specific approach behaviors by anyone who wants to relate intimately with them. In our Wisconsin Research[9] we learned to work with others who did not seek to relate closely with us and who had no real idea, in advance, of what such relating would be. They seemed not to know that one could articulate and communicate one's feelings about living in the typical way we are familiar with from psychotherapy. In a very different context, we see now that the same methods are needed with the parents of children in play therapy whenever the parents do not seek psychotherapy for themselves. In short, identified here is a category of therapist behavior, and a category of client behavior, both cutting right across the usual categories of individual psychopathology. Of course, much more specific subcategories are forthcoming.

The totally nonexpressive silent "schizophrenic" patient who sits immobile for hours and hours and is always found in the same chair in the hospital day room belongs in a different category for therapist behavior than the "schizophrenic" who, while always silent, is enormously expressive, reactive, and sensitive, and presents a different expressive behavior every moment. The therapist must use his experiencing differently with each. Again, this distinction cuts across the usual psychopathology, and again different ways of approaching a person must be specified for each.

This is the age in which we are becoming scientifically aware of ourselves. Just as 300 years ago we began to develop a vocabulary of nature, we will now develop a vocabulary of man's experience. As we develop this science of experience facilitation, we will thereby make the teaching of it in school much more practical and effective.

REFERENCES

1. Bowen, M. Family participation in schizophrenia. In R. D. Jackson (Ed.), *The etiology of schizophrenia*. New York: Basic Books, 1960.
2. Fenichel, O. *The Psychoanalytic Theory of Neurosis,* New York: W. W. Norton & Co., 1945.
3. Gendlin, E. T. Initiating psychotherapy with "unmotivated" patients. *Psychiatric Quarterly,* 1961, *1*, 34.
4. Gendlin, E. T. *Experiencing and the creation of meaning.* New York: Free Press, 1962.
5. Gendlin, E. T. Expressive meanings. In J. M. Edic (Ed.), *Invitation to phenomenology.* Chicago: Quadrangle Books, 1965.
6. Gendlin, E. T. In J. T. Hart & T. M. Tomlinson (Eds.), *New directions in client-centered therapy.* Boston: Houghton Mifflin, 1970.
7. Gendlin, E. T., Kelly, J. J., Raulinaitis, V. B., & Spaner, F. E. Volunteers as a major asset in the treatment program. *Mental Hygiene,* 1966, *50,* 421–427.
8. Kirtner, W. & Cartwright, D. Success and failure in client-centered therapy as a function of initial in-therapy behavior. *Journal of Consulting Psychology,* 1958, 22, 329–333.
9. Rogers, C. R. (Ed.) *The therapeutic relationship and its impact.* Madison, Wisc.: University of Wisconsin Press, 1967.

4. EXISTENTIAL PSYCHOTHERAPY

Existential Factors in (Group) Psychotherapy

Irvin D. Yalom, M.D.

The face of group therapy has changed dramatically over the past two decades. Many factors have participated in this evolution: the growing importance of interpersonal theory; the impact of the sensitivity training movement on psychotherapy; and the burgeoning of such new treatment approaches as Transactional Analysis, Gestalt Therapy, and Humanistic Psychology.

Underlying much of this change and likely to continue to exert considerable influence is a doctrine or set of principles loosely referred to as the "existential approach." It is a curious but commonplace phenomenon that many therapists find themselves ascribing to existential tenets without being certain of how or when they arrived at these beliefs. This has been true for me, and in this essay I shall discuss the role and meaning of existential factors in therapy by using myself as an illustrative example and tracing the development of existential trends in my work.

Several years ago, in an effort to understand the mechanisms of change in group therapy, my students and I studied a series of group patients who had had a highly successful course of therapy. We interviewed them informally about their group experience, inquired about significant incidents and factors in their therapy, and then, to make the entire procedure properly and officially "scientific," we asked each patient to do a 60-item Q-sort. This test consisted of a forced normal distribution sort of 60 statements about the mechanism of group therapy into several categories, each labeled according to its relevance to the change process—the labels ranged from "most helpful to me" to "least helpful to me."

How did we choose which mechanisms of change should be represented in this Q-sort? We drew on our own clinical experience, surveyed the literature of psychotherapy, and consulted with a number of highly experienced clinicians. All of these inquiries resulted in 11 primary clusters of change (or "curative factors"), e.g., Group Cohesiveness, Catharsis, Interpersonal Learning, Genetic Insight, Universality, Identification, Recapitulation and Re-evaluation of the Primary Family Experience, etc.

EXISTENTIAL FACTORS

Next we composed 5 statements describing each of the 11 factors. This done, we felt the instrument looked neat and precise but somehow incomplete. Something was missing. Certain sentiments expressed by patients and therapists had not been represented and, therefore, dutifully but with little conviction we included one other factor consisting of these five statements:

1. Recognizing that life is at times unfair and unjust.
2. Recognizing that ultimately there is no escape from some of life's pain and from death.
3. Recognizing that no matter how close I get to other people, I still face life alone.
4. Facing the basic issues of my life and death, and thus living my life more honestly and being less caught up in trivialities.
5. Learning that I must take ultimate responsibility for the way I live my life no matter how much guidance and support I get from others.

What to label this cluster? We finally settled, with much hesitation, on "Existential Factors." I didn't care for the word "existential"—it had become embedded in its own mystique; it meant something to everyone yet nothing precise to anyone. The term reminded me of an old academic patriarch, the Professor Emeritus who, bedecked in resplendent crimson academic gown, is wheeled in to bestow dignity to any occasion.

The patients responded otherwise! Despite my lack of conviction, the existential items struck some very responsive chords in the patients, and many cited some of these five statements as having been crucially important to them. In fact, the entire category of Existential Factors (the mean score of the five items) was ranked highly by the patients, ahead of such highly valued modes of change as Universality, Recapitulation of the Primary Family Experience, Identification, and Instillation of Hope. One of the items—"Learning that I must take ultimate responsibility for the way I live my life no matter how much guidance and support I get from others"—was very highly ranked by the patients, and its mean score ranked it fifth of the entire 60 items.

I used these 12 curative factors as a central organizing focus for a book that I wrote on the theory and practice of group therapy. I devoted sections or entire chapters to 11 of these 12 factors, but frankly I didn't know what to do with the 12th category, Existential Factors. My book was to be a clinical text grounded in empirical research, but there is no research about such "soft" concerns as responsibility, purpose in life, resoluteness, facing basic issues of life. I must have assumed that since the area was not one easily measurable by our usual truth-assaying instruments, it therefore contained little truth or importance. My final answer was to bypass the matter by presenting the findings in a cumbersome table but to ignore them in the text. Thus I dismissed the issue, but with a promissory note to my conscience to return to it some day.

The promissory note came due in 1974 when I undertook to revise this book on group therapy. I found myself struggling again with the concept of existential factors—there is no "hard" data and the existential language is very nebulous and often sanctimonious. Nevertheless, the patients, and I, too, had a deep conviction that these were crucially important factors in therapy.

What is true for myself and for the therapists in my study is the experience of most therapists: covertly, often unbeknownst to ourselves, we are existentially oriented. We often use psychoanalytically derived techniques, but inwardly we eschew or, at best, disregard much fundamental mechanistic analytic theory.

THE HELMHOLTZ SCHOOL

Psychoanalytic theory is, quite explicitly, based on a specific view of the nature of man. When Freud was 75 years old, he was asked who had been the most important influence upon him. Without hesitation he responded Brücke. Brücke, who had been Freud's physiology mentor in medical school and during his brief career as a researcher in Neurophysiology, was one of the original architects and founders of the Helmholtz School, an ideological school that dominated Western European medical and basic research in the latter part of the nineteenth century. The basic Helmholtzian doctrine was, simply stated:

> No other forces than the common physical–chemical ones are active within the organism; that, in those cases which cannot at the time be explained by these forces one has either to find the specific way or form of their action by means of the physical–mathematical method, or to assume new forces equal in dignity to the chemical–physical forces inherent in matter, reducible to the force of attraction and repulsion.

Freud never swerved from his allegiance to this postulate and to its implications about man's nature; many of his more cumbersome, more relentless formulations (for example, the dual instinct theory, the theory of libidinal energy conservation and transformation) were the result of his unceasing attempts to fit man and man's behavior to Helmholtzian rules. These doctrines insist that man is precisely the sum of his parts; they are deterministic, antivitalistic, and materialistic in that they attempt to explain the higher by the lower. The Helmholtzian manifesto constitutes a negative definition of the existential approach to man. If you feel restricted by its definition of you and you feel that there's something missing, that the doctrine has no place for some of the central features that make us human—purpose, responsibility, sentience, values, courage, will—then to that degree you are an existentialist.

EXISTENTIAL THOUGHT AND THERAPY

Other reasons exist for paying serious attention to the existential position in therapy. If one is interested in staying abreast of the field of psychotherapy, in making sense of the disparate new developments in technique and theory, then there is no better personal preparation than a thorough grounding in the origins, meaning, and meter of existential thought. The major psychotherapeutic revisionists, such figures as Horney, Adler, Fromm, Goldstein, Fromm-Reichman, Maslow, Rogers, May, and Perls, are all grounded squarely in an existential tradition.

The philosophic roots of modern existential thought and therapy are grounded in two traditions—one is substantive and the other methodological. It is well known that philosophers have dwelled upon the substantive issues of existence since the beginnings of written thought. Though a host of thinkers from Socrates onward examined basic existential themes, perhaps the most important modern philosopher was Soren Kierkegaard, who, in his penetrating discussions of the individual, of choice, of dread, and of paradox, explicated the fundamental problems for a philosophy of existence that were to be pursued by the major existentialists who have followed him: Nietsche, Heidegger, Ortega-y-Gasset, Jaspers, Buber, and Sartre.

However, it was when this substantive tradition merged with a new methodological one that the movement began to bear directly upon the field of psychotherapy. The methodological tradition, phenomenology, began with a deep questioning of Cartesian duality—the sundering of the world into consciousness and matter. The subject–object dichotomy which ruled that the self be kept out of its world as it investigated the world has made possible the advancement of modern scientific method but, so argues the phenomenological thesis, this dichotomy has been a disaster for the study and understanding of man as man. The leading architect of the phenomenological movement, Edward Husserl—who, incidentally, was a contemporary of Freud in Vienna and a student, as was Freud, of the philosopher Franz Brentano—rejected the subject–object split; he did not seek to discover anything of the natural world. Instead he made his realm of study the essence of phenomena as they were experienced by consciousness. Sartre put it most clearly with his maxim "Existence precedes Essence," asserting that nothing exists except insofar as we create it by our choices. The study of man, then, is the study of consciousness. Consciousness is always intentional, i.e., it is always consciousness *of* something, thus rendering object and subject inseparable. Understanding from a phenomenological sense can only take place from within, by bracketing the natural world and attending instead to our own experience.

Husserl's student, Heidegger, applied the phenomenological method to the oldest of questions—the nature of being—and developed with exquisite profundity (and obscurity) the view of man as Dasein: the being that is there by virtue of his constitution of the world, the being that is simultaneously a constituted and constituting ego. Heidegger outlined many of the tenets that reappear so often in modern psychotherapeutic tracts. For example, Heidegger describes "inauthenticity" as the way we ordinarily exist. By inauthenticity he means a way of life in which we lose ourselves in "Das Mann," in chatter, in the diversions of life. Inauthenticity is the avoidance of responsibility (i.e., the knowledge that we have constituted our world). Heidegger writes of the call of the inner voice harkening one back to authentic existence, of the presence of basic ontological *Angst* as our guide to authenticity, of our anxious awareness of our thrownness, our contingency, our constitution of the world (and, therefore, the possibility of no further possibility, of death and nothingness). He describes authentic being as not avoiding *Angst* but of taking ontological anxiety into oneself and living resolutely, of accepting our tragic condition, of living "with knowledge of" and "in spite of."

THE "THIRD FORCE"

Traditional Heideggerian existential thought and its application to psychotherapy has always been more acceptable, more resonant to the European therapeutic community than to the American one. The European philosophical tradition, the geographic and ethnic confinement, the greater familiarity with limits, war, death, and uncertain existence all favored the spread of the Heideggerian influence. The American *Zeitgeist* of expansiveness, optimism, limitless horizons, and pragmatism embraced instead the Scientific Positivism proferred by a mechanistic Freudian metaphysics or a hyperrational, empirical behaviorism.

Until recently! A major development in psychotherapy in the past two decades has been the emergence of what has come to be known as the "third force" in American psychology (third after Analysis and Behaviorism). The movement, commonly known as Humanistic Psychology, seems far flung; the troops hie from so many different ideological colonies and are so often bedecked in exotic garb that, to many, the entire discipline seems to have a generous, big tent, all inclusive carnival quality. Yet the movement is more than that; it has a professional organization, a viable journal, and an annual convention that in 1974 attracted 2000 professionals. Though members individually speak such strange languages as Gestalt, Sufi, Psychosynthesis, Horneyian, Adlerian, Encounter Groupese, they nevertheless can all converse in an existential Esperanto.

An importation and an Americanization of existential thought and therapeutic procedure has occurred. The frame is European but the accent is unmistakably New World-ish. The European focus is on the tragic dimensions of existence, on limits, on facing and taking into oneself the anxiety of uncertainty and nonbeing. The humanistic psychologists, on the other hand, speak less of limits and contingency than of development of potential, less of acceptance than of awareness, less of anxiety than of peak experiences and oceanic oneness, less of life meaning than self-realization, less of apartness and basic isolation than of I–thou and encounter.

Of course, when one has a basic doctrine with a number of postulates and the accent of each postulate is systematically altered in a specific direction, then there is significant risk of mutation of the original doctrine. To some extent this change has occurred and some humanistic psychologists have lost touch with their existential roots. The existential approach in therapy is not a set of technical procedures but basically an attitude toward man, his concerns, and his change; despite this nontechnical emphasis, there has been an overconcern, a reverence of technique to the extent that there has been an erosion of the theoretic foundation upon which all technique must rest.

What I shall attempt to do in the remainder of this presentation is to heap some flesh upon these abstract formulations by describing some clinical material from some of my therapy groups.

I feel on firmer ground by avoiding the accented, derivative phenomena and working with more traditional concepts; consequently, I have organized this material around a few basic existential concerns—responsibility, choice, will, meaning or purpose, the role of extreme experience, and, finally, encounter and mutuality.

RESPONSIBILITY

Responsibility has many meanings: legal, moral, ethical. I shall use it in Heidegger's sense, in which one is responsible for by "being the basis of," by being the cause, author, or even the occasion of something. In the strictest sense, as in Sartre's view, for example, one is responsible for his life, his future, his past, and for the whole world, since he is the author of his world.

A fundamental concept in group therapy, as I see it, is that the group is a social microcosm for each of the members. Often in my formulations I've drawn on this phenomenon for its interpersonal implications in that each member recapitulates, in the here-and-now of the group, his maladaptive modes of interpersonal interaction. His behavior and the other member's perception of and relation to his behavior is thus anhistoric, noninferential, and highly immediate. The early sequence (highly schematized) in the group therapeutic process is as follows: each patient (through feedback and self-observation) obtains a view of what his behavior is; next he learns of the impact of his behavior on others' feelings, then of the impact on others' evaluation of him, and then of the impact of these developments upon his own self-regard. Once this sequence is operational and apparent to the patient, the group leader has sufficient leverage to begin the crunch of therapeutic change by confronting him with the question, "Are you satisfied with this?"

I would suggest that we broaden the concept of microcosm to encompass more than interpersonal relations, to encompass as well the individual's posture toward his basic responsibility. I suggest nothing more than that we make explicit what is implicit in the dynamic process: when patients who are distressed by their relationship to the world about them (and I refer to their complete world or, in May's terminology,[1] their *Umwelt* [natural world], *Mitwelt* [interpersonal world] and *Eigenwelt* [personal world]) are brought to the point of understanding, in a deeply meaningful way, that they are totally responsible for this world, then and only then does it begin to be possible for them to will their change.

One of the most fascinating aspects of group therapy is that everyone is born again, born together, in the group. Each member starts off on an equal footing. Each, in view of the others (and, if the therapist does his job, in view of himself), gradually scoops out and shapes his own life space in the group. Each is responsible for this space and for the sequence of events which will occur to him in the group. Once the patient truly appreciates this responsibility, then it follows that he must accept, too, that there is no hope for change unless he changes. Others will not change him for him, change will not occur to him, the therapist will not infuse him with change. He is responsible for his past and present in the group (as well as in life) and he is similarly and totally responsible for his future.

Resistance never fails to occur, often in cunning guise: "This group is sick, how can I trust or value their opinion?" "I don't care about the people in this group—that's not why I sought therapy, all I want is to shake this depression." Never be tempted to accept this! Of course each group is unique; nevertheless, the behavior of the members in the group is representative of their general behavior and way of being in the world.

ILLUSTRATIONS FROM GROUP PROCESS

I recall vividly two group therapy patients, whom I shall call Jan and Bill, whose therapy rotated almost entirely around the axis of responsibility. Their course of treatment was enormously complex; during their stay in the group they had a sexual affair which complicated life for themselves and for the rest of the group. Nevertheless they managed to stay in the group and to work through important implications of their roles of relating to one another. To clarify the material at hand I shall select certain important aspects of this relationship and shall, of course, have to omit other features of their therapy, including their relationships with other members of the group.

Bill was a dashing young man who sought therapy because of chronic anxiety, episodic depressions and a nagging, distant feeling of guilt and unworthiness. Life felt empty and meaningless: his job seemed sterile and static, he had no male friends and related for the most part to women in a Don Juan pattern. Though he had been living with one woman for a few months, he felt, for reasons he could not explain, no commitment to her and regarded the relationship as highly tenuous. He had been in the therapy group for approximately eight months. It so happened that three female members had simultaneously completed therapy and a small nucleus—Bill and three other men—had been meeting for several sessions awaiting the addition of new members. A strong, close, virile Saturday-night, male-bonded subculture was established with all members sharing deeply and relating deeply. At this point two young women were added to the group and never have I seen a well-established culture disintegrate so quickly. The Saturday-night comaraderie was swept away by a wave of male dominance behavior and Bill, boldly and shamelessly, jettisoned his relationship with the other men and rode the crest of that wave by competing not for one but for both of the women.

Jan, a young divorcée, sought therapy for depression, self-hatred, infanticidal obsession, and loneliness, punctuated by frequent evanescent sexual liaisons. She could not say no to an attractive man. Men paid brief house calls and used her sexually but would not spend time with her in the daylight. Because of poor judgment she was in deep financial trouble and was flirting with the idea of prostitution. If others used her, why not cash in on them?

Bill's behavior changed radically with the entrance of the women. He lost sight of his primary task in the group and gave himself up to secondary gratification. For example, he no longer welcomed the therapist's interventions of interpretations; quite the contrary, he resented them for he felt they made him look weak or needy in the eyes of the women.

As time went by, despite the therapist's and other members' admonitions, Bill and Jan moved ever closer to a sexual liaison. Neither could seriously imagine foregoing the opportunity. For Bill, the sexual chase supplied meaning or, better, stuffing for his life. Whenever he had been between chases he had had a deep and terrifying sense of emptiness and purposelessness; consequently he did not permit the chase to languish very long. Jan never even considered the possibility of a choice in the matter; àfter all, she knew she could never say no. Besides, it was, to both Jan and Bill, a unique opportunity—an attractive young man, a beautiful helpless woman (not to mention such fringe attractions as the opportunity for besting the group and defeating the therapists).

I was reminded at the time of an episode Viktor Frankl, the existential analyst, once told me of involving a patient who consulted him on the eve of his marriage. He had had a sexual invitation from a strikingly beautiful woman, his fiancé's best friend, and felt he could not pass this up. When would such an opportunity come his way again? It was, in fact, a unique once-in-a-lifetime opportunity. Dr. Frankl, quite elegantly I think, pointed out that he did indeed have a unique opportunity and indeed it was one that would never come again; and that was the opportunity to say "no" in the service of his own self-regard and his relationship to his chosen mate! However, in the case of Bill and Jan, no argument was very effective against the onrushing libidinal locomotive; what would happen in the future was, they preferred to think, unrelated to their present choice and, anyway, in the hands of capricious fate. So they began a sexual relationship that was destined to lay bare their basic modes of relating to others and to themselves. (Space does not permit a thorough discussion of the implications of such sexual pairing for the course of the group in general. Generally such a development is exceedingly destructive to the group. Only rarely, as was true in this instance, with an extremely high energy diversion from other group members can such an event be harnessed in the service of growth).

It began ostensibly with neither expecting nor promising anything from the other: Jan wanted Bill's sexual presence approximately once a month, Bill wanted Jan's wanting his sexual gifts.

Life in the group became very complex for Bill. For one thing, he was still interested in seducing the other woman in the group. Each meeting therefore posed such fundamental problems for him as how to walk out of the group room at the end of the session and converse with the other woman without Jan's knowledge. Furthermore, he now only pretended to offer help to the other men in the group. In truth he wanted to defeat them not aid them; they became inanimate for him, a screen or background against which he could display himself to best sexual advantage.

Soon he was immersed in a sticky web of duplicity very similar to the web with which he had always criss-crossed his central core of emptiness.

To insure that he kept Jan available to him, he made faint innuendoes to the effect that his relationship to the girl with whom he lived was deteriorating, thus planting a seed of marital hope in Jan's breast. Bill's innuendoes colluded with Jan's enormous capacity for self-deception: she alone of any of the group members considered marriage a serious possibility. When the group confronted her with the reality they perceived, she grew defensively angry and considered leaving the group. I persuaded her to stay by reminding her that if she left now, she would have learned nothing, in fact accomplished nothing, except to hage repeated the same pattern that brought her to therapy; here was a unique opportunity to understand and, for once, to stay with a relationship and to play the drama through to its end.

After a couple of months the blush was off the rose; the relationship began to flounder. Jan came under much pressure: she lost her job and ran out of money, her children developed severe behavioral disorders, and she soon lapsed into a severe depression. She tore up her contract with Bill; no longer was a once-a-month contact sufficient. Now it was, "If Bill cares for me as much as he claims, where is he when I really need him?" She reinforced her new demands with some self-destructive accident proneness designed, it appeared, to evoke guilt in Bill.

Where, indeed, was Bill? As Jan grew more depressed he re-experienced his familiar feelings of dis-ease with himself, a gnawing anxiety and sense of worthlessness. It was all free floating, "out there" somewhere, unrelated in any way to his own choice and behavior. As Jan's depression deepened, the group confronted him with the question, "Had you known in advance the outcome (for Jan and for yourself) of the adventure, would you have done anything differently?" Bill said he would not have. "If I do not look after my own pleasure, who will?" he rejoined. The other members of the group, and now Jan, too, attacked him for his self-indulgence and his lack of responsibility for others. Bill pondered on this confrontation only to advance a series of rationalizations at the subsequent meeting. He was not irresponsible; he was high spirited, impish, a life-loving Peer Gynt. Life contains little enough pleasure; why is he not entitled to take what he can? He insisted that the group members and therapists, guilefully dressed in the robes of responsibility, were, in fact trying to rob him of his freedom. (I think of Viktor Frankl's comment that what is needed in America is a Statue of Responsibility on the West Coast to balance the Statue of Liberty on the East.)

Relentlessly the group honed in on the issues of love, freedom, and responsibility. Bill wanted Jan's creature comforts but he wanted to deny temporal continuity; to rip asunder the present and the future, to deny that his choices had a sequel.

Camus, in *The Fall,* creates a character who has an uncanny similarity to Bill:

> My sensuality was so real that even for a ten minute adventure I'd have disowned father and mother, even were I to regret it bitterly. Indeed—*especially* for a ten minute adventure and even more so if I were sure it was to have no sequel.

The group therapist, if he was to help Bill, had to make certain that Bill grew to understand that there was always a sequel to his choices. The therapeutic task was to help him recognize his responsibility for his relationship to his personal and interpersonal world.

Bill did not want to be burdened with Jan's depression. He had women in various cities around the country who loved him (and whose love made him feel alive); yet for him these women did not have an independent existence. In Heidegger's language they were not co-Daseins but instead, were objects present-at-hand, equipment in the world for his use; they came to life only when he summoned them. To quote Camus again:

> I could live happily only on condition that all the individuals on earth, or the greatest possible number, were turned toward me, eternally in suspense, devoid of independent life and ready to answer my call at any moment, doomed in short to sterility until the day I should deign to favor them. In short, for me to live happily it was essential for the creatures I chose not to live at all. They must receive their life, sporadically, only at my bidding."

Jan pressed him relentlessly. She told him that there was another man who was seriously interested in her and she pleaded with Bill to level with her, to be honest about his feelings to her, to set her free. By now Bill was quite certain that he no longer desired Jan. (In fact, as we were to learn later, he had been gradually increasing his commitment to the girl with whom he lived.) Yet he could not allow the words to pass through his lips. It was a strange type of freedom that he had then, as Bill himself gradually grew to understand: the freedom to take but not the freedom to relinquish. (Camus said, "Believe me, for certain men at least, not taking what one doesn't desire is the hardest thing in the world!") He insisted to be granted the freedom to choose his pleasures, yet, as he came to see, he had not the freedom to choose for himself. His choice was almost invariably one which resulted in his thinking less well of himself; and the greater his self-hatred, the more compulsive, the less free, was his mindless pursuit of sexual conquests that afforded him only an evanescent balm.

Jan's pathology was equally patent. She ceded her freedom to Bill (a logical paradox); only he had to power to set her free. The therapist confronted her with her pervasive refusal to accept her freedom: Why could she not say "no" to a man? How could men use her sexually unless she chose to allow them to do so?

Though Jan and Bill cound not confront these issues fully, neither could they ignore or avoid them. Eventually, through a relentless cyclotherapy, they came to terms with their basic responsibility. For Bill it was no longer a mystery that his relationship with the woman he lived with was "somehow" tenuous. He grew to understand that he chose to make and to keep it tenuous so as to provide himself with the excuse and rationale for other sexual chases. His gnawing guilt and feeling of unworthiness was self-determined; as long as he related to the world and to himself inauthentically he would never develop a sense of pride or inner comfort, he would never love himself. His choices alone were responsible for the creation and, therefore, for the transmutation of his world. The realization was similar for Jan. She grew to see that she could say no as well as yes. She realized that she chose to regard and present herself as helpless in the futile hope that somehow, someday, someone would rescue her from adulthood.

I hope to have illustrated with this vignette the fundamental role of responsibility and freedom in therapy. Bill and Jan eventually arrived at the somewhat obvious but hard truth that they are sentenced to freedom, it cannot be ceded away, it cannot be passively neglected; and freedom in the present stretches into the future, one's choices always have sequels.

DETERMINISM VERSUS CHOICE

In my account of the therapy of Jan and Bill there is a conspicuous absence of any focus on causality, especially traditional genetic approaches to causal explanation. Our goal in therapy must be change, and change, at some level, is always willful change. Any undue deterministic emphasis on an explanation of how one got to be this way may provide an apologia and undermine the mobilization of will. The past may be far less important in the change process than the present and future tenses. Nor must explanation, if one must explain, lie in the past: our behavior is as influenced by our future, by our goals, ideals, and purpose in life, by a host of abstract factors that pull us from the "not yet" rather than push us from the "already been." Nor would the existential therapist consider past influences as more definite, firm, or real. Our conception of the past changes as we alter our present and future. Some, for example, Sartre, would go yet farther to insist that since nothing exists besides consciousness, since we at every moment constitute the world—past, present and future—that we are not only responsible for our past but may, through our choices, alter it.

WILL

Though we as therapists do not often think or write about will, our ultimate goal in therapy is always, in one fashion or another, to influence will. We do it by encouragement and exhortation not unlike a second in the corner of a boxing ring. We undermine the rationalization that we are doomed to act as we do because of what has been enacted upon us in the past. We influence will as I did with Jan and Bill by bringing patients to the realization that they have authored their world, and, if they are dissatisfied with their product, they and only they can change it.

Often, however, these efforts are not sufficient and the therapist must apply additional leverage on the fulcrum of the will. One common method is to attack and undermine the obstacles to the will. If the previous step was "only *you* can change the world you have created," this step is "there is no danger in change."

An Illustration

A patient named Gail comes to mind—a 25-year-old perpetual student who complained of depression, loneliness, purposelessness, and severe gastric distress for which no organic cause could be found. In her initial session she lamented repetitively, "I don't know what's going on!" I could not discover what precisely she meant by this and since it was embedded in a lengthy litany of self-accusations, I soon forgot it. However, in the group too she did not understand what happened to her: she could not understand why others were so uninterested in her, why she developed a conversion paralysis, why she entered sexually masochistic relationships, why she became so infatuated with the therapist.

Once again I can only select a few illustrative themes from a long complex course of therapy. More than anything else, Gail was boring, dull, and absolutely predictable in the group. Before every utterance she scanned the sea of faces in the group looking for clues to what others wanted, what they expected. She was willing to be almost anything to avoid offense, to avoid affronting others and driving them away from her. (Of course, it resulted in her driving others away not from anger but from boredom; but that is another interpersonal facet of her therapy which I shall not describe here.) Gail was in chronic retreat from life and the group tried endless approaches to halt the retreat, to find Gail within the cocoon of compliance she had spun about herself.

However, no progress occurred until the group stopped encouraging Gail, stopped attempting to force her to socialize, to study, to write papers, to pay bills, to buy clothes, to groom herself, but instead urged her to consider the blessing of failure. What was there in failure that was so seductive and so rewarding? Quite a bit, it turned out! Failing kept her young, kept her protected, kept her from deciding. Being infatuated with the therapist served the same purpose. Help was "out there." He knew the answers; her job in therapy was to enfeeble herself to the point where the therapist could not in all good conscience withhold his royal touch.

A critical event occurred when she had a biopsy performed on an enlarged axillary node. She feared cancer and came to the group that day still awaiting the results of the biopsy (which ultimately proved to be benign). She had never been so near to her own death before and we helped Gail plunge into the terrifying loneliness she experienced. There are two kinds of loneliness the existential, primordial loneliness that Gail confronted then, and a social loneliness, an inability to "be with." The second, the social loneliness, is commonly and easily worked with in a group therapeutic setting. Basic loneliness is more rarely faced: groups often confuse the two and try to take away one's basic loneliness; but it cannot be taken away, it cannot be resolved, it can only be known. No one can die our death for us or with us. When one truly encounters this aloneness, the foundations of life are stripped to bare scaffolding and the view is dizzying and terrifying.

Rather quickly, then, many things came together for Gail. Far-strewn bits fell into place. She began to make decisions and to take over the helm of her life. She commented, "I think I know what's going on" (I had long forgotten her initial complaint). More than anything else, she had been trying to avoid the specter of loneliness. I think she tried to elude it by staying young, by avoiding choice and decision, by perpetuating the myth that there would always be someone who would choose for her, would accompany her, would always be there for her. Choice and freedom invariably imply loneliness, and as Fromm pointed out long ago, tyranny holds less terror for us than freedom.

Recall the Q-sort item that so many patients found important: "Learning that I must take ultimate responsibility for the way I live my life, no matter how much guidance and support I get from others." In a sense this is a double-edged factor: in a therapy group one learns what one *cannot* obtain from others. It is a harsh lesson and leads both to despair and to strength. One cannot stare at the sun very long and Gail on many occasions looked away and avoided her dread. Always she came back to it, however, and by the end of therapy she had made major shifts within herself. At the end of her very last group meeting she confessed that she still had little shreds of belief that, if I only would, I could cure everything with one sentence. I asked her to dictate the sentence she would like me to say. She did and then grinned gamely as I said goodbye by echoing her own words back to her.

Therapy groups often tend to water down the tragedy of life. Their natural currency is interpersonal theory and if care is not taken, they will make the error of translating existential concerns into interpersonal ones that are more easily grasped in the group. For example, as Gail's case illustrated, existential loneliness may be erroneously translated into social loneliness. Another incorrect translation occurs when we mistake feelings of powerlessness arising from awareness of our basic contingency for a powerlessness based on a sense of social inferiority. The group misses the point completely if it attempts to deal with the first, the fundamental feeling of powerlessness, by attempting to increase the individual's sense of social adequacy.

An extreme experience, for example, Gail's encounter with a possibly malignant lymph node, brings us sharply back to reality and places our concerns in their proper perspective. Extreme experience, however, occurs only rarely during the course of the therapy group. Some group leaders attempt to generate extreme experience by using a form of existential shock therapy. With a variety of techniques they try to bring patients to the edge of the abyss of their existence. I have seen leaders begin groups, for example, by asking each patient to compose the epitaph of their tombstone. "Destination labs" may begin with each member drawing their lifeline and marking upon it their present position: how far are they from their births, how close to their deaths? However, our capacity for denial is enormous and it is the rare group that perseveres, that does not slip back into less threatening concerns. Natural events in the course of a group—illness, death of others, and termination and loss—may jolt the group back but always temporarily.

ENCOUNTER AND MUTUALITY

Some time ago I began a group composed of patients who lived continuously in the midst of urgent experience. All the members had a terminal illness, generally metastatic carcinoma, and all were entirely aware of the nature and implications of their illness. I learned a great deal from that group; I especially learned about the fundamental but concealed issues of life that are so frequently neglected in traditional psychotherapy.

A great many very moving and very profound events occurred in that group. The first meeting set the tone of much that was to follow. Five doomed, if you will, desperately anxious women filed into the room and sat down. One of them, an extraordinary woman who had been the prime force in organizing the group and my mentor for many months in helping me face her death as well as my own, began the group by passing out copies of this old Hassidic tale:

> A rabbi had a conversation with the Lord about Heaven and Hell. "I will show you Hell," said the Lord and led the Rabbi into a room in the middle of which was a very big round table. The people sitting at it were famished and desperate. In the middle of the table there was a large pot of stew, enough and more for everyone. The smell of the stew was delicious and made the Rabbi's mouth water. The people round the table were holding spoons with very long handles. Each one found that it was just possible to reach the pot to take a spoonful of the stew, but because the handle of his spoon was longer than a man's arm, he could not get the food back into his mouth. The Rabbi saw that their suffering was terrible. "Now I will show you Heaven," said the Lord, and they went into another room exactly the same as the first. There was the same big round table and the same pot of stew. The people, as before, were equipped with the same long-handled spoons—but here they were well nourished and plump, laughing and talking. At first the Rabbi could not understand. "It is simple, but it requires a certain skill," said the Lord. "You see, they have learned to feed each other."

Many forms of nourishment were to flow from the feeding of one another in this group. It was extraordinarily helpful for them to be helpful to one another. Offering help so as to receive it in reciprocal fashion was only one and not the most important aspect of the benefits to be gained. Being useful to someone else draws the patients out of a morbid self-absorption and provides them with a sense of purpose and meaning. Almost every terminally ill person I have spoken to has expressed deep fear of a helpless immobility—not only of being a burden to others and being unable to care for oneself but of being useless, without value to others. Living, then becomes reduced to survival and the individual searches within even more deeply for meaning. However, as Viktor Frankl has argued so compellingly, a search that is inwardly focused is always futile. Happiness, fulfillment, self-actualization can never be intentionally captured; these life qualities ensue, but cannot be pursued.

The support offered one to the other was considerable and varied. They offered one another transportation to meetings, they maintained telephone vigils when a member was in deep despair, they shared their methods of coping and of gaining strength. One, for example, taught the group meditational procedures and every meeting thereafter ended with the group, in darkness, meditating over a lighted candle to ease their minds of pain and dread. In a number of ways the group provided the members power to transcend themselves, to extend themselves into others. They welcomed student observers and community interest. They were anxious to teach and to share their experiences.

They began the group with a common bond of enmity toward the medical profession. Much time was devoted to disentangling the threads of this anger. Some of the anger was displaced and irrational—anger at fate, envious anger at the living, anger at doctors for not being all knowing, all powerful, and all protecting. Some of the anger was entirely justified—anger at the doctors' lack of sensitivity, at their impersonality, their lack of time, their unwillingness to keep the patient fully informed and to include them in all important management decisions. We attempted to understand the irrational anger and place it where it belonged—on our basic thrownness and on the contingency of our existence. We faced the justifiable anger and attempted to cope with it by striving for effectance, by, for example, inviting oncologists and medical students to the group and by participating in medical school classes and conferences.

All of these approaches, these avenues to the outside of oneself, can, if well travelled, lead to increased meaning and purpose as well as to an increased ability to bear what cannot be changed. Nietszche, long ago, wrote: "He who has a 'why' to live can bear with almost any 'how'."

It is clear to me that the members of this group who have plunged most deeply into themselves, who have confronted their fate most openly and resolutely, have passed into a mode of existence that is richer than that prior to their illness. Their life perspective is radically altered; the trivial, inconsequential diversions of life are seen for what they are. There is a fuller appreciation of the more elemental features of living: the changing seasons, the last spring, falling leaves, the loving of others. Rather than resignation, powerlessness, and restriction, some have experienced a great sense of liberation and autonomy. Most of the group members carry their own time bomb, they keep themselves alive by taking some form of medication, generally a steroid, and thus make a decision daily whether to live or to die. No one takes his life with absolute seriousness until he fully comes to terms with his power to end his life.

We are all very familiar with the centrality of the quality of the therapeutic relationship in the process of change. In group therapy a sound, trusting relationship between the therapist and the patients and between the patients themselves is a necessary mediating condition: it enhances trust, risk taking, self-disclosure, feedback, constructive conflict, working through problems centering around intimacy, etc. In addition to these mediating functions, the basic, intimate encounter has an intrinsic value, a value in itself and for itself.

THE THERAPEUTIC RELATIONSHIP

Nowhere have I seen this benefit more clearly illustrated than in this particular group. The dying patient feels terrifyingly alone, alone with his existential loneliness but alone also because he feels cut off and shunned by the world of the living. I agree with Kübler-Ross that the question is not whether to tell the patient but how to tell the patient honestly and openly since the living, by their demeanor, by their shrinking away, always inform the patient of his dying. Many physicians who work with the dying quite consciously cut themselves off because they feel it is necessary to their own self-preservation, that it would be unbearable to so involve themselves that they die with each patient. I have never seen this more poignantly illustrated than in Ingmar Bergman's film, *Cries and Whispers,* in which a recently dead woman cries for a living person to stay with her; but her sisters shrink away in horror from touching their own destiny.

What can the therapist do in the face of the inevitable? I think that the answer lies in the verb "to be." He does by being, by being there with the patient. "Presence" is the hidden agent of help in all forms of therapy. When patients look back on their therapy they rarely remember a single interpretation of the therapist, but they always remember his presence, that he was there with them. It asks a great deal of the therapist to join this group, yet it is hypocrisy not to join. The group configuration is not the therapist and, then, the dying, but it is we, we who are dying, we who are banding together in the face of our common condition. The group so well demonstrates the double meaning of the word apartness: we are separate, lonely, apart *from* but also a part *of*. One of my members put it elegantly when she described herself as a lonely ship in the dark. Even though no physical mooring could be made, it was nonetheless enormously comforting to see the lights of other ships sailing the same water.

REFERENCE

1.   May, R. Contributions of existential psychotherapy. In May, R., Angel, E. & Ellenberger, H. (Eds.), *Existence: A new dimension in psychiatry and psychology.* New York: Basic Books, Inc., 1958, pg. 61.

PART TWO

Behavior Analysis and Biofeedback

Prologue

As we look to the future of psychotherapy and behavior change from the vantage point of behavior analysis and psychophysiological treatment models, it seems possible to visualize a range of applications at several interrelated levels or stages of the therapeutic process. At the most fundamental conditioning or reconditioning level, the rationale and methodologies emerging from the rapidly expanding research on biofeedback appear to portend important advances in the application of psychophysiological approaches to health problems. Similarly, a new perspective on the use of more strictly defined behavioral conditioning procedures, particularly those of the aversive or noxious variety, has been signalled in the most sophisiticated approaches to research and practice involving "total context" programs. Indeed, conditioning methodologies of the Pavlovian sort, which depend upon pairing procedures involving antecedent stimulus events and the elicitation of consequent response interactions, will obviously continue to provide a useful point of departure for some basic behavior therapy maneuvers. However, a more selective range of applications appears to be developing as refinements in methodology become evident and ethical sensitivities become more prominent.

At more advanced levels of research inquiry, the scope and complexity of the problems involved focus mainly upon the role of verbal behavior in the control of therapeutically important repertoires. Here, a scientific and functional analysis within the framework of an operant conditioning model emphasizing behavioral consequences as controlling factors in determining both the form and frequency of a response would appear to provide a clear advantage over the mentalistic and subjective language of more cognitive orientations. Indeed, if there is any hope for the future development of a therapeutic technology in this perplexing and poignant domain incorporating the understanding and management of behavior problems, it seems most likely to emerge from the coalescence of clinical and experimental activities directed toward an analysis of human conduct. The three papers that constitute this section of the volume epitomize such a coalescence at several of the interrelated levels in the therapeutic process.

JOSEPH V. BRADY, Ph.D.
Professor of Behavioral Biology
The Johns Hopkins University School of Medicine
Baltimore, Maryland

5. REINFORCEMENT THERAPY

The Role of Behavior Analysis in Understanding and Managing Problems of Human Conduct

Charles B. Ferster, Ph.D.

An experimental analysis of clinical phenomena inevitably raises the question of the relation between clinical and experimental psychology. The position I take is that the roles of the experimental psychologist and the clinician are complementary rather than competitive. I will make a distinction between behaviorism as a concept of human nature based on the traditions of biology and natural science and behavior modification as a particular way to influence human conduct. I will address the assumption that all human interactions modify behavior whether influenced by a psychoanalyst, a behavior modifier, or a member of a legislative body. We like some forms of social influence better than others, but science is not in a good position to choose one form of behavioral influence as better than another. It can, however, expose and make clear how our conduct is being affected by our social, political, physical, and biological environment.

BEHAVIORAL ANALYSIS–A "LINGUA FRANCA"

The usefulness of behavioral psychology is as a language about human conduct, a lingua franca, that is an alternative to the mentalistic and subjective language of psychodynamic psychology. Experts in the clinical fields seem to be able to communicate successfully to other experts who already know what they are saying, but the difficult questions are how to train new people and how to talk about experiences that are new. The situation is illustrated by an anecdote about communication in a prison. A visitor to the prison heard sounds that came from someone banging on the plumbing pipes. There were patterns of knocks followed by laughter throughout the prison. The visitor learned that funny stories or jokes were told this way. Each pattern of knocks indicated a particular joke. Then suddenly another pattern of knocks was heard followed by silence instead of the usual burst of laughter. The visitor got the explanation that, "that fellow never could tell a funny story properly." I sense that the problems of training and communication among members of the mental health profession are very serious. Expert clinicians spend many years learning the practice of their profession. The training is arduous and the difficulty of communicating what they do to apprentices seems to depend on giving them the identical experience. Behavioral language has the same advantage in clinical work as the objective language used in other fields of natural science. The basic principle of a behavioral description is a separation of human conduct into the act itself and the change in the environment it produces, whether this change is on the external environment, within his own skin, an effect on another person, or a social effect.

THE COMPLEMENTARY ROLES OF SCIENCE
AND CLINICAL PRACTICE

Reinforcement, as the instant immediate consequence of a performance, is the cornerstone of a scientific language about behavior. It allows us to observe the constant details of a complex activity in addition to its total effect. Many clinicians complain that describing the fine details of a complex act loses the essential human quality of it. There is reason to share that concern, for the tension between the fine detail and the overall picture illustrates the complementary roles of science and practice. The one side is illustrated by the metaphor of the Ph.D. scholar as a person who knows more and more about less and less. The other side is the practitioner as a source of knowledge about the substance of human conduct which has been gained by day-to-day interactions with the problems of human existence. As an experimental psychologist I have always found that clinical practitioners are an important source of data for me about what the important phenomena of human existence are. I have found it useful to look beyond the particular epistemology of the clinical, or colloquial, or mentalistic language to the events that prompted the clinician to speak. I assume that an effective practitioner has seen something of importance that moves him to speak. For me the ability to observe and formulate human conduct behaviorally and functionally provides an opportunity to go beyond the clinician's language to the details of the human event he has observed. From this point of view I have discovered that effective clinicians can be articulate, objective observers of their own clinical practice, with very good memories for the small details of their experience with the patient. Undoubtedly this memory is due, in large part, to their sensitivity to fine nuances. This attitude toward the clinician gives me access to the wealth of knowledge that the proven clinician has. It provides, for an experimental psychologist, the significant phenomena of human conduct that are important to understand and to formulate scientifically. Otherwise, how might we know what specimen to put under the microscope?

VERBAL BEHAVIOR–NEXUS BETWEEN
BEHAVIORISM AND PRACTICE

A characterisitc of a good clinician is his very good memory for the observations he makes. His ability to use clinical theories goes hand and glove with fluency and facility of observation with the patient and the ability to keep his findings in mind and work with them in his own thoughts. I have discovered, with enough probing through the mentalistic language, that even the most mentalistic and Freudian theorists operating in the "here and now" do deal with the immediate behavior of the patient, no matter what language or conceptual scheme they use to describe it. I think the unique aspect of behaviorism that brings it into contact with clinical practice is Skinner's analysis in *Verbal Behavior*. Ultimately the contact between the science of human behavior and clinical practice is the study of verbal behavior, and it is unfortunate that so many behavior therapies have tended to focus so much on nonverbal aspects. Clearly, nonverbal aspects of the interaction with the patient are important, but in so many cases the activity we observe in behavior therapies is a patient and therapist talking to each other. There is a conceptual jump when we go from the immediate events of the interview to the overt mode of conduct somewhere else; in some ways it is often as mystical and disconnected as the mentalisms and metaphorical leaps that are sometimes attributable to Freudian practice.

CONTROL

Reinforcement therapies, of course, are closely tied to the issue of control. For most reinforcement therapists, at least according to the literature, the primary event in their training, the experience of conditioning a pigeon, tends to induce a sense of power or control. The conditioner presses a button at the end of a cord and produces an immediate change in the frequency of the pigeon's behavior. When he stops pressing the button the frequency declines. He presses the button and within moments the pigeon begins to do complicated and different things. The work of operant conditioners with schedules of reinforcement has the same characteristic. The control that is achieved over the pigeon is dramatic and heady. Hundreds of yards of graphs emerge, representing hundreds and thousands of pecks; every change in rate is so predictable that the patterns repeat with geometric symmetry as on wallpaper. The sense of control is powerful. However, I think it is a mistake to confuse this kind of control with behavior theory, although the association is commonly made, I think, in the mental health field. The word "control" really has two connotations for behaviorists. One sense of the word is a functional relation between what the organism does and the antecedent conditions. In that sense, Freud also looked for control in the form of a functional relation between the organism's conduct and the antecedent conditions. The other sense of control is pejorative—one person coercing another.

The pejorative sense of control, in the sense of one person controlling another, like rape, is by no means a necessary association or corollary of behavioral theory. This association only occurs when behavioral science is thought of as a method, as a technique of controling, of managing, of changing people, rather than as a language or as a conceptual scheme that directs our attention to the key aspects of the human condition in considerably more detail than any other useful theories. One of the major advantages of behavior theory is that it provides a technical way to distinguish between control as understandable and control as exertion. One type of control, the arbitrary one, is for the purposes of the controller—the therapist, the teacher, the policeman, or some special agent. The other type of control involves the natural process of a person interacting in his own life. Both types are properly called control, but there are important differences between them. One sense of control is technical; the other concerns ethics and values and how we govern each other.

A CONCLUDING EXAMPLE

I will close with an example from my current work in education. Consider a student who is studying and learning, reading a textbook, talking with people, thinking, talking to himself, suffering discomfort from thoughts, suffering from discomforts at not having thoughts, and undergoing that complicated process that produces new competence and thoughts. We have progressed far enough in our understanding of the behaviors of thinking and learning to describe the processes technically and rather accurately by talking about many of the conditions that govern these behaviors. I've added to this understanding. Another type of student can be described by behavioral control: he comes to school because his parents have said he has to, he doesn't really know why he's there and doesn't think about it; he undertakes the examination because if he doesn't, they'll throw him out of school, and he will put anything the professor asks for on the examination or will copy from another student. I think the difference between these two students suggests the role of behavioral science for understanding and dealing with problems of human conduct. A behavioral analysis of the component processes makes it very clear that although the behaviors are orderly and predictable in the two cases, the quality of the result is very different.

6. AVERSIVE CONDITIONING

Clockwork Orange Revisited: Travesty and Truth About Aversive Conditioning

Cyril M. Franks, Ph.D.

Aversive conditioning is not an entity per se; it is one small, very rarely necessary part of the complex and sophisticated approach to psychotherapy and behavior change known as behavior therapy. This rare use was not always the case: in its early days it was regarded as a sufficient form of treatment in itself. I will try to show how aversive conditioning arose, what its assets and deficits are, and how it evolved from simplistic and therapeutically largely futile beginnings to its present highly limited potential for occasional and calculated integration into certain behaviorally oriented therapeutic regimes. I will also try to point out some of the physical and societal hazards that can arise with the use of direct or indirect aversive controls and suggest tentative remedies. Finally, with much diffidence, I shall make some forecasts about—to paraphrase slightly the title of H. G. Well's epic novel—the shaping of the things to come as they relate to the place of aversive conditioning in behavior therapy.

THE ORIGINS AND NATURE OF AVERSIVE CONDITIONING

In essence, aversion therapy is a special application of aversive conditioning in which the attempt is to develop a lasting association between an undesired behavior—be it simple or complex, overt or covert, externally observable or a primarily private event such as a thought or an affect—and an unpleasant stimulation.[8] This is classical or Pavlovian conditioning, a matter of Aristotelian association by contiguity. Alternatively, aversive conditioning can take the form of an attempt to make the unpleasant stimulation a *consequence* of the undesired behavior. This is known as instrumental or operant conditioning. In either situation, the intent is to develop a learned or acquired connection between the undesired behavior and the unpleasant stimulation. It is hoped that the establishment of this connection will be therapeutically beneficial in that there will be a reduction or even cessation of the undesired target behavior. Modern advocates of the therapeutic use of aversive conditioning, when it is used at all, view this aspiration as one small part of that complex form of treatment known as behavior therapy. As we shall see, this was not always so. When developed some four decades ago—primarily for the treatment of alcoholism—it was all too often prescribed as an autonomous treatment in itself. For reasons that will shortly become apparent, it fell into disuse and disrepute, and the revival of interest in its use with alcoholics and other groups is a comparatively recent phenomenon.

Aversive conditioning in the form of brutal punishment (e.g., cutting off a hand for stealing) or constructively intended therapy (e.g., having an alcoholic drink a glass of wine into which he or she had just seen squeezed a putrid spider) has been practiced for literally thousands of years.[1] However, it was not until the advent of Pavlov, who first subjected the various phenomena of conditioning to intensive, systematic, and controlled investigation, that the parameters of aversive conditioning began to be delineated. Slowly and painstakingly, as part of the comprehensive attempt by Pavlov and his group to elucidate the principles of cortical functioning—or higher nervous activity, to use Pavlov's term—the laws governing the conditioning process were formulated. Pavlov's concern was not primarily with conditioning per se, but with central nervous system activity and the mode of functioning of the brain in relation to what lay outside it, both within the body and the external world. At that time—around the turn of the century—the techniques developed by Pavlov and his associates were the best that were available for this purpose. Neither the electroencephalogram nor sophisticated techniques of direct electrode implantation existed, and Pavlov was forced to infer what happened centrally from a study of peripheral processes such as salivation. It is perhaps unfortunate that, while Pavlov recognized that conditioning is a means to an end—the understanding of how the brain functions—and not necessarily an end in itself, many of the early behavior therapists seemed to hold quite a different view.[2]

Whereas Pavlov explicitly recognized individual differences, genetic factors, and constitutional limitations, many of the early behavior therapists—somewhat naively to our present way of thinking—seemed to view the whole world as one vast conditioning process in which constitutional and genetic factors could safely be ignored. Perhaps most important of all, Pavlov explicitly differentiated men from animals: man possessed the "second signal system," involving speech, abstraction, cognition, and all the complexities that go with these faculties. Early behaviorists and behavior therapists overlooked factors of which Pavlov was well aware! A conditioned avoidance response to a glass of water could be developed in man by the skillful application of an aversive conditioning strategy involving electric shock and many trials—but it could be accomplished far more effortlessly in one trial with no apparatus whatsoever by merely whispering in the subject's ear that the glass of water contains typhoid germs!

While Pavlov seems to have been the first to note the ability to induce a conditioned aversion in a dog to a neutral tone by pairing it with the effects of an injection of apomorphine, the first formally documented attempt to use aversive conditioning in a therapeutic situation seems to be that of Kantorovich in 1930 in the Soviet Union.[4] He treated 20 alcoholics with electrical aversion therapy and claimed that, thereafter, most of them did not use alcohol for months. In the West, one of the earliest accounts of the use of aversion therapy is provided by Max,[5] who employed faradic stimulation to reduce a homosexual fixation to a fetish object.

Despite such apparent success with electrically induced aversion, and despite the extensive use made of electrical stimulation in experimental psychology—upon which behavior therapy is supposedly based—it was nausea-inducing drugs that were used in aversive conditioning, primarily in the treatment of alcoholism, in the 1930s and 1940s in both Europe and North America. Unfortunately, with a few notable exceptions, such as the systematic and relatively rigorous work of Voëgtlin and his colleagues at the Shadel Sanatorium, most of these projects were of extraordinarily poor scientific quality. Crucial data were either not reported or reported in a useless form, control groups were at best inappropriate, follow-up was inadequate, and, by and large, even the elements of research design were virtually nonexistent. Under these circumstances, the success rates reported in these early studies, ranging from 100 percent success to 100 percent failure, are largely meaningless.

Many of these early therapists, primarily clinicians pressured by service demands, failed to make use of research findings that were readily available to them had they had both the time and the initiative to delve into the experimental literature. For example, it was known by the 1930s and 1940s, from the work of Pavlov and others, that backward conditioning was difficult to establish; the conditioned stimulus should precede the unconditioned stimulus in time, and the sight, touch, feel, taste, smell, and/or sound of the alcohol in the glass should precede the onset of the aversion—be it chemical or electrical. All too often, since it is difficult to pinpoint the onset of intense nausea, the busy therapist, doing other things perhaps, exposed his patients to the alcohol stimulus *after* that crucial onset of nausea. To take another example, although it was well established by the 1930s and 1940s that central nervous system sedatives such as the barbiturates and bromides impair the ability to form and maintain conditioned reflexes, alcoholic patients, understandably complaining of stress at the prospect of having to undergo aversion therapy, were sedated beforehand by their well-meaning therapists. No wonder, then, that aversive conditioning as a method of treating alcoholics fell into disrepute and disuse, but the fault hardly lay with the principles of aversive conditioning. As Bernard Shaw is alleged to have said about Christianity: "Maybe it hasn't worked because it hasn't been tried!"

FROM AVERSIVE CONDITIONING TO BEHAVIOR THERAPY

The resurgence of interest in aversion therapy in the late 1950s and afterward can be traced to a variety of causes. First, there was the burgeoning emphasis upon sophistication in research design as applied to clinical situations, with behavioral scientists emerging from the laboratory into the clinic and then, much later, into the natural environment. Second, there was the rise of behavior therapy as a viable entity, with its uniquely integrated combination of expertise in matters clinical and scientific. Actually, this combination of sophisticated clinician cum behavioral scientist reflects an ideal that we are only now in the mid-seventies beginning to attain.

With the immediate postwar emphasis upon doctoral programs in experimental–clinical psychology, the scientist–practitioner model and the rise of numerous departments of Behavioral Science in schools of medicine and psychology alike, a new breed of clinically oriented experimentalists arose. These experimentally sophisticated individuals knew well the parameters of effective aversive conditioning: partial rather than 100 percent reinforcement was used under optimal conditions; and rather than the unquantifiable amorphous nausea, they employed the far more precisely controllable electric shock—only, as scientists of course, they had to call it "faradic stimulation."

With all these advantages, one might reasonably expect to hear that they were highly successful in the treatment of alcoholism by aversive conditioning and that the number of alcoholics in the country was drastically reduced. Far from it. Their success rates were hardly any better than those of their predecessors, with the consequence that the more probing of these behavioral scientists dabbling in clinical matters began to ask why. Two developments occurred at this stage: First, as behavioral scientists, they began systematically to explore additional parameters. For example, operant and classical conditioning procedures were combined, with rewards for selecting a nonalcoholic beverage and cessation of punishment for relinquishing an alcoholic beverage being skillfully incorporated into a design that also included the establishment of a direct conditioned aversion to alcohol. Unfortunately, while such strategies produced somewhat better results, the success rate was still less than satisfactory and the problem of alcoholism remained.

Second, behavior therapy was emerging as a viable and alternative therapeutic modality, and it was the experimentally trained *clinician* who came into prominence rather than the clinically oriented experimentalist, as hitherto. Such individuals, while deriving their strategies, conceptual framework, and choice of techniques from experimental psychology in general, and the experimental psychology of learning in particular, were also very much attuned to the complexities of man and the exquisite differences (as well as similarities) between people and poodles. As Pavlov knew well, men don't jump off cliffs for the same reasons that dogs salivate to bells!

Increasingly, those behavior therapists who made use of aversive conditioning began to recognize the complexity and the uniqueness of man. Conceivably, aversive conditioning *might* be effective and even sufficient in the elimination of some relatively circumscribed learned habit, such as smoking, in the case of the otherwise functionally intact individual. But to apply such a rationale to an alcoholic was clearly absurd. Thus, for all but the most circumscribed of disorders, behavior therapists generally learned to adopt a multidimensional, albeit thoroughly behavioral, strategy. Such procedures range from aversive conditioning through various methods involving positive reinforcement, through covert processes in which the subject is trained to imagine aversive situations as vividly as possible, to modeling and cognitive therapy, to biofeedback, to the development of techniques of self-control and environmental manipulation. Whatever the procedure, its deployment has to be a collaborative process emerging from informed discussion with the patient of various possibilities, why they are suggested, and their probable outcomes. In this respect, behavior therapy actually increases the patient's choice of response repertories, puts *him* in control, fosters *self*-management procedures, and is utterly devoid of mystique or subterfuge. The emphasis is usually upon the patient's total life style rather than any one aspect. For example, no behavior therapist worthy of the name would assume that something called "homosexuality" was, by definition, pathological and therefore something to be treated. Were he to consider aversive conditioning at all, it would unquestionably be as a small part of a total picture in which positive features were given the major prominence; heterosexuality, *if* this be the goal, is not to be viewed as something that automatically rushes in to fill the vacuum caused by the extinction of homosexual behavior, thoughts, and feelings.

THE OUTCRY AGAINST AVERSIVE CONDITIONING

The preceding description may give the impression that the therapeutic millenium has arrived, and well may you wonder how it is that all therapists are not behavior therapists and how it is that there is such an outcry against aversive conditioning if it is indeed practiced as I have described. Before I go on to explain how this seemingly impossible state of affairs has come about, let me say a little more about aversive conditioning.

While the search for noxious stimuli antedates the growth of scientific psychology by at least 2000 or 3000 years, aversion therapy—modern style—had, until recently, depended upon either electrical or chemical noxious stimulation. Proponents and critics of each have spelled out on many occasions their respective methodological, psychological, and physical advantages and disadvantages, the hazards that each entails and how they may be circumvented. However, it is possible to list a variety of additional procedures now available that either directly fall into the category of aversive stimulation—such as noxious odors, smoke inhalation, high-intensity auditory signals, and traumatic respiratory drug-induced paralysis—or may be classified as indirectly aversive—such as time out from positive reinforcement, curtailment of liberty or privileges, deprivation of rights earned, locking a child in his room, fines, social condemnation, and so forth.

Much human learning, as Roos[9] points out, is the result of aversive conditioning occurring in the natural course of events—fire burns, falling beams, provoked dog bites—and many of our social systems function by the judicious use of aversive consequences—parents and magistrates punish, laws are enforced, pay is docked. Electroconvulsive shock treatment can be an aversive consequence of depression, sociopaths may be institutionalized, the intake of alcohol by alcoholics prescribed Antabuse is highly aversive in its consequences, nonpayment of the therapist's fee can result in termination, in the Soviet Union deviant political views can have involuntary and indeterminate incarceration in a mental hospital as a consequence. Forms of therapy other than behavior therapy practice aversive conditioning in some fashion. Aversive conditioning, as practiced selectively by discriminating behavior therapists, differs from such procedures primarily in that its limited usage is merely one small part of a judiciously planned and informed application of learning theory principles.

If aversive conditioning, then, is one tiny unit in an enlightened program of behavior therapy, if it is used at all, and if aversive principles, in one form or another, underlie the very fabric of our society and permeate many other forms of therapy, again we may ask: How is it that there is such an outcry—sometimes in thoughtful and constructive fashion and sometimes in the less welcome form of a diatribe—against aversive conditioning per se, and how is it that it is identified primarily with behavior therapists?

No one now seriously questions the viability of conditioning principles. When behavior modification was in doubt, it was not feared. Now that its efficacy (circumstances being appropriate) has been demonstrated beyond doubt, it assumes the potential for becoming something to be feared, distorted, and misinterpreted, wittingly or otherwise—a thing to develop folk legends and mythology about. Of all the areas of behavior therapy, aversive conditioning, for obvious reasons, is most likely to evoke apprehension.

The public image of our "power" (i.e., our ability to "control" people's minds and actions) is readily prone to exaggeration. The popular film, *A Clockwork Orange,* in which the ultraviolent hero is conditioned into a state of abject passivity, is an excellent example of this process at work. This film, all the more harmful because of its widespread appeal as technically excellent "cinema," is a product of common misconceptions regarding the power of behavior therapy and the "sinister" intent of behavior therapists. Perhaps even more important, it has become a public symbol of behavior therapy and a rallying point for the justification and strengthening of even more misconceptions.

THE RESOLUTION OF THE DILEMMA

Clearly, the responsibility for such a climate lies, in part, with behavior therapists. If public attitudes are to change, then a first step might be where necessary, for behavior therapists to modify their own attitudes and behavior—shades of "Physician, heal thyself?" Fortunately, as contemporary developments within the Association for Advancement of Behavior Therapy and elsewhere testify, behavior therapists are acutely sensitive and responsive to such needs.

Some of the more damaging publicity occasionally comes from behavior therapists themselves; a prime example is an article in *Psychology Today* by McConnell. He states, among other things:

> I believe the day has come when we can combine sensory deprivation with drugs, hypnosis, and astute manipulation of reward and punishment to gain almost absolute control over an individual's behavior. . . . We'd assume that a felony was clear evidence that the criminal had somehow acquired a full-blown social neurosis. . . . We'd send him to a rehabilitation center where he'd undergo positive brainwashing. . . . We should reshape our society so that we all would be trained from birth to do what society wants us to do. We have techniques now to do it. . . . The techniques of behavioral control make even the hydrogen bomb look like a child's toy.[6]

As behavior therapists, we may respond to McConnell's outrageous statements by declaring that in no way does he represent the thinking of the majority of behaviorists. We can point to articles in behavior therapy journals that emphasize the importance of freely given informed consent to treatment, the inalienable rights of the client, and the need for restrictions on even the clearly therapeutic use of aversive conditioning. However, the public doesn't read professional journals; the public reads *Psychology Today*. It does not, for example, read McConnell's admirably honest retractions, clarification, and correction in such professional publications as the *APA Monitor*.[7]

If we are to appreciate public reaction to behavior therapy, we must try to see it from the public's point of view. The average lay person has little or no knowledge of learning theory; his or her exposure to behavior therapy is often limited to a magazine article or popular movie in which aversive control is presented with either incorrect or no explanation and usually in the worst possible light. With this background, it is understandable that so many people are attacking behavior therapy, particularly aversive conditioning.

Aldous Huxley's *Brave New World* and Anthony Burgess's *Clockwork Orange* were set in the future—a future, if Toffler[10] is correct, of accelerating change, excitement, uncertainty, and anxiety. However, the future is generated by the present, and thus it is to present concerns that we must address ourselves as a first step to the future. For example, it is deplorable but conceivable that certain misguided individuals within state facilities and correctional institutions could sometimes misuse various facets of the token economy or aversive conditioning paradigm. While the "Clockwork Orange Syndrome" is indeed a travesty of all that enlightened and humanistic behavior therapists cherish, abuses can occur, and it behooves us to set our own house in order—for if we don't, someone else will! (An extended discussion of this point and related topics can be found elsewhere.[3])

For the future, aversive conditioning techniques will continue to be used—but only when there is little or no alternative (as in cases of extreme self-destructive behavior). They will be used within the context of a total behavioral program, as outlined above, involving constant monitoring and the active, informed, and considered consent of the individuals or groups concerned. The aim will be to foster behavioral *self*-control rather than control by others. Throughout, we will constantly be addressing ourselves to ethical and legal implications, and the thoughtful implementation of precedents and standards. This consideration will include such issues as the demonstrated physical safety and validity of a particular procedure, and the incremental success added by this procedure, if any. Is it worth it? Do nonaversive alternatives exist? Is the use of aversive therapy implicitly or explicitly meeting some personal needs of the therapist rather than those of the patient? Do the ends really warrent the means? Have we presented the issues squarely and fairly to all concerned, including the patient and the public? By what rights and criteria can any one group of individuals decide what is "good" for society at large?

Under these stringent circumstances, aversion therapy will be used less and less in the future and this curtailment will almost certainly be a good thing. Nevertheless, there will, at least in the foreseeable future, always be those very rare occasions when its use seems to be beneficial and even essential—the example of the individual unswervingly bent on self-destructive behavior is a case in point. Is it better to use electric shock to prevent such an individual from plucking his eyes out? Or is it better to keep him in a straight jacket or severely tranquilized all day? It is up to us to ensure that the necessary safeguards are met. By all the indications, these are the directions modern behavior therapy is taking rather than the dangerously misleading travesty as outlined in such popular culture as *A Clockwork Orange*.

REFERENCES

1. Franks, C. M. Conditioning and conditioned aversion therapies in the treatment of the alcoholic. *International Journal of the Addictions, 1966, 1,* 61–98.
2. Franks, C. M. Behavior therapy and its Pavlovian origins: Review and perspectives. In C. M. Franks (Ed.), *Behavior therapy: Appraisal and status.* New York: McGraw-Hill, 1969, pp. 1–26.
3. Franks, C. M., & Wilson, G. T. W. Commentary. In C. M. Franks & G. T. W. Wilson (Eds.), *Annual review of behavior therapy: Theory and practice* (Vol. 2). New York: Brunner/Mazel, 1974, pp. 1–9.
4. Kantorovich, N. V. [An attempt at associative reflex therapy in alcoholism.] *Nov. Refl. Fiziol Nerv. Sist. 1929, 3,* 436–447. *Psychological Abstracts, 1930, 4,* 493, No. 4283.
5. Max, L. Breaking up a homosexual fixation by the conditioned reaction technique. *Psychological Bulletin, 1935, 32,* 734. (Abstract)
6. McConnell, J. V. Stimulus/response: Criminals can be brainwashed—now. *Psychology Today,* (14)8, 1974.
7. McConnell, J. V. Behavior modification. *American Psychological Association Monitor,* August 2–3, 1974, 5, (8). (Letter)
8. Rachman, S. & Teasdale, J. *Aversion therapy and behavior disorders.* London: Chaucer Press, 1969.
9. Roos, P. Human rights and behavior modification. Mental Retardation, 1976, 12, 48–66.
10. Toffler, A. *Future shock.* New York: Random House, 1970.

7. BIOFEEDBACK

Psychosomatic Self-Regulation and Volition

Elmer E. Green, Ph.D.
and Alyce M. Green

Biofeedback training for migraine relief quickly caught the attention of the public and there was a subsequent expectation and demand for many applications of biofeedback to health problems. Though this demand has not been accompanied by adequate "supply," professionals are increasingly looking into the potentialities of biofeedback for building, restoring and maintaining health. It is useful, therefore, to focus attention on biofeedback rationale, methodology, and applications, and on the significance of physiological self-regulation skills of unusual people such as yogis. Biofeedback devices, meditation, and yogic techniques for self-regulation are tools that clearly can be put to professional use. The sense of self-mastery that accompanies the development of self-regulation skills seems to be a potent factor in increasing the value and meaning of life for many individuals.

Biofeedback is the immediate presentation to a person of information about his or her own physiological processes, such as muscle tension, temperature, heart rate, blood pressure, brainwaves, etc. Information is usually "fed back" by a needle on a meter, a light, or a tone. Biofeedback *training* is making use of the information to gain voluntary control of such processes.

VOLITION

Although a variety of self-regulation subjects are referred to in this paper, we hope it will be clear that in our estimation the important factor they have in common is volition. Many physical and psychological variables already intensively studied enter into, or must combine, to produce a healthy body and mind, but the contribution of volition has been almost entirely ignored. Although the explicit focus of our "voluntary controls" research almost always involves biofeedback, the implicit focus always includes volition, and how to "mobilize" it for mind–body coordination.

Without the exercise of volition, we are passive acceptors of (1) our genetic predispositions and (2) our cultural and environmental impacts and conditionings. Such passive acceptance is unnecessary, however. Some of our most successful people are those who learned in some way to shape their minds and bodies to their wills, against odds. Franklin D. Roosevelt is one example. Ben Hogan, one of the all-time champion golfers, is another good example of the effectiveness of volition. When an automobile accident put him out of action, one leg being so severely damaged that doctors wanted to amputate, it was his volition that indirectly saved his leg, developed a "new" vascular network, and made him Masters Champion. His will to play golf would not let him stay down. That galvanizing impulse guided by his *visualization* (of playing golf), governed his physical effort and physiological processes and resulted in a "yogic" accomplishment of the highest level. In one sense you could say that Ben Hogan "told his body" what he wanted it do do, insisted that it do it, and the body complied. The question for everyone who wants to master a mental, emotional, or physical problem is, of course, "How do you make it happen?"

British medical doctors have known for a long time that some of the Indian yogis could demonstrate voluntary control of physiological processes that are, by definition, involuntary. It was reported by medics in the last century, for instance, that certain yogis could stop their hearts, or could be buried underground for days, sometimes weeks, and when dug up would "come back" to life. These reports were probably not believed at first, but as decades passed and more reports came in, and the phenomena of hypnosis came to Western medical attention, it became clear that the normally involuntary section of the psychophysiological apparatus could be manipulated in some unexplainable way by cognitive instructions plus volition.

AUTOGENIC TRAINING

About 70 years ago the latent ability to regulate one's own physiological self began to be brought to Western attention by Johannes Schultz, M.D., through his self-regulation system called Autogenic Training, self-generated, or self-motivated training.[18] [26] Although Schultz worked at first with hypnosis, he was also interested in yoga. Perhaps it was the volitional aspect of yoga that especially appealed to him, but in any event he felt that the failures of hypnosis were in part related to the fact that the patient either became too passive and dependent and did not take enough self-responsibility, or unconsciously blocked the doctor's hypnotic programming.

In his medical practice, Schultz noticed that "good" hypnotic subjects often reported a feeling of heaviness throughout the body and warmth in the limbs before a successful therapeutic attempt, so he decided to teach patients to first "put" themselves into the state of physiological quietness through the silent repetition of phrases associated with heaviness and warmth. After that, they could tell their bodies what to do, using "organ-specific" formulas. This self-regulation is in sharp contrast to hypnosis in one particular way, even though the same physiological "final common path" processes are involved. In hypnosis, the doctor quiets the patient by suggestion, rather than the patient quieting himself, and then the doctor suggests what the patient's body and psyche should do. The patient is "programmed" by the doctor rather than by himself.

Schultz' idea of *self*-instruction during a relaxed, receptive state was a simple brilliant insight, the significance of which can hardly be overestimated. Our bodies usually do not "listen" to our own instructions because usually we do not put the body into the listening mode, so to speak. In one way, at least, the body acts like a tape recorder. Before recording on magnetic tape we put the machine into the "listening" mode, the record mode, because it will not record while in the active playback mode. Similarly, the body must be quieted before it can take instruction.

Bodies may not be as unresponsive as mules, but in both cases distractions must be eliminated and attention must be focused before they can be told what to do. That was what the Missouri farmer said about his mule when he hit it on the head with a plank, before telling it to go into the barn.

AUTOGENIC FEEDBACK TRAINING

When we began work at The Menninger Foundation in 1964, it seemed that one of the simplest ways to test self-regulation would be to record physiological changes during autogenic training. As soon as the Psychophysiology Laboratory in the Research Department was constructed we designed a demonstration "experiment" in which 33 women volunteers from the community used autogenic-like exercises (verbal phrases) for two weeks, with special attention on the feeling of warmth in the right hand. The hand-warmth response was tested in the lab during a first training session and again two weeks later in another lab session. In the interim, between lab sessions, the subjects practiced autogenic exercises at home twice a day for 15 minutes, morning and evening. After two weeks, two of the women were able to warm their hands 10°F at will, apparently without involvement of striate muscles. A few others could raise their temperatures 3° to 4°F.

We were impressed. According to medical textbooks the autonomic nervous system, which controls blood flow and temperature in the hands, is involuntary. Although subjects were not aware of changes in blood flow, some of them were able gradually to become aware of temperature change, a sensory variable in the hands that is related to blood flow almost perfectly, though temperature change usually lags blood flow change by 15 to 20 seconds. Encouraged by these results, we decided to attempt, with the help of our colleague, Dale Walters, a more elaborate experiment with college students, using biofeedback devices combined with autogenic phrases for temperature training, muscle tension reduction, and increase in percentage of alpha. There is not space to discuss this research effort except to say that most students learned in a few hours of training, spread over five weeks, to control one or two of the variables to some degree, including the production of eyes-open alpha while carrying on a quiet conversation. From that research we developed several procedures that were later useful in conducting research in greater depth with brainwave training. That study, also with college students, was called the Reverie and Imagery Project.[9]

Gardner Murphy, Director of the Research Department of The Menninger Foundation during the study of autogenic training for control of hand temperature, was very much interested in the *feedback* of muscle tension for control of striate problems. He felt certain that abnormal involuntary tension in large muscle bundles could be brought under voluntary control if it were displayed on an unusually sensitive meter, a meter that would tell whether or not miniscule but significant changes were being made in response to one's efforts. Murphy had felt for a long time that self-confrontation was necessary for successfully changing one's own psychological and physiological states. That is, in order to bring about some desired change one needs feedback of information about one's own self. In the striate domain, self-confrontation would logically consist of feedback of information about striate processes. Davidowitz et al.[5] and Hefferline[16] had already demonstrated feedback methods for control of striate processes, and so had Basmajian.[1] Murphy felt that the technique could have great therapeutic significance.

Subsequent research indicated that biofeedback could be remarkably effective for rapid learning of striate control,[15] but we (the present writers) felt that the feedback idea could be generalized and also applied to autonomic behavior. Some yogis had apparently developed control of a number of autonomic processes, and if such control was truly possible, then perhaps the learning of it could be accelerated with feedback. Especially intriguing was the yogic postulate that *all* physiological processes could be influenced by psychological processes, and we hypothesized that if autogenic training were coupled with appropriate feedback training, it would facilitate conscious control of both striate and autonomic sections of the nervous system.

From research in many laboratories it now seems clear that both striate and autonomic processes can be voluntarily controlled, and it is also apparent that "autogenic feedback training" is more effective in learning self-regulation than either autogenic training or biofeedback training alone.

AUTOGENIC FEEDBACK TRAINING FOR MIGRAINE CONTROL

Research in migraine self-regulation resulted from an observation we made of one of the subjects who tried autogenic phrases for hand warmth. This woman told us, during the first lab session, that she developed a migraine-like headache as soon as she began listening to the autogenic phrases. She had a history of migraine, she said, and in this case the headache was precipitated by anxiety associated with the possibility of failure to warm her hands. We consoled her by saying she might do better after two weeks of autogenic practice at home, but during the second lab session she got another headache. The polygraph record revealed a severe decrease in blood flow in her hands (measured by photoplethysmographs) and a drop of 10°F when she tried to *raise* the temperature of her hands. Fifteen minutes later, still "wired up," while she was in a relaxed, restful, nondemanding phase of the experiment, the blood flow suddenly increased in both hands and the temperature shot up 10°F in two minutes. At the end of that phase of the session, in response to the question, "What happened to you two minutes ago?" she said, "How did you know my headache went away?"

Her startling question raised the possibility that training in control of hand temperature (peripheral blood flow control) might help other migraine sufferers. It is known that (1) migraine headache is associated with vascular dysfunction in the head—scalp arteries dilate too much and each pulse becomes a wave of pain, and (2) data from the Soviet Union[23] indicate that vasodilation in the scalp is generally associated with vasoconstriction in the hands. Word of this "migraine relief" reached a headache victim, and using a temperature feedback machine (that we had developed to help train subjects to control hand temperature) an unusually successful trial was made to change chronic blood flow behavior in her hands. Using autogenic feedback training for voluntary increase of hand warmth, this "patient" eliminated her headaches and the need for drugs in about two weeks. She has been free from headache since the training experience ten years ago.

These findings interested Joseph Sargent, an internist at The Menninger Foundation and he has since demonstrated, in a clinical research setting, migraine amelioration in about 120 out of 150 patients.[24] [25] Some might say that Sargent "treated" these patients, but "treated" does not seem to be an appropriate word. When biofeedback is used the doctor teaches, rather than treats. The feedback machine does not do anything *to* the patient, of course, it merely tells him the result of what he himself is doing. It is a passive indicator of what is going on inside the skin.

The neurological processes involved in voluntary control of blood flow in the hands have not been traced by neuroanatomists, but it can be inferred that the "fight or flight" system (the sympathetic section of the autonomic nervous system) is being controlled. There is no significant parasympathetic inervation of smooth muscles in the walls of blood vessels in the hands, and the muscles either constrict in response to increased sympathetic outflow to the hands, or they dilate in response to a decrease in sympathetic outflow. In order to voluntarily increase hand temperature, therefore, it is necessary to voluntarily reduce sympathetic outflow to the hand. Since sympathetic outflow is regulated from a hypothalamic control center, however, it really means that a person in some way voluntarily modifies the behavior of a section of the hypothalamus, as described in the section on rationale below.

When the conscious or unconscious psychological stress that results in cold hands in migraine patients is properly handled, as indicated by an increase in hand temperature—which means relaxation in the sympathetic nervous system, and restoration of proper hypothalamic homeostasis—then the improper blood flow behavior in the head is "wiped out," apparently as a side effect.

Biofeedback can also be of value in cases in which the physiological variable brought under control is seemingly not related to a patient's problem, as in hand temperature training for alcoholics. Biofeedback shows immediately, without any dogma or doctrine, without any need for belief or faith, that one can successfully learn to control some normally unconscious processes. Such a demonstration means much to a psychosomatic victim who knows that his unconscious reaction to stress is killing him, but who can do nothing about it, and who may be "living on pills" with only the hope that a new drug will save him before it is too late. When he discovers that he can make changes in "involuntary" behavior, the scales often begin to tip toward recovery and psychosomatic health. Paul Kurtz, in particular, has demonstrated this phenomenon in alcoholics and drug addicts.[14] [17]

Other researchers and clinicians who have successfully used biofeedback include Engel with heart problems,[7] Budzynski et al. with insomnia and tension headaches,[3] [4] Gladman and Estrada with patients who received both psychosomatic and psychotherapeutic benefits,[8] Poirier[22] and Sterman[27] with epilepsy, and Brudny[2] and his group with many neurological problems using electromyographic feedback. In addition, there is a host of professional, paraprofessional, and graduate student members of the Biofeedback Research Society, too numerous to mention, who have demonstrated in one way or another that biofeedback helps to implement volition.

Brudny told us a short time ago that 42 torticollis patients had been helped, 30 percent with essentially complete success, using electro-myographic feedback for learning voluntary control of muscle tension. Other cases included voluntary muscle tension *increases*. Certain paraly-sis victims increased their control of intact nerve and muscle fibers whose normal tension levels had been below the threshold of consciousness (that is, the biocybernetic loop discussed below was not closed) so that noth-ing could be learned. After awareness developed "in the muscles," so to speak, voluntary control was enhanced and the feedback devices could be discontinued.

BIOFEEDBACK RATIONALE

At this point someone might say, "This is interesting, and may possibly be true, but what does this have to do with volition? What is volition, and how does it get into the nervous system?" Although volition cannot yet be adequately defined, it seems phenomenologically self-evident that, whatever it is, it can modify and control various kinds of neurological behavior. Before discussing volition, however, it is useful to consider what is already known about control circuits in the central nervous system and to question how biofeedback works. For instance, how can knowledge about what is going on inside the skin (through biofeedback) make it possible to self-regulate physiological processes that have traditionally been thought to be involuntary?

Figure 7-1 is a highly simplified representation of processes that occur in the voluntary and involuntary neurological domain, and simultaneously in the conscious and unconscious psychological domain. The upper half of the diagram represents the normal domain of *conscious* processes, that is, processes of which we normally have awareness when we wish it. The lower half of the diagram represents the normal domain of *unconscious* processes. The normal neurological locus for conscious processes seems to be in the cerebral cortex and the craniospinal apparatus. The normal locus for unconscious processes appears to be in the subcortical brain and in the autonomic nervous system. Apropos of these ideas, someone at a meeting of the American Medical Association called the cerebral cortex "the screen of consciousness." If that description is appropriate, then the subcortex and other normally involuntary parts of the nervous system might be called "the screen of the unconscious."

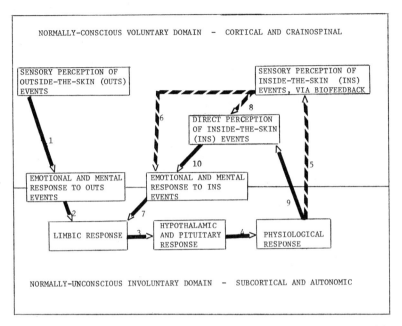

Fig. 7-1. Simplified operational diagram of self-regulation of psychophysiological events and processes. Excerpted from Green, E. E., and Green, A. *Biofeedback and Volition,* a paper given at a symposium titled, "New Dimensions of Habilitation for the Handicapped" (University of Florida, Gainesville, June 1974), presented jointly by the State of Florida, Department of Health and Rehabilitative Services, Divison of Retardation, and The Academy of Parapsychology and Medicine, Los Altos, Calif.

Electrophysiological studies have shown that every perception of outside-the-skin (OUTS) events (see upper left-hand box of the diagram) has associated with it (arrow 1) electrical activity in both conscious and unconscious structures, those neural mechanisms involved in emotional and mental responses. The boxes labelled "Emotional and Mental Responses . . ." have been placed on the midline of the diagram, divided by the horizontal centerline into conscious and unconscious parts, in order to show their two-domain nature. The next box, called "Limbic Response," (arrow 2) is placed entirely in the unconscious section of the diagram, though some neural pathways lead from limbic structures directly to cortical regions, implying that "information" from limbic processes can reach consciousness.

The limbic system has been intensely studied in both animals and humans in the years since Papez' historic paper[21] outlined the functions of the limbic system in emotional responses. MacLean coined the phrase "visceral brain" for the limbic system,[19] and others have referred to it as the emotional brain, but the important point is that emotional states are reflected in, or correlated with, electrophysiological activity in the limbic system.

Of major significance to a proper rationale is the fact that the limbic system is connected by many pathways (arrow 3) to the central "control panel" of the brain, the hypothalamus. Though the hypothalamus weighs only about 4 grams, it regulates a large part of the body's automatic neural machinery and has control functions over the pituitary gland. The pituitary, the so-called "king gland" of the body, is at the top of the hormonal hierarchy and its action precipitates or triggers off *changes* in the homeostatic balances of other glandular structures. With these concepts in mind, it is easy to see how news from a telephone message can cause a person to faint, or to suddenly have a surge of high blood pressure. The perception of OUTS events leads to limbic–hypothalamic–glandular responses, and, of course, physiological changes are the inevitable consequence (arrow 4).

This information is not "news" to a neurologist; what is news is the fact that if a physiological change from the "Physiological Response" box (at the lower right) in the diagram is "picked up" by a sensitive electrical transducer and displayed to the person (arrow 5) on a meter, or made audible by a tone in order to feed back physiological information, then there ensues (arrow 6) a "new" emotional response, a response to normally unconscious INS information. The new emotional response is associated with a "new" limbic response (arrow 7). It combines with, replaces, or modifies the original limbic response (arrow 2). This new limbic response in turn develops a "new" pattern of hypothalamic firing and pituitary secretion, and a "new" physiological state ensues. Thus, a cybernetic control loop is completed, a biocybernetic control loop, as a result of providing the conscious cortex with information about normally unconscious INS processes. Closing the biocybernetic lool bridges the normal gap between conscious and unconscious processes—voluntary and involuntary processes.

In learning voluntary control of normally unconscious processes, we do not become directly aware of the neural and hormonal pathways involved any more than we become aware of what cerebral and subcerebral nerves are involved in hitting a golf ball. However, as in the golf ball case, when we get external objective feedback we can learn to modify the internal "set up" so as to bring about changes in the desired direction. It is worth noting that everything that is learned, without exception, is learned with feedback of some kind, whether it involves the corticostriate system or the corticosubcorticoautonomic system.

BIOFEEDBACK AND THE BIOCYBERNETIC LOOP

It is useful to focus attention especially on arrows 5, 6, 8, 9, and 10 of the diagram. Biofeedback information, along arrow 5 and then arrow 6, is often not needed for more than a few weeks. Biofeedback is not addictive, it seems, because voluntary internal control, rather than dependence on an external agency, is established. In this, biofeedback differs considerably from drugs. Drugs often are addictive and almost always dosages must be increased as time passes in order to overcome the body's natural habituation. With biofeedback, however, sensitivity to subtle internal cues is increased, rather than decreased. This increased sensitivity, indicated by arrow 8, is an essential step in closing the internal cybernetic loop, so that the use of feedback devices need be only temporary. As sensitivity increases, the patient becomes aware of what is going on inside the skin and eventually does not need feedback. In addition, this increased sense of internal awareness seems to come under conscious control and can be "turned on" and "turned off" at will.

This process of enhanced awareness was well illustrated in one of Engel's tachycardia patients, who, after some months of biofeedback practice, said that she did not need his machine anymore in order to know how fast her heart was beating. She was aware of her heartrate any time she turned her attention to it. In terms of the diagram, she used only arrows 5 and 6 at first. Gradually arrow 8 developed, accompanied by the formation of arrows 9 and 10. When these two were well developed she no longer needed arrows 5, 6, and 8, and the machine could be turned off. The internal loop, arrows 9–10–7–3–4–9, had been established. She could now modify her own dynamic equilibrium without external aids. She could "adjust" the homeostatic balance point involving heart rate at will, by making the needed internal changes ("choosing" the psychophysiological states that were productive, such as a certain mood, a certain kind of breathing that goes along with mood control, and a certain response, or lack of response, to environmental stress).

It is an important empirical finding that in regulating a physiological response to psychological stress the biofeedback patient apparently learns to handle the stress itself in a satisfactory way. We know of almost no cases of symptom substitution in autogenic feedback training. This result probably stems from the fact, first recognized by Schultz, that when a patient's motivation and volition bring about his own recovery, there is little "need" for another symptom. Another way of putting it is to say that when autogenic feedback training is used it seems as if the symptomatic problem is erased from the synaptic control patterns of brain structures. The patient has apparently deconditioned himself, psychologically and physiologically.

We often point out to trainees who suffer from psychosomatic ills that it is not life that kills us, but our reaction to it. We probably cannot change life to any great extent—it will probably continue to "beat on us" in the customary way—but we can do something about our reaction to it, and biofeedback shows a "way." After the way is learned, and becomes a way of life, we can let the whole matter become automatic—with little conscious attention—allowing normally unconscious homeostasis to maintain the new dynamic equilibrium.

YOGA

One reason we have been interested in unusual people, such as yogis, is because they have learned to "turn off" as well as "turn on" physiological behaviors that in the average person would be called psychosomatic diseases. When a yogi induces at will an unusual heart behavior, and then returns the heart to normal, it is clear that his control goes both ways. Thousands of ordinary people have "demonstrated" peculiar heart rhythms (though not intentionally) by allowing a stress reaction to become chronic, but they "know" only one-half of the process. Because they cannot "turn it off" they are called patients, rather than yogis.

As previously reported,[11] we have had an opportunity to observe two unusual persons in our psychophysiology laboratory, an Indian yogi, Swami Rama, and a "Western Sufi" from Holland, Jack Schwarz. Without going into the details of his demonstrations, Swami Rama demonstrated voluntary control of his heart by causing it to cease pumping blood for 17 seconds, putting it into a state of atrial flutter.[10] He also demonstrated control of the major arteries in his wrist and hand, causing a temperature change of 9°F between two spots on the palm of his hand, two inches apart. One half of his palm turned pink and the other half gray. There was no physiological evidence of striate muscular involvement.

Jack Schwarz demonstrated that he could stop the bleeding of wounds from a sailmaker's needle driven through his biceps (in two seconds after he said, "Now it stops"), and that he could prevent bleeding entirely from such wounds.[13] He also demonstrated "pain control" by showing no significant physiological responses (heart rate, galvanic skin response changes, etc.) in three trials when burning cigarettes were held against his forearm for as long as 25 seconds. In addition to their physiological demonstrations, both Swami Rama and Jack Schwarz demonstrated on numerous occasions the Edgar Cayce-like ability to report on mental, emotional, and physical conditions of persons whom they did not know and had not seen before being asked for their "perceptions" of these people.

The importance of these demonstrations by Swami Rama and Jack Schwarz does not lie in the physiological records per se, but in their understanding, or "feeling" of how it is done. After much discussion and narrowing to essentials, the most succinct concept we have been able to obtain is that "all of the body is in the mind, but not all of the mind is in the body." That is, everything that is demonstrated in the body is in actuality accomplished in the mind. This is the basic position, it seems, in the Yoga Sutras of Pantanjali, dating back some 1500 years.[28] This concept has an important bearing on the idea of mind as an energy structure and provides a useful insight, or theory, in light of which volition can be studied anew.

VOLITION RECONSIDERED

One way volition could "get into" the nervous sytem is to be there already, as a chemiconeurological discharge system in unconscious structures whose behavior automatically programs us, in the same way that random processes and certain preset restrictions and contingencies make "computer music." That view is, of course, the hard-line behaviorist position. There is, however, an interesting diametrically opposed alternative.

If we carefully examine the Indo-Gnostic theory in modern terms, we can hypothesize that mind is an energy structure whose densest section is the physical body. This concept makes a place in theory for parapsychology and its crucially important psychokinetic phenomena. In this model, volition directs a normally imponderable psychophysical energy, such as the energy hypothesized 100 years ago by Gustav Fechner in order to account for parapsychological phenomena.

A satisfactory operational definition of volition may not be found for decades, but if it is a fact that mind includes or appears as a normally imponderable energy that can directly modify OUTS events, as psychokinesis studies indicate, then it seems reasonable to assume that the same normally imponderable energy could be directed to influence INS events.[15] That is, a person could "manipulate" by metacontrol his own cortical and subcortical firing patterns; could modify his own neurological and hormonal behavior from "inside." In essence, such a metacontrol of brain tissue was hypothesized by Myers as long ago as 1901[20] and was also proposed (in a somewhat modified form) by Eccles.[6]

This idea of "mind contains body" is the reverse of the behaviorist position, but it makes it possible to conceive of humans as open "field" entities (whose multidimensional nature has been only slightly studied). The unusual people of all ages are, in this open-ended view, "regular" people who have discovered how to use some of their volitional capacities. Their control of both INS and OUTS phenomena are extrapolations of what all of us do to a degree, all of the time. In other words, all "coincidences" are not necessarily coincidental in the sense of "random congruence."

Although the idea of self-selection of neurological firing patterns may seem strange, biofeedback data certainly do not contradict it. For instance, research in at least four laboratories, starting with Sterman's work, has shown that epilepsy can be modified by self-selection of brain rhythms.[27] Since brain rhythms per se have no known sensory correlates, what seem to be selected in actuality are emotional and mental states (psychological states, mind states, states of consciousness) whose correlates are particular brain rhythms.

As previously mentioned, the behaviorist position maintains that the psychological state itself is the consequence of preceding biochemical brain processes, but there is no "hard" evidence to support this idea, even though it is a kind of faith with some. The more general hypothesis, that both mind and body are states of an energy continuum in which mind is a normally imponderable substance or energy, with extraphysiological extensions, has, however, at least three supports. Two of the supports listed below are inferential, but the third is empirical and qualifies as hard evidence: (1) "nonsensory" self-regulation, that is, brainwave feedback studies; (2) the simple phenomenological gestalt of human awareness in which we "feel" we make choices; (3) the OUTS data from psychokinetic studies.

Every important human experience incorporates the feeling of choice, of free will, whether it is to perceive, to act, or merely to be. A limited behaviorist position is not without merit, however. No doubt most of our "choices" are not fully free, but are in fact predetermined to a large extent by unconscious neurological potentials and biochemical gradients. However, of vital significance is the fraction of opportunities for "choice" that exist—the extent, however tiny, to which "metachoices" can successfully be made, that is, choices made by a person from outside the neurochemical system like a rower who dips his oars in the river to control his boat, but who is not himself part of the otherwise "predetermined" river/and/boat system.

For those who already feel that humans have a choice, this discussion is perhaps academic, but it may be useful for those who are depressed by circumstances or who feel that they are already beaten, as many paralysis victims, psychosomatic casualties, mental patients, alcoholics, and drug addicts seem to feel. Perhaps the first step for them is to accept the possibility, however difficult to implement, that through the use of volition one can learn to modify mind–body processes.

VOLITION AND THE
PSYCHOPHYSIOLOGICAL PRINCIPLE

The psychophysiological principle has been stated as follows:

Every change in the physiological state is accompanied by an appropriate change in the mental–emotional state, conscious or unconscious; and conversely, every change in the mental–emotional state, conscious or unconscious, is accompanied by an appropriate change in the physiological state.[12]

This "closed" principle, when coupled with the idea of volition acting as a metaforce (from outside the "closed" system) makes possible the concept of psychosomatic *self*-regulation. Scientifically, much data remain to be gathered, but the psychophysiological principle, and its manipulation by volition, "feels" right; and, above all, it seems to work.

William James discovered this principle when he was depressed to the point of considering suicide. He read that if you first assume that you have some volitional power over yourself and circumstances, and then try to assert that power (by acting *as if* you have it), it beings to "work;" you and your circumstances change. James tried it because he could think of no alternative, and it "worked." He recovered from the depression that his "scientific" behaviorist logic had plunged him into and went on to reach a high level of creativity and production.

Whether volition enters the rationale diagram as a change in the emotional and mental matrix, or as a metaforce manipulation of limbic or hypothalamic structures, cannot yet be determined, but we anticipate that a new psychophysical science, corresponding with some of Fechner's original concepts, will result from research on volition with respect to yoga, biofeedback, autogenic training, psychokinesis, and parapsychology in general.

REFERENCES

1. Basmajian, J. V. *Muscles alive: Their function revealed by electromyography.* Baltimore, Md.: Williams & Wilkins, 1962.
2. Brudny, J. New sensory feedback therapy unit established in ICD's medical school. *ICD News,* 1973, 9, 1–2.
3. Budzynski, T. H. Biofeedback procedures in the clinic. *Seminars in Psychiatry,* 1973, 5, 537–547.
4. Budzynski, T. H., Stoyva, J. M., Adler, C. S., & Mullaney, D. J. EMG biofeedback and tension headache: A controlled outcome study. *Psychosomatic Medicine,* 1973, 35, 484–496.
5. Davidowitz, J., Browne-Mayers, A. N., Kohl, R., Welch, L., & Hayes, R. An electromyographic study of muscular tension. *The Journal of Psychology,* 1955, 40, 85–94.
6. Eccles, J. C. *The neurophysiological basis of mind.* Oxford: Clarendon Press, 1953.
7. Engel, B. T. Clinical applications of operant conditioning techniques in the control of the cardiac arrhythmias. *Seminars in Psychiatry,* 1973, 5, 433–438.
8. Gladman, A. J., & Estrada, N. Biofeedback: A useful adjunct in the treatment of psychosomatic illness. Paper presented at symposium on Biofeedback for Counseling and Psychotherapy, V.A. Hospital and the Menninger Foundation, Topeka, Kans., October 10, 1973.
9. Green, A. M., Green, E. E., & Walters, E. D. Brainwave training, imagery, creativity and integrative experiences. Paper presented at the Biofeedback Research Society Conference, February 1974.
10. Green, E. E., Ferguson, D. W., Green, A. M., & Walters, E. D. *Preliminary report on Voluntary Controls Project, Swami Rama.* The Menninger Foundation, Topeka, Kans., June 1970.
11. Green, E. E., & Green, A. M. The ins and outs of mind–body energy. *Science Year, 1974* (World Book Science Annual). Chicago: Field Enterprises Educational Corporation, 1973.
12. Green, E. E., Green, A. M., & Walters E. D. Self regulation of internal states. In J. Rose (Ed.), *Progress of cybernetics: Proceedings of the International Congress of Cybernetics,* London, 1969. London: Gordon and Breach, 1970.
13. Green, E. E., Green, A. M., & Walters, E. D. *A demonstration of voluntary control of bleeding and pain.* The Menninger Foundation, Topeka, Kans. March 1972.

14. Green, E. E., Green, A. M., & Walters, E. D. Biofeedback training for anxiety tension reduction. *Annals of the New York Academy of Sciences,* 1974, *233,* 157–161.
15. Green, E. E., Walters, E. D., Green, A. M., & Murphy, G. Feedback technique for deep relaxation. *Psychophysiology,* 1969, *6,* 371–377.
16. Hefferline, R. F. Learning theory and clinical psychology—An eventual symbiosis? In A. F. Bachrach (Ed.), *Experimental foundations of clinical psychology.* New York: Basic Books, 1962.
17. Kurtz, P. S. Turning on without chemicals. *The Journal of Bio-Feedback,* 1973, *1,* 88–105.
18. Luthe, W. (Ed.). *Autogenic therapy,* (Vol. 1–6). New York: Grune & Stratton, 1969.
19. MacLean, P. D. Psychosomatic disease and the "visceral brain": Recent developments bearing on the Papez theory of emotion. *Psychosomatic Medicine,* 1949, *11,* 338–353.
20. Myers, F. W. H. *Human personality and its survival of bodily death.* New York: Longmas, Green, 1953.
21. Papez, J. W. A proposed mechanism of emotion. *Archives of Neurological Psychiatry,* 1937, *38,* 725–743.
22. Poirier, F. Traitement del epilepsie par retro-action sonore. *La Clinique D'Epilepsie de Montreal* (unpublished report), September 1972.
23. Razran, G. Excerpts from "The observable unconscious and the inferable conscious in current Soviet psychophysiology." *Psychology Review,* 1961, *68,* 81–147.
24. Sargent, J. D., Green, E. E., & Walters, E. D. The use of autogenic feedback training in a pilot study of migraine and tension headaches. *Headache,* 1972, *12,* 120–124.
25. Sargent, J. D., Walters, E. D., Green, E. E. Psychosomatic self-regulation of migraine headaches. *Seminars in Psychiatry,* 1973, *5,* 415–428.
26. Schultz, J. H., & Luthe, W. *Autogenic training: A psychophysiologic approach in psychotherapy.* New York: Grune & Stratton, 1959.
27. Sterman, M. B. Neurophysiologic and clinical studies of sensorimotor EEG biofeedback training: Some effects on epilepsy. *Seminars in Psychiatry,* 1974, *5,* 507–525.
28. Taimni, I. K. *The science of Yoga.* Wheaton, Illinois: The Theosophical Publishing House, 1961.

PART THREE

Neurosurgical and Pharmacological Intervention

Prologue

In recent years, the physical manipulation of the brain to modify behavior has become a highly controversial issue with social as well as scientific and medical implications. The term "psychosurgery," which denotes this branch of neurosurgery, has taken on a rather negative connotation. Euphemisms such as "psychiatric surgery" or "functional neurosurgery" have done little to quell the tempest. Regardless of the terminology, this form of surgical intervention consists of selective destruction of small areas of brain tissue for the primary purpose of altering disordered behavior or mental states. Less destructive techniques of localized electrical stimulation have also been employed. Similar techniques of ablation or stimulation are being used in the management of other conditions such as pain, epilepsy, or movement disorders. Although there is scientific and medical controversy concerning the management of the latter conditions, there is little question regarding the social or ethical propriety of neurosurgical intervention. The current controversy surrounding psychosurgery is therefore not a matter of the techniques employed but rather a question of their application to behavioral or emotional disorders. The issues here relate not only to scientific documentation of therapeutic efficacy, but particularly to ethical considerations.

To set the stage historically for this discussion, we look back to the 1930s when Fulton and Jacobsen* observed the tranquilizing or sedative effect of frontal lobe lesions in monkey and chimpanzee. Egas Moniz†, a Portuguese neurologist, applied these observations to mental illness in man and introduced the technique of "frontal lobotomy," which consisted of cutting the prefrontal connections to the thalamus. Lobotomy rapidly became an accepted technique in mental institutions, with the remarkable effect of making agitated psychotic patients docile and manageable. Unfortunately, some patients were reduced to an apathetic, listless state which caused concern regarding the moral justification of the procedure. Frontal lobotomy fell by the wayside in the late 1950s with the introduction of the phenothiazine tranquilizers that appeared to be a miraculous "chemical scalpel" and revolutionized psychiatric treatment.** Although vast numbers of patients were benefitted by these psychoactive drugs, it became clear in the early 1960s that there remained a hard-core group of patients who failed to respond to these agents. In addition, a proportion of patients manifested toxic side effects such as dyskinesias and metabolic dysfunctions. In the past decade, faced with the dilemma of intractable mental or behavioral disorders, some clinicians turned once more to psychosurgery. Improvements in stereotaxic technique enabled lesions to be restricted to a matter of millimeters rather than the large crude lesions of the "lobotomy era." Increased precision permitted a shift in targets from the frontal lobe to the limbic system. Despite these technological refinements, questions have been raised in the

---

* Fulton, J. F., & Jacobsen, F. The functions of the frontal lobes. A comparative study in monkey, chimpanzee and man. *Second International Neurological Congress*. London, 1935, pp. 70–71.

† Moniz, E. Les premieres tentatives opératoires dans le traitement de certaines psychoses. *L'Encéphale,* 1936, *91,* pp. 1–29.

** Davis, J. M., & Kline, N. S. Therapeutic efficacy of the phenothiazines and other antipsychotic agents. In P. Black (Ed.), *Drugs and the brain.* Baltimore, Md.: Johns Hopkins Press, 1969, pp. 173–184.

past few years regarding the scientific validity of psychosurgical intervention, and the ethical issues of "tampering with the essence of human life." Early in the 1970s, as a result of this debate, a virtual moratorium on such procedures was called in the United States and Japan; there has also been considerable public pressure against these procedures in some European countries.

In considering the further exploration of psychosurgery as a therapeutic modality, the issues may be addressed as four questions:

1. The first issue concerns the scientific validity of the theory that local destruction or interruption of pathways or electrical circuits in the brain can modify, hopefully beneficially, human behavior. Furthermore, how specific is the relationship between lesions in a given area of the brain and particular behavioral or mental processes?

2. The ethical considerations must also be confronted. Primary among these is the problem of informed consent. It has been argued that informed consent in patients suffering from behavioral or emotional disorders is impossible on the grounds that the "organ of consent," the brain, is already impaired.

3. Then there are the social implications. Among the considerations here is the matter of how society can be protected against abuse of psychosurgery for political repression of dissenters.

4. Can guidelines be established to regulate psychosurgery such that *both* individual liberty and society can be protected, while at the same time promoting further scientific study of this modality—in the laboratory and in clinical trials? Implied in this question is the assumption that the potential therapeutic benefits of psychosurgery warrant further study so that a more definitive decision may be made regarding its future application.

In the United States, in the latter part of the 1970s, guidelines are evolving whereby it seems likely that psychosurgery may once again be considered in the management of certain psychiatric disorders that have been refractory to other forms of therapy. The application of surgical techniques to psychiatric conditions draws public attention, partly because of the associated "physical invasion" of a presumably "normal brain," as well as the irreversibility of a psychosurgical lesion. While less dramatic than surgery, the use of psychoactive agents to control behavior and the emotions also poses ethical questions, as well as the risk of side effects and potentially irreversible damage to the brain. The papers in this section deal with these neurosurgical and pharmacological issues, and include some consideration of "risk–benefit" factors affecting the individual and society.

PERRY BLACK, M.D., C.M.
Associate Professor of Neurological Surgery
Associate Professor of Psychiatry
The Johns Hopkins University School of Medicine
Baltimore, Maryland

8. TECHNIQUES OF NEUROSURGERY

Therapeutic Potential and Risks of Limited Frontal Leucotomy

William H. Sweet, M.D., D.Sc.

During my third and fourth years of medical school, I wanted to be a psychiatrist and appraised the appeal of this choice while working in the laboratory of the Boston Psychopathic Hospital. It was then that I became completely discouraged at what seemed to me to be an absolutely hopeless morass of ignorance with no promising avenues of exploration. There were and are no animal models for the diseases under consideration. I did not have the courage displayed by many to continue in this difficult field. It was against that bleak background, especially the poor prognosis associated with the serious psychoses, that the operation of bilateral frontal leucotomy and its various major modifications were introduced in the late 1930s.

STANDARD PSYCHIATRIC–SURGICAL PROCEDURES

Figure 8-1 illustrates the site of incision in the so-called standard lobotomy operations. In the earliest operations, the surgeon divided virtually all of the white matter in the coronal plane just anterior to the anterior tip of the lateral ventricle. This operation was done on many different types of serious psychoses; however, there was only one systematic study done with the procedure applied to a significant number of patients. This was a randomized, controlled investigation conducted in six United States Veterans Administration Hospitals. It is not only the sole extant randomized study of the standard type of bilateral frontal lobotomy, but also the only controlled study of any other form of psychiatric surgery conducted since then. This investigation was initiated by Drs. Jenkins and Holsopple, and was interrupted temporarily by Holsopple's death. The final publication in a series of seven was a long-term follow-up study by Ball et al.[2] Of 188 experimental (prefrontal lobotomy) patients and 185 matched controls, all but 12 (6 experimental and 6 controls) were schizophrenics, the diagnostic group regarded today as probably the most difficult to treat with psychiatric surgery. Quantitative assessments of 13 factors related to the disorder were made before surgery, three months after, and each year thereafter for five years. In most of the 11 measures of the illness, as well as in overall morbidity, 140 surgical patients were shown to have more severe symptoms before but less after the operation than the controls. Specifically, the postoperative group was described as manifesting "less restiveness, paranoid projection, melancholic agitation, perceptual distortion, motor disturbance, belligerence, withdrawal, and conceptual disorganization than the controls."[2] By the fourth postoperative year, considerably more of the extensive surgical patients had been discharged from the hospital than the controls. The percentages were 9.7 percent of the controls discharged versus 17.8 percent of those with the standard operation.

Later in the course of the study, the surgeons performed a less extensive procedure of bimedial leucotomy. The result was that 23.1 percent of the 26 patients with that operation were discharged from the hospital. The beneficial results in both operated groups were statistically significant ($p \le .05$). The investigators concluded:

The community adjustment of these discharged patients, although below average to marginal, was rated as better for those who had been lobotomized than for the controls. The standard and bimedial lobotomized patients remaining in the hospital show improvement over the controls in terms of rating scale scores as early as three months after the operation. The improvement was maintained in most respects throughout the five years of study.[2]

I call particular attention to this study to indicate that thoughtful, conscientious psychiatrists throughout the world had sound reasons for recommending as many lobotomies as they did in the 1940s and early

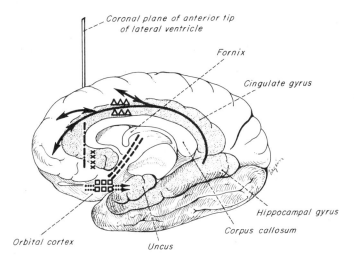

Coronal plane of anterior tip of lateral ventricle

Fornix

Cingulate gyrus

Hippocampal gyrus

Corpus callosum

Orbital cortex

Uncus

—·—·— CORONAL PLANE OF:
     BIMEDIAL LEUCOTOMY (FALCONER-SCHURR, JACKSON)
     INFERIOR-MEDIAL LEUCOTOMY (BAKER et al)

△△△
△△△ CINGULOTOMY: (BALLANTINE et al)
                  (MEYER et al)

ⅹ
ⅹ SITE OF LEUCOTOMY: (BAILEY et al)
ⅹ

□□□
□□□ SITE OF ^{90}Y LESION OF KNIGHT (IN SUBCORTICAL WHITE MATTER)

·········▶ CONNECTIONS ORBITAL CORTEX TO UNCUS (VAN HOESEN et al)

◀━━▶ RECIPROCAL CONNECTIONS FRONTAL GRANULAR CORTEX◀━▶GYRUS
     CINGULI (NAUTA)

════ THALAMO-FRONTAL RADIATION – MEDIAL PART OF DORSO-MEDIAL
     NUCLEUS THALAMUS TO MEDIAL PART OF ORBITAL FRONTAL CORTEX

Fig. 8-1.   Site of surgical incision in common leucotomy operations. (Reproduced with permission from W. H. Sweet: Special Article. Treatment of medically intractable mental disease by limited frontal leucotomy—Justifiable? _New England Journal of Medicine_, 1973, _289_, 1117–1125.)

1950s. By the late 1950s, when the final report was published, new and obviously superior drugs dominated the therapy of psychotic patients. This carefully designed and executed study was largely ignored or overlooked, perhaps because of its publication in a comparatively obscure journal. Some psychiatrists speak with shame of this period when their colleagues submitted so many of their patients to this type of procedure. It should be known that they advised this operation because they were grossly dissatisfied with other therapeutic alternatives at that time.

In my own group at the McLean and Massachusetts General Hospital, Dr. Paul Howard was largely responsible for such cases. Dr. Jason Mixter and I operated on about 75 seriously ill psychotic patients back in the late 1940s and early 1950s. Howard recently has told me that of those 75, about one-third were sufficiently improved to be discharged from the hospital; one-third were distinctly improved, though kept in the hospital; and one-third were unimproved. He thought none of the 75 was worse. Parenthetically, several years later one patient in our series was doing creditable work as a student at one of the graduate schools in Harvard University. She came to him distraught after having been to a lecture where she had been told that people who were lobotomized became vegetables, and she wondered if she were in this category. Although I have had my doubts sometimes about some of the graduate schools at Harvard, I do feel that Howard was justified in reassuring her that she was not a vegetable.

IMPROVED SURGICAL TECHNIQUES

Two significant developments have occurred in the past two decades. Not only were new drugs introduced in the middle 1950s, but the biochemical and physiological understanding of the psychoses has improved, and avenues for research in these areas are opening up to such a degree that any mode of therapy is going to be necessarily assessed against any other mode of therapy in a critical fashion.

The curious thing about the surgery in this disorder has been that it has proved possible to make much smaller lesions, producing much less in the way of an undesirable deficit. Yet such lesions have yielded what has seemed to me to be an astonishing percentage of improvement in the very seriously ill patients. Indeed, the techniques by which these lesions are made entail a lower risk and less unwanted deficit than almost any of the other forms of major surgery in the intracranial cavity that we have to offer for any of the disorders we treat neurosurgically.

Small Lesion Operations

I would like to document some of these statements regarding the small lesion operations, in particular the stereotactic procedures. These involve the introduction into the brain of either electrodes, cold probes, or yttrium-90 seeds, on the assumption that some cerebral component of the

limbic system is the appropriate target for destructive lesions. These
lesions have been made in the gyrus cinguli in the white matter lateral to it,
or in the white matter of the posteromedial orbital cortex, just below the
head of the caudate nucleus.

The largest series of inferomedial frontal lesions is that of Geoffrey
Knight.[8] In 1960 he initiated the procedure of inserting two rows of
yttrium-90 seeds into the area on each side. Others inserted electrodes into
this region beneath the frontal horn of the lateral ventricle as shown in
Figure 8-2. A sagittal projection of the same electrodes (Fig. 8-3) shows
that they lie just far enough lateral to the midline to miss the medial gray

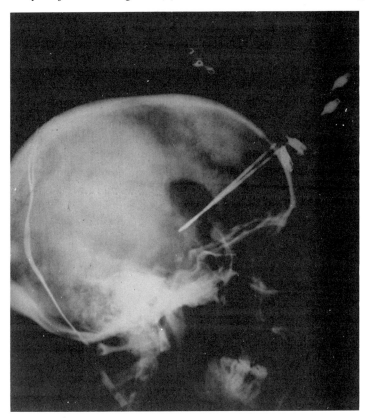

Fig. 8-2. Stereotactic radiofrequency inferior frontomedial leucotomy, lateral
view. One-centimeter electrodes lie with their tips just in front of the third ventricle
and beneath the frontal horns of the lateral ventricles. The ventricular air is injected
via one of the openings used for insertion. Wires and metal electrode sheaths are
insulated.

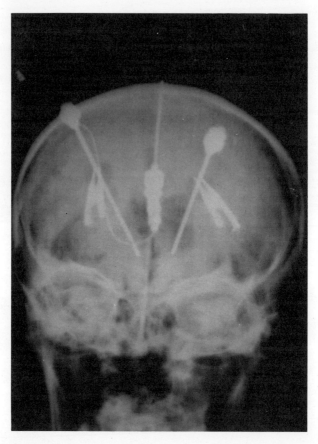

Fig. 8-3.   Sagittal view of same electrode placement as shown on
Figure 8-2.

matter and make a lesion in the white matter. Figure 8-4 illustrates in
coronal brain sections the lesions made anterior to the ventricles in a patient
who had intractable pain from an advancing cancer. (His pain was relieved
for two months until death.) The electrodes are metal rods 1 cm long and 1
mm in diameter. The coronal sections are each 1 cm apart, beginning at the
frontal pole; 3 cm posterior to that we begin to see the lesions, which
become maximal in size 4 cm behind the frontal pole. The lesions are not
seen in the 6-cm section through the anterior horns of the ventricles. On the
right of the illustration is the lesion made by one electrode. On the left side

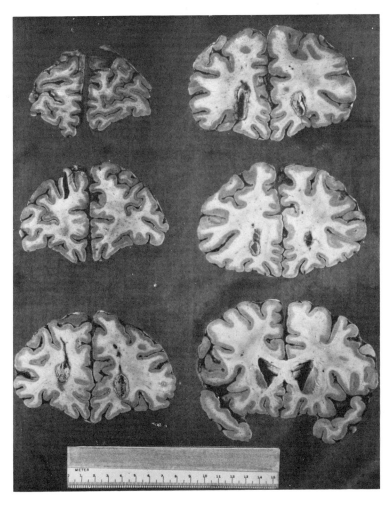

Fig. 8-4. Radiofrequency leucotomy: successive 1-cm coronal transections of frontal lobes post mortem. These sections show the position and extent of two lesions made on each side in patient who died two months after coagulation. This man, with carcinoma of the apex of the lung and severe pain in the chest and arm, remained at home, free of his former pain and the need for excessive narcotic dosage. (Reproduced with permission from J. C. White: Choice of surgical procedures for relief of pain in incurable diseases of chest and abdomen. *Surgical Clinics of North America*, 1958, *38*, 1373. Courtesy of W. B. Saunders.)

is a longer lesion made by a second placement of the electrode a week later, when the pain relief didn't continue after the first two lesions. These illustrations indicate the size of the lesion that we make these days in our efforts to control not only psychiatric problems but also pain.

Two nonsurgeons have been among the reporters on the Knight material. Ström-Olsen and Carlisle[12] reported on 210 of the patients who had lesions made with yttrium-90 seeds beneath the frontal horns. These patients had longstanding psychiatric illnesses and were operated on either at the Hammersmith Post Graduate Hospital or at the Brook General Hospital. The 150 patients who could at long-term follow-up be interviewed with their relatives by both authors formed the group for analyses: 66 percent were followed from 2 to 8 years; the remainder from 16 months to 2 years. Complete recovery from their illnesses occurred in 33 percent, with another 16 percent much improved. The latter group had only minor residual symptoms requiring no further treatment. Another 23 percent improved but still needed treatment. The authors conclude:

> The best results were obtained in the depressions, 56% recovered or much improved; the corresponding figures for obsessional neurosis were 50% and for anxiety states 41%. There were only 4 of 150 who developed troublesome lasting behavior change. One became irritable and aggressive, two sexually promiscuous, one pleasure seeking, neglecting her home.[12]

A report on similar lesions induced by yttrium-90 seeds focused upon a two- to nine-year follow-up of 44 psychiatric cases.[5] All of the patients had long illnesses refractory to other treatments. Following surgery, none of the patients developed a frontal lobe syndrome; however, one patient with obsessional neuroses had no relief of his problem and developed "new impulsivity and irritability." The poorest results were obtained in those with schizophrenia, psychopathic personality, or character neurosis. For example, in those patients categorized, "agitation with mental deficit, encephalopathy, or dissociated hebephrenia," there were five failures, one recurrence, three with partial relief, and only one with major relief. Only 3 of the 44 patients were cured at once after operation and remained so. In 11, progressive amelioration led to cure. In five, there was no early improvement, but about six months later major amelioration began. These good results were concentrated largely in the intractable neuroses and depressions. Lempérière and Gutmann,[9] after further observation of the same patients, reviewed the world literature and concluded in an editorial in 1970 in the *Presse Médicale* that "psychosurgery is justified after the failure of other treatment by the results at times spectacular which are obtained in certain cases."

Lesions in the Supracallosal Portion of the Gyrus Cinguli or Its Subcortical White Matter

These operations were first carried out as open procedures in which portions of this part of the brain were removed. Mild but definite personality and behavioral changes ensued following this operation by a number of neurosurgeons in various parts of the world. Seeking to reduce sequelae, Ballantine began in 1962 to make sterotactic lesions in this area. In 1967 he and his psychiatric colleagues reported on 40 psychiatric patients judged to be intractably ill (of 2500).[3, 4] The procedure involves making a pair of radiofrequency cylindrical lesions. Figure 8-5 reveals, in the lateral and sagittal projections of ventriculograms, the electrodes lying in the white matter immediately above the anterior parts of the bodies of the lateral ventricles. Ballantine and his colleagues selected a total of 121 psychiatric patients for this operation. These patients suffered from such mood disturbances as depression, hypomania, alcoholic depression, obsessive compulsive neurosis, anxiety neurosis, and anorexia nervosa. Of 66 patients in this group, cared for by one group of psychiatrists, 49 percent changed after one such bilateral operation from a preoperative state of total disability to either the well or the markedly improved category. The total in these two categories was increased to 79 percent following the

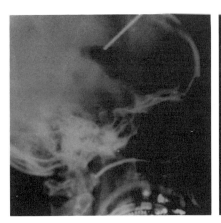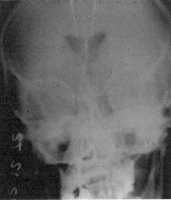

Fig. 8-5. Placement of needle electrodes for production of cingulate lesions under ventriculographic control. Left, lateral radiograph; right, anteroposterior radiograph. (Reproduced with permission from R. W. Hurt and H. T. Ballentine: Stereotactic anterior cingulate lesions for persistent pain: A report on 68 cases. *Clinical Neurosurgery,* 1974, *21,* 336. Courtesy Williams & Wilkins.)

making of a second pair of lesions in the cingulum in 28 of the patients who had had an unsatisfactory result after the first operation. An important feature of these small lesions was that the goal of no significant psychiatric or surgical complications was achieved.

A group of psychiatrists, psychologists, and a neurosurgeon at the University of Texas have recently reported[10] much more comprehensive pre- and postoperative evaluations of this operation in 53 patients in alcoholic, depressive, and schizophrenic groups. Absence of complications and relatively encouraging results characterized the communication. From Sidney, Australia, has come another report[1] by two psychiatrists, a psychologist, and a neurosurgeon on the results of anterior cingulotomy in 48 patients whose severe depressive illness had been treated intensively for five or more years before operation. At surgery, under direct vision, an incision 2 or 3 cm wide was made in the white matter, deep to the lower part of the gyrus cinguli. A few patients with the 3-cm incision developed "a marked and sometimes prolonged state of anergia with negativistic components. This always reversed." This temporary side effect was successfully obviated in the later cases by an incision extending no more than 2 cm laterally. A battery of 17 different psychometric tests was given before and after the operation, revealing "in nearly every case a significant degree of improvement in intellectual and emotional measures after operation." The numbers with each diagnosis were 26 manic depressives, 7 schizo-affectives (predominantly affective), 7 anxiety-phobic depressives, 7 obsessive-compulsives, and 3 puerperal depressed. "A remission of all symptoms and ability to work at the pre-illness level or better" was reported in 88 percent of the patients. They said there were no instances of impairment of social awareness or deterioration in ethical–moral behavior after the operation. The authors emphasized what they described as the life-saving usefulness of this type of psychosurgery. I have published much more extensive documentation elsewhere.[14]

RATIONALE FOR SURGICAL TARGETS

Both anatomical and physiological studies in animals have shown that the white fibers almost encircling the corpus callosum include the major pathways in the cerebral hemisphere for expression of emotion. They constitute the hemispheral portion of the limbic system (Fig. 8-1). Also included in this limbic system are deeper nuclei in the thalamus and in the hypothalamus. Figure 8-1 also indicates (dashed lines) that part of the thalamofrontal radiation extending from the medial part of the dorsal medial nucleus of the thalamus to the medial half of the cortex on the orbital surface of the frontal lobe. By empirical trials and correlation with postmortem studies, it has also been found that lesions outside this limbic system have less effect on psychotic symptoms. For example, of eight elderly patients who died of causes unrelated to the operation of Knight,[8] Corsellis found accurate inferoposteromedial positioning of the yttrium-90 seeds on late postmortem examinations in the four patients who had recovered or improved. Conversely, in the four patients whose illnesses were unchanged, the seeds were too far forward and too far lateral on one side or both. Evans[6] also has reported on two depressed patients who failed to improve and committed suicide after a psycho-surgical procedure. Their brains showed that at the open leucotomy the thalamofrontal radiations had not been cut as planned. Conversely, Ström-Olsen and Northfield[13] found in a late postmortem, after clinically and anatomically successful orbital leucotomy, the appropriate degeneration of the medial part of the dorsal and medial thalamic nucleus. Ballantine et al. have also noted that when the lesions were largely above the cingulum, instead of in it as planned, the clinical results were worse.[4] Thus there are a few isolated anatomicoclinical correlations indicating that gyrus cinguli and inferomedial thalamofrontal radiations may well be appropriate targets in intractable affective disorders.

Newly discovered pathways originate from the full circumference of the gyrus cinguli, projecting to the neocortical granular parts of the frontal lobes. In Figure 8-1 they are indicated by double-ended arrows. The second end, the end pointing back toward the gyrus cinguli, indicates that reciprocal projections extended from those neocortical granular parts of the frontal lobes back to the gyrus cinguli. Nauta[11] has suggested that via such connections the frontal cortex both monitors and modulates limbic mechanisms. Another neocortical limbic pathway has recently been described by Van Hoesen,[15] and there are others from the orbital cortex to the uncus, also indicated in Figure 8-1.

I emphasize that the psychiatric disorders which appear to respond best to surgery of this limbic system are those characterized by stereotypy of an excessive and futile emotional response: that is to say, the phobias, anxieties, obsessions, depressions, and the affective component of schizophrenia. One thinks of the analogy of the uncontrolled feedback on a public address system that begins to howl. An interesting feature of this concept is that the chronic, intractable, diffuse pains that we have attempted to treat by operations in the frontal lobes are most effectively treated by essentially the identical types of operations. Here, too, chronic intractable pain associated, for example, with malignant disease is an excessive and futile response.

CONCLUSION

Few well-controlled studies have been conducted in the United States. Psychiatrists and neurosurgeons in this country are lagging behind those of several other nations in intelligently appraising the bases for interaction between their two disciplines. That such bases exist has been amply demonstrated by many distinguished men and institutions, especially in Great Britain. The vastly increased therapeutic armamentarium now available to psychiatrists means that only a small fraction of the large number of patients with mental illness without identifiable organic brain disease need be considered for cerebral surgery. However, the evidence now at hand indicates, in my view, that those who have not responded to appropriately protracted medical management should be appraised as possible candidates for psychiatric surgery.

REFERENCES

1. Bailey, H. R., Dowling, J. L., Swanton, C. H., et al. Studies in depression. I. Cingulo-tractotomy in the treatment of severe affective illness. *Medical Journal of Australia,* 1971, *1,* 8–12.
2. Ball, J., Klett, C. J., & Gresock, C. J. The Veterans Administration study of prefrontal lobotomy. *Journal of Clinical Experimental Psychopathology Quarterly Review Psychiatric Neurology,* 1959, *20,* 205–217.
3. Ballantine, H. T., Cassidy, W. L., Flanagan, N. B., et al. Stereotaxic anterior cingulotomy for neuropsychiatric illness and intractable pain. *Journal of Neurosurgery,* 1967, *26,* 488–495.
4. Ballantine, H. T., Cassidy, W. L., Brodeur, J., et al. Frontal cingulotomy for mood disturbance. In E. Hitchcock, L. V. Laitinen, & K. Vaernet (Eds.), *Psychosurgery.* Springfield, Ill. Charles C Thomas, 1972, pp. 221–229.
5. Bonis, A., Covello, L., Lempérière, Th., et al. Etude critique des indications d'interventions psychochirurgicales. *Encèphale,* 1968, *57,* 439–473, 525–563.
6. Evans P. Failed leucotomy with misplaced cuts: A clinico-anatomical study of two cases. *British Journal of Psychiatry,* 1971, *118,* 165–170.
7. Hurt, R. W., & Ballantine, H. T. Stereotactic anterior cingulate lesions for persistent pain: A report on 68 cases. *Clinical Neurosurgery,* 1974, *21,* 334–351.
8. Knight, G. Stereotactic tractotomy in the surgical treatment of mental illness. *Journal of Neurology, Neurosurgery, and Psychiatry.* 1965, *28,* 304–310.

9. Lempérière, T., & Gutmann, A. Indications et résultats de la psycho-chirurgie. *Presse Medicale,* 1970, *78,* 1813–1816.

10. Meyer, G. A., Martin, W. L., McGrawl, C. P., et al. *Stereotactic cingulotomy.* Paper presented at the Third World Congress of Psychosurgery, Cambridge, England, August 14–18, 1972.

11. Nauta, W. J. H. Some efferent connections of the prefrontal cortex in the monkey. In J. M. Warren & K. Akert (Eds.): *Frontal granular cortex and behavior.* New York: McGraw-Hill, 1964, pp. 397–409.

12. Ström-Olsen, R., & Carlisle, S. Bi-frontal stereotactic tractotomy: A follow-up study of its effects on 210 patients. *British Journal of Psychiatry,* 1971, *118,* 141–154.

13. Ström-Olsen, R., & Northfield, D. W. C. Undercutting of orbital cortex in chronic neurotic and psychotic tension states. *Lancet,* 1955, *1,* 986–991.

14. Sweet, W. H. Special Article. Treatment of medically intractable mental disease by limited frontal leucotomy—Justifiable? *New England Journal of Medicine,* 1973, *289,* 1117–1125.

15. Van Hoesen, G. W., Pandya D. N., & Butters, N. Cortical afferents to the entorhenal cortex of the rhesus monkey. *Science,* 1972, *175,* 1471–1473.

9. IMPLICATIONS OF NEUROSURGERY

Physical Intervention into the Human Brain: Ethical and Scientific Considerations

Elliot S. Valenstein, Ph.D.

Although the new techniques for physically modifying the brain are fascinating to almost everyone, they have also produced a great amount of anxiety and fear and even a little paranoia over the way these techniques might be used.* The topic can hardly be avoided, as we have all been bombarded by popular accounts in newspapers, magazines, novels, television shows, movies, science fiction stories, etc., depicting the great power of electrical and chemical brain stimulation to control behavior, emotions, and even thoughts. Michael Crichton's *The Terminal Man*[4] will probably have a greater impact than Mary Shelley's *Frankenstein* due to the many people who believe that behavior can be controlled by electrical stimulation of the brain. A story in a popular magazine even described a future government, an *electroligarchy,* in which the social classes would be distinguished by the number of brain electrodes implanted.[18] The members of the lowest class, for instance, would have 500 electrodes

*Only a few aspects of this complex subject can be discussed here. I have tried to present a readable and unbiased description of the major historical, scientific, and ethical considerations in *Brain Control: A Critical Examination of Brain Stimulation and Psychosurgery* (Wiley, 1973).

inserted, no free will, and would in fact be completely robotized. According to the story, "they could dig ditches all day and love every minute of it."

Of course many of these stories are only meant for our amusement, but that intention does not stop even these, in time, from having a profound influence. It is not uncommon, for example, for psychiatric patients to claim that their thoughts and emotions are being controlled by devices implanted in their brains while they slept. These paranoid thoughts are not very different from what many normal people now think is possible, including some whose education and position might lead us to expect they would be more critical and sophisticated than the average person. One prominent professor of psychology, for example, has described the power of electrical stimulation of the brain in the following manner:

> The number of activities connected to specific places and processes in the brain . . . is simply huge. Animals and men can be oriented toward each with emotions ranging from stark terror or morbidity to passionate affection and sexual desire . . . Eating, drinking, sleeping, moving of bowels or limbs or organs of sensation gracefully or in spastic comedy, can all be managed on electrical demand by puppeteers whose flawless strings are pulled from miles away by the unseen call of radio and whose puppets, made of flesh and blood, look like "electronic toys" so little self-direction do they seem to have.[9]

It would not be difficult to provide many similar examples from widely read books and even college texts. Such exaggerated and distorted descriptions of the power of electrical stimulation and other physical techniques used in brain research have produced not only fears about their possible misuse, but they have also led to proposals for applying this presumed power to the solution of social problems. The belief that brain interventions might achieve desirable social goals was expressed by the social psychologist Kenneth Clark in his Presidential Address at the American Psychological Association Convention in 1971. Clark startled the large number of people in the audience by his statement that

> . . . [We] might be on the threshold of that type of scientific biochemical intervention which would stabilize and make dominant the moral and ethical propensities of man and subordinate, if not eliminate, his negative and primitive behavioral tendencies.[3]

Clark also suggested at the time that political leaders should be required to

> . . . accept and use the earliest perfected form of psychotechnological, biochemical intervention which would assure their positive use of power and reduce or block the possibility of using power destructively.[3]

The fact that such a suggestion came from a social scientist—a member of a group that has traditionally favored environmental rather than biological explanations—is an indication of the extent of the influence of these many distorted portrayals of behavior control by physical manipulation of the brain.

In addition to the optimism and anxiety about potential social application of brain interventions there is also a controversy currently raging over the "resurgence of psychosurgery" as a means of treating the mentally ill. This controversy has raised a multitude of ethical and social concerns about how to protect patients and our civil liberties but not block all experimentation and progress in science and medicine.

SEPARATION OF FACT FROM FANTASY

If the problems raised by these new brain techniques are to be discussed realistically, it is essential at the outset to separate fact from fantasy as best we can. A distorted conception of the power of brain interventions can lead to legislative and other protective remedies that may not be addressed to the right problem and may in the long run be quite harmful. A closer examination of some typical animal experiments may be the best way to illustrate some of the misconceptions.

Several years ago, José Delgado (at that time a professor at Yale University) described the results of a demonstration of the use of brain stimulation on wild bulls. Although there was little information that was scientifically useful in this demonstration, because of the drama of the situation the results have been described over and over in the popular media and in psychology textbooks. The following account is very representative:

Dr. Delgado implanted a radio-controlled device deep within the brain of a *brave bull,* a variety bred to respond with a raging charge when it sees any human being. But when Dr. Delgado pressed a button on a transmitter, sending a signal to a battery-powered receiver attached to the bull's horns, an impulse went into the bull's brain and the animal would cease his charge. After several stimulations, the bull's naturally aggressive behavior disappeared. It was as placid as Ferdinand.[13]

Although the interpretation implied in the above quotation is commonly accepted, there is actually little evidence supporting the conclusion that the stimulation had a specific effect on the bull's aggressive tendencies. It is immediately apparent to almost everyone who has had an opportunity to view the film record of this demonstration that every time the bull charged it was forced by the stimulation to turn in circles. After a number of such repetitions the confused bull stopped charging for a short period. None of this behavior is at all surprising to anyone knowledgeable about the nervous system because the stimulating electrode had been placed in a brain structure (the caudate nucleus) known to play an important role in regulating bodily movements. Patients receiving stimulation in this brain structure typically display various types of stereotyped motor responses.[21] Movement disorders such as the spasticity and tremors seen in Parkinson's disease have frequently been linked to pathology in the caudate nucleus. No convincing evidence has been presented to support the belief that the bull was pacified in any significant way by the stimulation. Rather, it seemed confused and perhaps frustrated. Certainly, it is misleading to convey the impression that the brain stimulation was modifying aggression exclusively.

Aggression is certainly not controlled exclusively by the caudate nucleus or even the hypothalamus, a brain area where electrical stimulation can provoke normally peaceful cats to kill rats. Experimental destruction of either of these brain areas does not eliminate natural aggressiveness unless the region destroyed is so extensive the animal becomes generally incapable of almost all behavior. The interpretation of these demonstrations can be quite complex, but it is clear that they do not point to any practical way to eliminate aggression while leaving other behaviors undisturbed. The conclusion that many regions of the brain play a role in regulating aggressiveness, and that each of these regions plays a role in a great number of different behaviors, is inescapable.

Another example illustrates a similar point, but from a somewhat different perspective. The power of brain stimulation to control behavior is often exaggerated due to the belief that it is possible to arouse distinct motivational states by stimulating specific areas of the brain. It is often claimed that the fact that brain stimulation causes animals to eat, drink, carry young, engage in sexual behavior, and so forth demonstrates the possibility of turning such appetites as hunger, thirst, and sex on and off with a great amount of reliability and selectivity. It is important to examine this conclusion more critically.

In my laboratory we have shown in many different ways that brain stimulation does not duplicate natural motivational states.[23, 25] It now seems unlikely that the animal that eats, for example, in response to brain stimulation does so because the stimulation has evoked a natural state of hunger. For instance, although a rat may start to eat food when its brain is stimulated, it usually eats only one type of food and not another. The stimulated animal may not even eat the same food after it has been changed in shape or texture. A particular difficulty in the usual interpretation of these events is the fact that the behavior evoked by identical brain stimulation can change over time. Initially, a rat may only eat when stimulated. Later, however, it may drink when the same brain area is stimulated, or it may engage in some other behavior. Moreover, changes in the animal's environment often result in very different behaviors being evoked by the brain stimulation. In view of these facts it is not possible to maintain that the stimulation reliably produces the same behavior or motivational state all the time.

If the response to brain stimulation is variable in inbred rats, it is certainly much more variable in monkeys, apes, and man. In humans, stimulation may evoke general emotional states that are somewhat predictable in that the activation of certain brain areas tends to produce unpleasant feelings while the activation of other areas tends to produce pleasant emotional states. In response to brain stimulation, patients may report feeling tension, fear, or anger, or they may describe feeling relaxed and on occasion even become sexually aroused. However, patients differ in their emotional response to stimulation of the same brain area and the same person may have very different responses to identical stimulation administered at different times. It simply is not true that stimulation of brain structure in humans evokes the identical emotional state repeatedly.

Stimulation of a particular brain area does not always evoke the same emotional state and it clearly does not always produce the same behavior. It may be convenient and dramatic to speak about the correspondence of brain areas to complex behaviors, but as usually stated a much more direct relationship is implied than actually exists. The behavior that is expressed in response to even the same emotional state will vary with the personality of the subject and the situational determinants that are operating at the time. One person may lash out at the world when angry, while another person may simmer quietly or redirect the anger into constructive behavior. Certainly there is no simple correspondence between discrete brain areas and the desirability of a behavior for our social needs. We may be concerned about aggression, but it should be obvious that a concept such as aggression is a man-made abstraction that does not exist as a separate entity in the brain. Much of what comprises aggressive behavior is undoubtedly also very essential to highly desirable behavior. The belief that we can modify the normal brain and selectively decrease the expression of asocial behavior without influencing desirable capacities and behaviors is completely unrealistic. This argument is not at all mitigated by the fact that there are people who became violent after brain damage and whose behavior was restored to normality following reparative neurosurgery.

Not everyone will be reassured by these arguments. There are those who would argue that in view of the progress made so far, it is likely that our ability to control behavior by physically altering the brain will be much more precise in the future. While anything is possible, the present data certainly do not suggest that precise and predictable control over behavior will be realized in the foreseeable future. Greater accuracy in placing electrodes in the brain, for example, is not likely to reduce the unpredictability of changes in complex behavior in response to stimulation. The behavior influenced by stimulating any brain structure (even a single nerve cell) will always depend upon ongoing activity in other brain areas. Undoubtedly, more efficient means will be developed to alter mood and to modify mental alertness and memory. This ability is very different, however, from controlling the specific content of thought processes or predicting how changes in mood or cognitive ability will be expressed in behavior.

The belief that there are brain techniques that can control behavior in highly predictable ways has produced two different reactions. On the one hand, the fear that this presumed power may be used as a political weapon has caused people to recommend some very hastily conceived and potentially dangerous legislative action.* On the other hand, others have tended to abandon the search for appropriate social remedies because of the belief that there are (or will soon be) biological solutions available.

*The fear that psychosurgery is primarily a behavior-control technique of potentially wide applicability to political and social problems has had a significant influence on legislation under consideration. For instance, a recently proposed federal law (H.R. 6852), which could outlaw psychosurgery, included the following definitions of these operations:

(A) modification or control of thoughts, feelings, actions, or behavior rather than the treatment of a known and diagnosed physical disease of the brain;
(B) modification of normal brain function or normal brain tissue in order to control thoughts, feelings, actions, or behavior.

The arguments are frequently couched in a political and social framework. The psychiatrist Peter Breggin has charged, for example, that "these brain studies are not oriented toward liberation of the patient. They are oriented toward law and order and control toward protecting society against the so-called radical individual." The unfounded speculation by Mark et al.[12] that the more violent participants in a race riot may have had some brain pathology has undoubtedly caused much anxiety about future applications. It is only fair to note, however, that their psychosurgical patients have all been white and have had demonstrable evidence of brain pathology.

It would be difficult to fabricate a better example of the distortions that can result from a preoccupation with biological techniques for controlling behavior than that contained in an article by Ingraham and Smith.[8] These two criminologists suggested that techniques are available for maintaining a surveillance on paroled prisoners and for controlling their behavior. They described implanted devices for monitoring the location and physiological state of a parolee and the possibility of using remotely operated brain stimulation to control undesirable behavior. Pictured in the article is the following scenario:

> A parolee with a past record of burglaries is tracked to a downtown shopping district (in fact, is exactly placed in a store known to be locked up for the night) and the physiological data reveal an increased respiration rate, a tension in the musculature and an increased flow of adrenalin. It would be a safe guess, certainly, that he was up to no good. The computer in this case, *weighing the possibilities,* would come to a decision and alert the police or parole officer so that they could hasten to the scene; or, if the subject were equipped with an implanted radiotelemeter, it would transmit an electrical signal which could block further action by the subject by causing him to forget or abandon his project.[8]

Even though it is highly unlikely that anyone would approve or fund Ingraham and Smith's proposal, the fact that they could make such a proposal demonstrates the impact of the many distorted representations of brain control techniques. If many criminologists are expending energy and funds on such unreal solutions it is little wonder our penal institutions are in such a dreadful state.

PSYCHOSURGERY

There is no doubt that there has been evidence in the past and there is some in the present to support the position that psychosurgery has produced serious deficits. It is also true that the majority of the postoperative studies have reported that a significant number of seemingly intractably ill patients have been improved by such operations. Almost all of the older studies, however, can be criticized on various methodological grounds such as the involvement of the evaluators with the success of the surgery or the insensitivity of the testing instruments to important changes in personality and intellect. Often the estimates of improvement gave too much weight to the elimination of "troublesome behavior" and placed much less emphasis on the qualitative level of the postoperative adjustment. Over the years the criteria for selection of the patients considered to be the best candidates for psychosurgery have changed and the surgical procedures themselves have been greatly refined. Only during the past few years have data applicable to current psychosurgical practice begun to accumulate. The evaluation of these complex data is clearly beyond the scope of the present chapter, but it seems appropriate to underscore the point that any evaluation of psychosurgery must be guided by the conviction that postoperative changes cannot be limited to a narrow behavior category.

In the past (and to some extent in the present), there has always been a certain percentage of those performing psychosurgery who have displayed a frightening tendency toward "tunnel vision." While quick to see possible clinical applicability in some of the results of studies of brain-lesioned animals, this group has often seemed oblivious to behavioral changes that should have cautioned them against the operation or at least influenced the procedures used for evaluating patients postoperatively. There are far too many instances in which the results of psychosurgery are described only in terms of the alleviation of some disruptive emotional problem with little or no reference to other consequences of the operation.

A few brief examples may help to illustrate this point. It is generally acknowledged that Egas Moniz, the Portuguese neurologist who received the Nobel Prize for initiating the prefrontal lobotomy, was greatly influenced by Carlyle Jacobsen's description of a chimpanzee that stopped throwing temper tantrums after destruction of its frontal lobes. The main point of Jacobsen's findings, however, seemed not to have influenced Moniz. Jacobsen had shown that monkeys and chimpanzees appear to permanently lose the capacity to solve certain types of problems following destruction of their frontal lobes.

One of the more striking illustrations of tunnel vision comes from a psychosurgical procedure used to treat pedophilic homosexuals—that is, men who seek out sexual opportunities with young boys. Roeder and his colleagues at the University of Göttingen have described their response to a film depicting the hypersexual behavior of cats after destruction of a brain region in the temporal lobes called the amygdala nucleus.[16] [17] They have written:

> . . . the behavior of male cats with lesions of the amygdala region in some respects closely approached that of human perversion. The films convinced us that there was a basis for a therapeutic, stereotaxic approach to this problem in man.[16]

Roeder and his colleagues were referring to the fact that there were reports that ventromedial hypothalamic lesions eliminate the hypersexuality previously produced by destruction of the amygdala. They proceeded to make stereotaxic lesions in the ventromedial hypothalamic nucleus in man. Based on experience with a relatively small patient population that has been described in only a cursory manner in the literature, they presented the following disquieting, if not shocking, conclusion about their surgical procedure.

. . . there is *no doubt* that experimental behavioral research has afforded us a basic method to eliminate or to control pedophilic homosexuality by means of an effective psychosurgical operation in the area of the *sex behavior center*.[17]

The reports from this group seem to be amazingly uninfluenced by the voluminous literature implicating the ventromedial hypothalamus in the regulation of hormonal balance, appetite, irritability, and many other functions as well. However, once the focus was directed at the sexual behavior changes the other important behavioral changes modified by this brain area were neglected.

Still another example of tunnel vision (from the many that could be offered) can be seen in a report by Quaade.[15] Quaade described the destruction of another part of the brain, the lateral hypothalamus, as a surgical treatment for very obese patients. This operation was undertaken because there were many reports that animals show marked decreases in food consumption after this brain region was destroyed. Once again, a large literature was apparently overlooked. There is very good evidence that destruction of the lateral hypothalamus in animals not only reduces appetite for food, but there seems to be a general decline in all motivation, as well as a decreased responsiveness to stimuli and an impairment in learning ability.

These examples of tunnel vision among some psychosurgeons is not meant to characterize all activity in this field. It is clear, though, that the critics as well as the supporters of psychosurgery and other physical interventions into the brain have often performed a disservice (if not great harm) by adopting an unrealistically oversimplified view of brain–behavior relationships.

PSYCHOSURGERY: INDIVIDUAL VERSUS SOCIAL THERAPY

It is most important that psychosurgery as an attempt to help intractably ill mental patients be distinguished from claims that it may contribute significantly to the solution of social problems. The latter possibility has been expressed by Mark and Ervin in their book, *Violence and the Brain.*[10] They have stressed the magnitude of violence in the United States and have strongly suggested that biological interventions can make a significant contribution toward a solution of that problem. Although the book contains perfunctory concessions to the possible contribution of environmental factors, these are more than counterbalanced by statements criticizing (often unfairly) the failure of such factors to explain the occurrence of violence or to suggest any helpful programs. By exaggerating the ineffectiveness of environmental programs—when actually they have not been tried in any serious way—the alternative biological solutions they offer appear to gain in attractiveness. Mark and Ervin make it very clear in the preface of their book that they "have written this book to stimulate a new and biologically oriented approach to the problem of human violence," and they remind us of the severity of the problem by indicating that

> in 1968 more Americans were the victims of murder and aggravated assault in the United States than were killed and wounded in seven-and-one-half years of the Vietnam War; and altogether almost half a million of us were the victims of homicide, rape, and assault.[10]

The impression that brain abnormalities may be a major cause of violence is conveyed early in the book:

> Most people consider brain disease to be a rare phenomenon. It is likely, however, that more than ten million Americans suffer from an obvious brain disease, and the brains of another five million have been subtly damaged.[10]

Because the statistics on brain abnormalities are so intimately coupled to descriptions of violent crimes, only the most critical reader will fail to draw the conclusion that brain pathology is a frequent cause of violent behavior.

Mark and Ervin argue that sudden, "episodic," violent behavior is frequently triggered by abnormal foci in a temporal lobe brain structure called the amygdala. Much of their argument is based on the belief that there is a strong relationship between violent behavior and temporal lobe epilepsy and even "convulsive disorders" without seizures. While there is some evidence to support this view, most current reviews of the literature have concluded that the relationship between temporal lobe epilepsy and violence has been exaggerated.[7] Whatever the true extent of the relationship, there is little justification for the position that a significant amount of the total violence in our society can be attributed to brain damage or that the increases in violence are related to increases in brain pathology.

Mark and Ervin's description of their psychosurgical procedure seems very straightforward and the rationale appears unassailable. It is especially important, therefore, to consider their arguments carefully. At the heart of their proposal is the claim that electrical stimulation is a reliable means of locating the exact focus in the brain that triggers the violent episodes of many persons who exhibit such behavior. Once this focus is located, they claim it can be destroyed with such precision that only a small brain area need be damaged and this area is likely to have been pathological anyway. Thus they have written that ". . . tiny electrodes are implanted in the brain and used to destroy a very small number of cells in a precisely determined manner."[10] They state: "To our knowledge, this is the first time that rage behavior was artificially produced by electrical stimulation in an abnormal brain and used to diagnose the proper placement for a therapeutic lesion."[10] It is important to look more closely at the claim that electrical stimulation is a reliable technique for determining the brain locus responsible for the behavior.

The experimental and clinical evidence clearly indicates that the behavior evoked by brain stimulation in animals and man is greatly influenced by the temperment or personality of the subject and the general emotional state aroused by the stimulation. If the brain stimulation evokes fear, anxiety, or pain and the subject is prone toward violence or aggression, then such behavior will very likely be expressed in response to stimulation at a great many brain sites that evoke such emotional states. Many animal studies support this conclusion. For example, Panksepp has concluded from a study in rats in which mouse killing was evoked by brain stimulation that the ability to evoke this behavior

interacted with the behavioral typology of individual animals—animals normally inclined to kill mice were more likely to kill during hypothalamic stimulation than nonkillers. Thus, the electrically elicited response was probably not determined by specific functions of the tissue under the electrode but by the personality of the rat.[14]

There is little justification for the belief that brain stimulation is a valid technique for locating discrete foci that trigger violence even if such foci exist.[22] In the assaultive patients described by Mark and Ervin, it is likely that violence can be triggered by stimulating a great number of brain sites and probably also by a hard pinching of the skin. It is clear that the ability of brain stimulation to ferret out a presumed critical focus of a behavioral trait has been grossly exaggerated. Moreover, the statement that only "a very small number of cells" are destroyed in this psychosurgical procedure is not supported by their own reports. Most of the operations destroy parts of the amygdala on both sides of the brain and the general practice has been to gradually increase the size of the lesion over a number of months until the troublesome violent behavior appears to have significantly diminished. Although Mark and Ervin have not been very complete in the description of their surgical procedure the information they have published strongly suggests that the area destroyed is much larger and less precisely defined than they have implied in their book.

An additional point that should be made is that *Violence and the Brain* conveyed the impression to many readers that the surgical techniques described are applicable to a great number of violent persons, including those who do not have clear evidence of temporal lobe epilepsy. This impression is given in spite of the fact that Mark and Ervin's own surgical population seems to have been restricted to epileptic patients or those with reasonably good evidence of brain pathology. In the court proceedings of the well-publicized John Doe case in Detroit, Mich., the neurologist, Dr. Ernst Rodin, indicated that the book had misled him into believing that the surgical technique had very broad applicability to behavior problems without demonstrable brain pathology.[6] Indeed, there seems to be little doubt that many other readers concluded that Mark and Ervin were suggesting that the behavior which characterized their "dyscontrol syndrome" might be sufficient grounds to justify surgery. It is only fair to note, however, that whatever his conviction prior to all the criticism of *Violence and the Brain,* Mark has made it very clear recently that he now believes that the neurosurgical treatment of violence should be used very cautiously and only if the evidence of brain pathology is convincing.[11]

It is hoped that the frustration over our inability to stop the spread of violence will not cause us to lose perspective of the problem. It is patently evident that, depending upon the social and physical environment, humans exhibit great differences in behavior. This variability is clearly not due primarily to biological differences between people, as the same people behave very differently under different conditions. The point is well illustrated in Colin Turnbull's[20] account of the transformation of the Ik, a friendly African people forced to change from a life of successful hunting to that of farming under the most difficult of circumstances. Within three generations their social organization had deteriorated and the struggle for individual survival made them hostile and as "generally mean as any people could be." This is the perspective that must be maintained above all else when we try to understand the current increases in violent behavior in our society.

Although it may not be easy to introduce appropriate social changes to decrease violent behavior, there is certainly no reason to believe that biological solutions will soon be available. While there will continue to be a few assaultive patients with clear brain pathology who may be significantly improved by surgical intervention, for the foreseeable future we should increase, rather than decrease, attempts to find social solutions for what are primarily social problems.

COMMENTS ON ETHICAL ISSUES

Over the past several years there has been a great amount of discussion of ethical issues related to physical interventions into the brain. There has been so much discussion, in fact, that it is a challenge to find anything new to say on the topic. It is clear that many of the considerations involve problems that are common to most areas of biomedical experimentation.* It is often argued, however, that operations on the brain present special ethical problems because of the irreversibility of brain damage and especially because the brain is the organ that is responsible for all that makes us human. My own view is that while there is merit to this concern it is frequently phrased in much too general a form to guide our ethical behavior. If it is meant only to imply that we should be very hesitant to operate on the brain the point is so obvious that it is almost trivial. Often, however, the argument takes the form of implying that any brain destruction produces devastating consequences for intellect, personality, and capacity for experiencing emotion. This notion is definitely not true. People who have undergone brain operations that are usually not considered controversial, such as those to remove tumors or to repair cerebral vascular damage, do not necessarily experience any great deficits in spite of brain damage. The results in any particular case depend on the area of the brain damaged and other factors. It is not at all helpful, therefore, to list all the human characteristics dependent on the whole brain. We must come to grips with the more meaningful problem of predicting the likely consequences of specific brain interventions on particular types of patients. This information should be evaluated against the background of the alternative therapeutic possibilities available to the patient under consideration.

There is a tendency these days to suggest a moratorium to review the evidence whenever there is a strong disagreement about some medical

*The term "experimental" often conjures up the image of human "guinea pigs." The use of the term is not meant to imply that the primary purpose is research not therapy, but rather to indicate that the results are not very predictable or that there is no clear consensus on the value of the treatment.

procedure. On the surface, no suggestion could seem more reasonable and moderate in spite of the fact that it may often only be a means of postponing a controversial decision. There is no doubt that there are situations in which a review of past experience and practice would be most helpful. It is questionable, however, whether psychosurgery is such an area. The evidence necessary for evaluating the newer psychosurgical procedures is just beginning to accumulate. It is unlikely that the evidence presently available will make it possible to reach a consensus. We are likely to remain frozen in a moratorium status while the more extreme protagonists continue to cite only that part of the inconclusive evidence which supports their views. A moratorium is most useful in those instances in which it is reasonable to expect that an objective review of the available data will provide answers to the questions raised. It should not be used as a device to obtain a de facto prohibition. Psychosurgery aside, the fact that there have been instances in the past in which patients have been deprived of effective treatment because of misguided objections should caution us against overuse of the moratorium "solution."

Rejecting the usefulness of a moratorium in this situation does not imply that anarchy should prevail in the field of psychosurgery. The recognition that a medical procedure is "experimental" implies the need for control. The process of reviewing proposed experimental procedures seems to be at the center of the problem of patient protection. Traditionally, review panels in hospitals have consisted of physicians reviewing the proposals of their colleagues from the same institution. This procedure has not been very effective in the past. Physicians, particularly those at the same institution, have often been very reluctant to criticize their colleagues for a number of obvious reasons. Moreover, review panel members are often too busy to critically evaluate the relevant literature or the adequacy of previous attempts to treat the patient by less "heroic" procedures. The solution to this problem is not easy, because it seems that people willing to contribute adequate time to serve on review panels often have strong biases that color their judgment. Some method must be established—perhaps, similar to the jury selection system—to obtain reasonably objective people to serve on review panels.

The question of who should serve on review panels is quite controversial. Many physicians feel quite strongly that the layman has no place on such panels. For example, M. Hunter Brown, a neurosurgeon practicing psychosurgery in California, has clearly stated his views on the subject:

Current proposals for surgical boards manned by lawyers, ethicists, consumer advocates, clergymen, etc., are arrant nonsense; lay persons would get into a scientific act in which they have no competence. An informed decision on target neurosurgery is not possible for uninformed people, particularly from those not acquainted with modern technology.[2]

Not everyone is persuaded by such arguments. Clearly, the present review practices often have not provided adequate protection for the patient. Moreover, it is a mistake to believe that the only responsibility of review panels is to consider technical aspects of proposals. Patient protection involves questions about the adequacy of the consent obtained from the patient or guardian, the thoroughness of previous attempts to treat the patient by more conservative therapies, and the legal status of the patient, as well as a number of other questions that can be answered more adequately by a heterogeneous review panel. It is also likely to be a more effective means of monitoring the rare, but real, problem of the physician who is irresponsible or whose ego may be involved in proving the value of a new technique. Heterogeneous review panels might also be better equipped to help in the systematic pooling of the data that would make it possible to be more objective in estimating the probability of success in the future.

It is clear that we must find a way to institute whatever changes are necessary to ensure that members of review panels take their job seriously. During the past few years there have been several reports of patients subjected to very questionable experimental procedures. Unfortunately, no one has asked the review committees in these instances to justify their approval. In the much publicized John Doe case in Detroit, a case involving a proposal to perform an amygdalectomy on an incarcerated patient, one of the review panel members failed to attend any of the meeting related to the proposed surgery. It was his view that

As a layman I am unqualified to comment on any of the technical aspects which are involved in the project. Therefore, we must all trust the good intentions and technical competence of the Hospital Medical Committee, psychologists, psychiatrists, neurologists, etc., who have reviewed and evaluated John Doe's case.

Such passivity, whether from laymen or physicians, is totally misplaced on review panels.

One recurrent problem concerns the ambiguity about which procedures are experimental. A given procedure may require a thorough review in one hospital because it is considered experimental. In another hospital the same technique—for example, implantation of brain-stimulating electrodes—may be classified as a diagnostic tool and may not be reviewed at all or may receive only a cursory review. It is obvious that some classification standardization would help protect patients. There are other reasons for differences between hospitals. The control over experimental medicine has commonly been regulated by the prerogative of the Department of Health, Education, and Welfare to withhold Federal funds. Some private hospitals that receive no such funding are relatively uncontrolled. Under the present system, a patient at a hospital receiving no Federal funds may be much more vulnerable than one at a hospital required by the Department of Health, Education, and Welfare to utilize an approved review procedure.

Briefly, we need to establish standards for classifying procedures as "experimental." Review panels must not serve as "rubber stamp" committees; the members must be made to realize that they may have to justify their decisions. There may actually be a legal precedent for this suggestion, as review panel members have been sued because of the claim that their decision was clearly not based on the best interest of the patient. Review panels should have multidimensional representation; some mechanism must be established for selecting reasonably unbiased members. Lastly, since the procedures in question are experimental, there must be adequate assessment procedures established beforehand, and there must be mechanisms for collecting, pooling, and disseminating information on the outcome.

THE ETHICAL BEHAVIOR OF ETHICISTS

Evidence of the increasing concern over the ethical and social implications of scientific developments is available almost everywhere. Symposia on ethical issues are now on the programs of meetings in almost all of the sciences and professions. This is a very healthy development, but it is not insulated from the influences that can distort every human endeavor in our society. While the motivation of most people concerned about ethical issues may be completely admirable, it would be a mistake to believe that all the good motives belong with those who espouse ethical causes and all the bad motives reside with those they criticize. Ethics is a rapidly expanding field and as a result it would be unrealistic to believe that its members are any more immune to the lure of prestige, power, position, and prosperity than are those engaged in research. Motives aside, the important issue is that criticisms based on ethical concerns can have a great impact on biomedical research and public policy, and often this impact is not adequately considered. Usually the researcher and the clinician are put on the defensive, while the criticism itself is seldom scrutinized. An example may help to illustrate this point.

Concerned individuals, probably with motives that could not be impugned, argued passionately for *indeterminate jail sentences* to remove the sentencing power from vindictive judges and to provide a means of releasing prisoners earlier if they reformed. Much evidence was brought forth to illustrate the capriciousness of some judges who consistently gave very long sentences. There was much less discussion, however, about the practicality of the solution, and Congress was persuaded to pass a resolution supporting the indeterminate sentence. The result, which might have been foreseen if more thought was given to the factors influencing decisions about releasing prisoners, is that prisoners receiving indeterminate sentences serve significantly longer average sentences than those who receive fixed sentences for the same crime. Moreover, they serve their time under the added psychological strain of uncertainty about when they will be released.

Obviously, it is not sufficient to have your "heart in the right place." The harm that is caused unintentionally still hurts. Moreover, where the consequences might have been anticipated—if the analysis of the problem had been a little more cortical and somewhat less visceral—there may be justification for assigning blame. Because concern with ethical issues and reforms does not guarantee beneficial results, it is more important to apply the same criteria to those who point out abuses and advocate reform as we do to those engaged in the practices being scrutinized. If we did this, we would find many instances of failure to meet these criteria, particularly when those concerned are convinced they are engaged in a moral crusade.

Psychosurgery is clearly one of the controversial issues that seems to spawn moral crusaders. Some consider this procedure nothing less than a criminal mutilation of the brain that changes human beings into emotional and intellectual "vegetables" in order to eliminate their troublesome behavior. Others, however, believe these brain operations are the only available means of alleviating some crippling mental illnesses and making it possible for otherwise wretched patients to live reasonably normal lives. The charges and countercharges are often quite heated.

Although we may understand why emotions enter into some controversies, the intensity of feelings does not justify biased, irresponsible, and even dishonest reporting of the evidence. Even after admitting that propaganda techniques may be justifiable under some circumstances, there is no justification for those posing as experts to mislead policy makers by quoting out of context or reporting only that data which supports a preconceived position. In the long run, the passive acceptance of such distortions as a way of life—or even the attempt to justify them on the basis of the goal that is served—will do greater harm than most of the practices that are being criticized.

For several years the Washington, D.C., psychiatrist, Peter Breggin, has been one of the leaders in the attack against psychosurgery. It is his prerogative and it is clearly his right to carry on whatever legal/political action he feels is justified. It should not be his prerogative, however, to pose as an authority while giving distorted testimony to Congressmen or in a courtroom.[19] It is very obvious that Breggin searches the literature only to find ammunition for his cause. Anyone who has objectively examined his statement published in the *Congressional Record*,[1] would have no trouble detecting numerous examples of all the classic ways of distorting evidence. He has selected data, quoted out of context, and resorted to demagogic accusations in order to raise emotions and secure allies. Later, while testifying before the Kennedy subcommittee, Breggin actually referred to this distorted document as his "research papers in the Congressional Records" (Hearings 359). In the *Congressional Record* Breggin accused Dr. O. J. Andy, a Mississippi neurosurgeon, of concealing the fact that he was operating mainly on blacks. This charge was picked up by many persons and repeated frequently. *Ebony* magazine, for example, published an article entitled, "Psychosurgery: A New Threat to Blacks."[1] Apparently no one bothered to check the facts, but at least according to a letter written in response to my enquiry, Andy claimed that of the 40 psychosurgical operations he had performed only 5 percent of the patients—that is, 2 cases—were black. This is very significantly below the percentage of blacks in Mississippi. More recently, I had an opportunity to survey psychosurgical practice in the United States for the U. S. Commission for the Protection of Human Subjects in Biomedical and Behavioral Research. It was found that blacks were clearly significantly underrepresented among the patients who received psychosurgery. For example, there was only 1 black patient among the 600 operated on during the past 20 years by the two neurosurgeons who have in recent times performed more of these procedure than anyone else in the United States. This statistic should not be surprising because the route of referral for psychosurgery is now almost always through private psychiatrists, whose patients have the demographic characteristics of those above the middle socioeconomic class. Hearing Breggin's charge, however, black Congressmen and Congresswomen became understandably concerned and were among the leaders in proposing legislation (H. R. 6852) to outlaw psychosurgery.

Leaving aside any evaluation of psychosurgery, it is likely that we will soon be in serious trouble if a precedent of passing hastily written legislation in response to political pressure based on distortions is established. It would be an especially serious mistake to use the legislative route as a means of resolving controversies over specific medical procedures. This is not to deny that Congress may play a useful role in establishing legal guidelines to protect patients.

Electroconvulsive shock treatment is another controversial procedure that is presently generating much heat. John Friedberg, a psychiatric resident in Oregon, has written an article on electroconvulsive therapy in *Psychology Today*. The article's tone is revealed by its title, "Let's Stop Blasting the Brain," and by such boldtype paragraph headings as "Shock Treatment Burns the Brain," "Beating Up the Insane," and by a text that is characterized by such statements as the following:

> Egas Moniz experimented with prefrontal lobotomies. In Rome, Ugo Cerletti developed electroconvulsive shock treatment. The Germans came up with a simple and final solution for mental illness; in the late 1930's, 275,000 inmates of German psychiatric institutions were starved, beaten, drugged, and gassed to death.[5]

Among other distortions, Friedberg's article clearly conveys the impression that studies by neuropathologists "consistently show severe brain damage" after electroshock treatment. Actually, there is no such clear evidence at all. Conceivably, new neuroanatomical techniques might reveal brain pathology, but there is no reliable evidence today that this is the case.

It is not unreasonable to expect scholarship, intellectual honesty, accurate treatment of data, and responsible behavior by those who claim to be arguing the ethical position as well as by those engaged in the controversial experimentation. It is indeed ironic that in the name of ethics, the study of moral behavior, so many questionable acts of morality have been committed. There is no justification for the situation that forces only the researcher to defend himself and leaves the self/appointed defenders of patients' rights—who often have an equally great impact on patient care—completely uncriticized. Important decisions should not be based on *demands, demagogy,* and *distortions,* nor can complex issues usually be reduced to the absurdly simplistic level of the "good guys versus the bad guys." Up to now there has been little criticism directed toward those who attempt to influence and coerce in this fashion because of the superficial belief that they are in the "service of the angels." Articles such as Friedberg's, however, have been instrumental in initiating legislation in several states which may prevent some patients from having what many (probably most) psychiatrists feel is the best available treatment—whatever its shortcomings—for some types of severe depression.

It is sad, but perhaps true, that confrontation may often be the only way to bring attention to a problem. Those who are unresponsive to more rationally presented arguments must bear much of the blame for this development. Unless means are found to increase the responsiveness of the decision makers, confrontation is likely to continue to be a way of life. However, the techniques that have become necessary to get problems about biomedical research into the open and on the agenda may be totally inappropriate for their resolution. We need muckrakers and gadflys, but the task of making policy in these complex areas can only be harmed by those who persist in distorting the evidence. Particularly great harm can be done by those who adopt the adversary posture of a moral crusader while posing as an "expert witness."

Although there have been some very positive results from the increased concern over practices in biomedical research, we should be sensitive to problems that may develop in this area. It might be useful to mention a few of these because up to now they have been relatively neglected. First, it is helpful to recognize that only a few of the so-called ethical questions in biomedical research actually involve disagreement about moral behavior. Those who disagree about psychosurgery, electroshock treatment, implanted electrodes, amphetamines for hyperkinetic children, and many other controversial therapies all claim to have the best interest of the patient in mind. Much of the controversy really is over the true estimate of risks and possible benefits. The resolution of the controversy, therefore, must depend to a great extent on a realistic appraisal of the evidence. If the evidence is not conclusive, then where it is appropriate and feasible the data required to make the best judgment should be obtained. We should recognize that ethicists do not have any set of agreed upon principles that can help us make the "right" decision even though they may serve the very useful purpose of sensitizing people to the existence of a problem.

The shortcomings of existing experimental procedures in medicine must be evaluated together with the practical alternative that exists. This is seldom done. It is much safer (and also easier) to criticize than to offer an alternative program. Moreover, those who do not have to face patients can afford the luxury of elaborating on our ignorance about the brain and behavior and the causes of mental illness. They are not confronted by a desperate patient and family and decisions that have to be made. The patient cannot always wait for our knowledge of the brain to increase or for society to become more just. Those who criticize electroshock treatment, for instance, seldom offer any suggestions about how to treat those seriously depressed patients—often suicidal—who do not respond to drugs, psychotherapy, or any other kind of treatment that is now available. There is a real danger that ethical discussions may become so elevated that the patient is no longer in the picture.

Finally, it is important to recognize that we must be concerned about protecting future patients as well as those in the present. There is a real danger that we might forget the future patients and create such a bureaucratic morass in order to protect patients from every conceivable abuse that the most imaginative and truly productive researchers will be driven out of every controversial field. The only ones left will be those who practice medicine defensively—continuing ineffective treatment simply because it is easier than spending all one's time with paperwork and committees and contending with long, frustrating delays.

REFERENCES

1. Breggin, P. R. The return of lobotomy and psychosurgery. *Congressional Record, 18,* (26), Feb. 24, 1972.
2. Brown, M. *The captive patient.* Unpublished manuscript.
3. Clark, K. Cited in the *APA Monitor,* October 1971, 2(1).
4. Crichton, M. *The Terminal Man.* New York: Alfred Knopf, 1972.
5. Friedberg, John. Let's stop blasting the brain. *Psychology Today,* August 1974.
6. Gass, R. S. Kaimowitz v. Department of Mental Health: The Detroit psychosurgery case. In W. Gaylin, J. Meister, & R. Neville (Eds.), *Operating on the mind. The psychosurgery conflict.* New York: Basic Books, 1975, pp. 73–86.
7. Goldstein, M. Brain research and violent behavior. *Archives of Neurology,* 1974, *30* 1–35.
8. Ingraham, B. L., & Smith, G. W. The use of electronics in the observation and control of human behavior and its possible use in rehabilitation and parole. *Issues in Criminology,* 1972, *7,* 35–53.
9. London, P. *Behavior control.* New York: Harper & Row, 1969.
10. Mark, V. H., & Ervin, F. R. *Violence and the brain.* New York: Harper & Row, 1970.
11. Mark, V. H., & Neville, R. Brain surgery in aggressive epileptics. *Journal of the American Medical Association,* 1973, *226,* 765–772.
12. Mark, V. H., Sweet, W. H., & Ervin, F. R. Role of brain diseases in riots and urban violence. *Journal of the American Medical Association,* 1967, *201,* 895. (Letter)

13. *The New York Times,* September 12, 1971.
14. Panskeep, J. Aggression elicited by electrical stimulation of the hypothalamus in albino rats. *Physiology and Behavior,* 1971,*6,* 321–329.
15. Quaade, F. Stereotaxy for obesity. *Lancet,* 1974,*1,* 267.
16. Roeder, F., Muller, D., & Orthner, H. Stereotaxic treatment of psychoses and neuroses. In W. Umbach (Ed.), *Special topics in stereotaxis.* Stuttgart: Hippokrates-Verlag, 1971, pp. 82–105.
17. Roeder, F., Orthner, H., & Muller, D. The stereotaxic treatment of pedophilic homosexuality and other sexual deviations. In E. Hitchcok, L. Laitinen, & K. Vaernet (Eds.), *Psychosurgery.* Springfield, Ill. Charles C Thomas, 1972, pp. 87–111.
18. Rorvik, D. Someone to watch over you (for less than two cents a day). *Esquire,* 1969, *72,* 164.
19. Shuman, S. I. The emotional, medical and legal reasons for the special concern about psychosurgery. In F. J. Ayd, Jr. (Ed.), *Medical, moral and legal issues in mental health care.* Baltimore, Md.: Williams & Wilkins, 1974, pp. 48–80.
20. Turnbull, C. M. *The mountain people.* New York: Simon & Shuster (Touchstone), 1972.
21. Van Buren, J. M. Evidence regarding a more precise localization of the posterior frontal-caudate arrest response in man. *Journal of Neurosurgery,* 1966,*24,* 416–417.
22. Valenstein, E. S. Brain stimulation and the origin of violent behavior. In W. L. Smith & A. Kling (Eds.), *Issues in brain/behavior control.* New York: Spectrum, 19$6, pp. 33–48.
23. Valenstein, E. S. Behavior elicited by hypothalamic stimulation. A prepotency hypothesis. *Brain, Behavior, Evolution,* 1969,*2,* 295–316.
24. Valenstein, E. S. *Brain control: A critical examination of brain stimulation and psychosurgery.* New York: Wiley, 1973.
25. Valenstein, E. S., Cox, V. C., & Kakolewski, J. W. Re-examination of the role of the hypothalamus in motivation. *Psychological Review,* 1970,*77,* 16–31.

10. PHARMACOTHERAPY

Wither Alchemy? The Future of Pharmacology

Nathan S. Kline, M.D.

The biological sciences today are in a state not unlike that of chemistry in the Middle Ages. Certainly to those working at the time, there was every reason to believe that their approach was the most avant garde and indisputably "scientific." Today we look back at the potpourri of astrology, numerology' demonology, and the beginnings of modern chemistry. It seems likely that we are beset by a similar set of myths—the difficulty is that one becomes aware of mythological properties only long after the fact.

We have borrowed all too freely from the methodology and explanatory concepts of the "hard" sciences, whereas in reality biology requires a radically different approach. Traditional methods such as holding all variables except one constant cannot possibly be applied to biological material which "squirms." In fact (as I have proposed), it would

This article was previously published in the *Journal of Social Issues* (1971, 27 (3), 73–87). It appears here with the kind permission of the author and the Society for the Psychological Study of Social Issues.

make more sense to try to hold one variable constant and determine what effect this would have on other relevant factors. Certainly compartment models are only the beginning in setting up a system that will allow us to interpret the not infinite but very complex relationships existing between the different components that appear relevant to the subject. In fact, as Wolfgang Koehler pointed out many years ago, "the last thing a science knows is what it is about."

Perhaps this paper, acknowledging the primitive state of the art, may provoke some response that will move things just a bit farther along.

Drugs have played an important role in man's experience for thousands of years, first in relation to religious and ritualistic functions, later for a variety of secular reasons as well. Social, psychological, and technological factors set the stage for today's drug problem. It is becoming increasingly clear that the problem is not drugs, but the manner and purpose of their use. Life styles can be altered by drugs, positively as well as negatively. Pharmacological treatment can provide relief for abnormal psychological states and correct potential pathology. New knowledge is also opening vistas for enlarging man's creative and productive capacities. Man himself remains the key determinant.

From times immemorial man has been plunged in a pharmacological environment and even today all but the most primitive tribes make quite extensive use of drugs. The growing concern about such drug use is usually misplaced onto the drugs themselves, whereas it is clear that the problem is the manner and purpose of their use. Drugs, like art, music, and dance, originally served primarily religious and ritual functions. Among the surviving peyote cults of Mexico[5] and the Ayuasqua users of Northern Peru, in the back country of Nepal,[20] as well as in numerous other places, it is the spirit of the plant or of some deity summoned through the drug taking which is the purpose of its use. The circumstances are almost always ceremonial and the expectations of response quite explicit. As traditions deteriorate (as when a tribe dweller migrates to a cosmopolitan city or a foreign worker violates, and encourages others to violate, "outworn" restrictions) the drugs are utilized for other purposes. In fact, some of the drugs never make the transition because of violent and disagreeable side effects that are accepted within the ritual context but not otherwise.

Setting aside the ritualistic purpose of inducing the spirits to favor us, what are the secular motives that lead us to use drugs that alter thinking, feeling, and behaving? Some of the reasons, obviously not all mutually exclusive, would be relief of psychological discomfort (guilt, insecurity, anxiety, regret, etc.), escape *from* emotional anaesthesia (lack of any or sufficient feeling, pleasant or unpleasant, of which boredom is one variant), escape *into* emotional anaesthesia, curiosity, rebellion or nonconformity, group pressure (belongingness, daring, etc.), pleasure seeking, search for "meaning," or provision of a rationalization for economic, social, and other forms of failure.

In viewing the users it is helpful to distinguish between various types: those who are unaware that they are using drugs (e.g., the nice old ladies who take "tonics" containing alcohol and opiates); the deliberate individual user who takes the drug for its own sake when the drug is legally and legitimately obtained (e.g., alcohol, caffeine) and when it is illicitly obtained; the group user for whom it serves some secondary purpose such as enhanced conviviality or more intimate feeling of relatedness; those who are prone to drug dependence and experience the continuing, periodic, or sporadic need to experience sensations produced by the drug or to relieve discomforts which might otherwise occur.

Other considerations which involve both initial and continued use are the properties of the drug (dependency development, duration of action, tolerance, sensitization, potentiation, sequelae, chromosome alterations, etc.), availability of the drug (cost, enforcement if illegal, medical channels, ease of manufacturing, etc.), and environmental inducements or restraints (warnings or "temptations" via media of mass communication, prestige of use, etc.).

Difficulties arise because of the vague border between disease and discomfort in the phychological universe. There are substantial areas of physical discomfort that are not regarded as disease, but the distinction is unclear in the mental and emotional field. The situation is further complicated because drugs have been used to ease such psychological discomfort under *non*medical sanction.

Life as we find it is too hard for us; it entails too much pain, too many disappointments, impossible tasks. We cannot dispense with auxiliary constructions. . . . There are perhaps three of these means: powerful diversions of interest which lead us to care little about our misery; substitutive gratifications which lessen it; and intoxicating substances which make us insensitive to it.[4]

The services rendered by intoxicating substances in the struggle for happiness and in warding off misery rank so highly as a benefit that both individuals and races have given them an established position within their libido-economy. It is not merely the immediate gain in pleasure which one owes to them but also a measure of that independence of the outer world which is so sorely craved.[4]

The medical use derives from religious–spiritual beginnings. As late as the Middle Ages, in our own Western medicine the generally accepted belief was that the zodiac sign under which an individual was born determined his individual response to particular drugs—as did the time of gathering and preparing them. Paracelsus, Newton, and others in the vanguard of secularism were generally accepting of this approach. In the refugee settlement established by the Dalai Lama of Tibet, the medical and astrological activities are combined.[16] We are inclined to regard the invocations for spiritual assistance in early medical texts (e.g., the Ebers papyrus of 1500 B.C.) as irrelevant concessions to current prejudice. The evidence, however, is that the medical practitioners were quite serious: without the spiritual influences how could one account for the success of an identical treatment in one case and its failure in another?

Although the conditions favoring its application had been present for a considerable time, it was the introduction of the synthetic products of chemistry (and the refinement of natural products) that set the stage for today's problem. Within the past century the conviction has become almost universal that through chemistry we will eventually succeed in finding treatment for all medical disorders. The insistence that emotional and mental disorders are medical has naturally led to their inclusion as amenable to pharmacological management—and in fact there have been some brilliant successes.

Even Freud is most moralistic about the use of drugs for such purposes since he adds to the quotation above: "In certain circumstances they are to blame when valuable energies which could have been used to improve the lot of humanity are uselessly wasted."[4]

Anxiety and depression are part of the human condition and without them we would be other than we are—for better or for worse. Most would argue that the very extremes of anxiety and depression should be treated, but where is the border to be drawn? Shall it differ from one individual to another depending on his or her tolerance? Shall different groups (based on age, sex, or occupation, for instance) be handled differently? The proposals that follow are in general not strictly medical since they do not deal with the rectification of pathology. Perhaps we should not "tinker with the levers which control eternity." However, since we do know that we are being influenced in our decisions and feelings and behavior, it is really not a question of avoiding influence but deciding whether we wish to leave the pressures to special interest groups or to random events, or whether we wish to attempt control of our own destinies—a more responsible but probably no less dangerous venture.

WAYS IN WHICH DRUGS CAN ALTER
LIFE PATTERNS

Correction of Existing Symptoms

There are a surprisingly large number of persons who suffer from diseases that affect their life style. High on such a list would be chronic depression, which may manifest itself in such forms as fatigue, underachievement, hypochondriasis, etc., as well as in its more obvious manifestations. Appropriate treatment can alter the total life pattern. As one patient put it, "Now for the first time I feel like I always knew I should feel."

Not only relief of abnormal psychological states (anxiety, phobias, obsessions, etc.) but also pharmacological treatment of physical pathology (hypothyroidism, diabetes, chronic prostatitis, colitis, etc.) can entail a radical alteration of life pattern.

Correction of Potential Pathology

The administration of drugs may prevent the development of conditions that would be severely disabling by supplying some missing ingredient as in pellagra, cretinism, and other endocrine-deficiency disorders. A curious reversal is phenylketonuria, in which the treatment is to subtract from the diet, as far as possible, the foods with phenylalanine since it cannot be appropriately metabolized. There are several similar amino acid and other inborn errors of metabolism whose correction radically alters the way the life pattern will develop.

Prevention of Acute Symptoms

Excruciating pain, uncontrolled euphoria, dementia, and deliria can abruptly precipitate irreversible changes. Thus prevention of such acute symptoms by anesthetics, tranquilizers, etc., may similarly alter a life pattern by preventing its disruption.

Prevention or Relief of Chronic Symptoms

Recurrent or continuing pathology ·such as angina, mucous colitis, hiccoughs, or depression can lead to profound alterations in how one feels, thinks, and acts. Thus drugs which prevent or relieve such states are profoundly life altering. The current interest in lithium (for recurrent affective disorders) illustrates the importance of this approach.

Acute Drug-Induced Pathology

At times alterations in life patterns can be produced by deliberate or accidental use of drugs on a single occasion. One of my most notable failures in treatment was a Ph.D. studying in London who attempted suicide with cyanide. The resultant impairment was an immutable and inseparable mixture of physical and psychological trauma that in no way damaged his intelligence but nevertheless made him hopelessly and retrogressively dependent.

In susceptible individuals, LSD and similarly acting drugs may produce permanent dissociation after a single administration.

Pathology Induced by Chronic Drug Use

The character of the Mad Hatter in *Alice in Wonderland* was drawn from life. In the preparation of felt for hats, mercury was commonly used and the fumes plus the quantity accidentally ingested produced a type of organic deterioration resulting eventually in dementia. Thus a sizeable number of hatters did become "mad" as a result of chronic mercury poisoning.

It may well be that chronic air pollution, chemical sprays of food, or radioactive fallout may someday be found to have had a similar effect on our own life patterns.

Minor Reality Relievers

Drugs are widely used to alter life patterns in ways other than the correction or production of gross pathology. In our own culture there are tens of millions of persons whose lives are markedly more happy because of the use of caffeine, alcohol, nicotine, and even amphetamines and barbiturates. Unfortunately, with some of these drugs (e.g., alcohol, amphetamines, barbiturates) a percentage of users become abusers; in other instances (e.g., nicotine) there may be unfortunate side effects such as heart disease and cancer; in others (e.g., coffee and tea) there are only very rarely undesirable consequences. There is some reason to be hopeful that methods of preventing addiction can be developed.

In different cultures other drugs have been used for similar purposes, e.g., cannabis sativa (whether as hashish, bhang, marijuana, or in some other form), qat (kat), or coca leaves.

Controlled use in one culture by no means guarantees that a drug can be imported "safely" into another culture. The introduction of alcohol to the American Indian or of opium to India and China had disastrous consequences. It is too early to tell what results cannabis use by the middle and upper classes will have here in the United States.

Induction of Transcendental States

The recorded use of drugs in conjunction with religious or mystical ecstasy dates back at least as far as the Eleusinian mysteries and probably even earlier, to the time of the Egyptian Middle Kingdom. The actual beginnings are lost in protohistory. From hashish use by the *hashashin* (assassins) under Hasan Sabah, to the hallucinogenic candles burned at the witches' Sabbaths, to current use of LSD to induce psychedelic states, there has always been a great value placed on the use of drugs to effect major conversions of life patterns. Drugs may produce dissociation and perceptual pathology (including hallucinations), but obviously a great deal more is involved in determining the result.

FACTORS DETERMINING HOW DRUGS INDUCE ALTERATIONS OF LIFE PATTERNS

Aside from the chemical structure of the drug itself and its expected action on the organism, there are other influences that determine what actually does happen.

HEREDITARY POTENTIALS

There was until fairly recently a great neglect of pharmacogenetic influence. The impetus to a good deal of this work was a demonstration in 1938 that atropine esterase occurred in some rabbits but not others, which explained the puzzling observation made in 1852 by Schroff, a Viennese physician, that some strains of rabbits enjoyed eating belladonna leaves that were fatal to other rabbits. McClearn and Rodgers[12] demonstrated clear and pronounced strain differences in alcohol preference of highly inbred groups. The possibility that the preference was due to learned behavior was ruled out since "pups cross-fostered on mothers of other strains showed preference patterns consistent with the genetic rather than the foster line."

Certain strains of mice will even drink to their own detriment. We thus conclude that we have demonstrated a close analogue to the condition of human alcoholism: specifically identifiable physiological changes of an undesirable sort, resulting from prolonged voluntary ingestion of alcohol by animals with alternating access to adequate diet, continued their level of ingestion following the physiological changes.[12]

The capacity of drugs to alter life patterns in one individual but not in another in many cases may be related to hereditary potentials.

Environmental Conditions

Physical environment has long been known to influence drug response. The amount of oxygen available (high or low altitude), the season, and the temperature of the environment are obvious factors.

Certain drugs such as barbiturates and alcohol are disinhibitors and resultant behavior depends strongly on the social environment. If given to an individual in a quiet room, they induce sleep, but if the individual is attending a noisy party there is usually overstimulation.

At times hereditary factors interplay with environmental circumstances. Stimulants such as the amphetamines are about eight times as toxic to mice crowded into one large cage as to litter mates caged singly. However, for certain strains of mice (DBA/2 or BDF mice) this susceptibility does not hold. Thus social environmental conditions as well as physical ones can be shown to influence drug response in animals as well as in humans.

Psychological Structure

Anxiety-prone individuals respond in a different way to medication than do those not so inclined.[2, 6-11, 13-15, 19] Introversion and extroversion tendencies are also important factors, as is intellectual capability.[18]

Expectations

To a surprising degree we derive from experience that which we anticipate and we live out our expectations of ourselves. The diversity of response to drugs is at least partially accounted for by the fact that many of the drugs cause dissociation. Once the always tenuous restraints of reality are further released, it is not difficult to see why events follow closely after the heart of desire or apprehension. The "revealed" state, once experienced, can produce a permanent conversion.

Physiological State

Hunger, sleep deprivation, and reduced oxygen supply brought on by hyperventilation or by retarded breathing (as in Yoga) usually accentuate the speed and depth of drug action. Reportedly, elevated blood sugar provides an extra depth of response with certain drugs (e.g., marijuana). The general state of nutrition, recent diet, the presence or absence of other drugs—even at times those used months before[3]—may alter responses. There are curious combinations. The use of Calabar beans in ritual trials is based on the fact that in the presence of high adrenalin the drug is poisonous, but otherwise it is relatively harmless.

Thus alterations in physiological states can determine the extent of a drug response and whether it will have any long-term or even short-term effects.

Timing

One of the most basic of biological phenomena is the constant waxings and wanings in addition to diurnal rhythms. Lack of appropriate techniques for measuring, storing, and analyzing data of this type led in the past to serious neglect of this problem. High-speed data collection techniques and computers with large enough memory cores have brought us within sight of dealing with this area, although the software (i.e., the programs) for analysis are still generally lacking.

Timing is crucial in at least three ways. First, it is important to know when in the life cycle the drug is given; there are often specific periods, prenatal as well as postpartum, when, and only when, the fetus or neonate is suceptible. Second, the effect of a drug on a specific parameter or even the total organism may differ depending on whether that specific parameter is ebbing or flowing; this factor in turn may determine whether there is or is not a permanent alteration in the life pattern. Finally, for some, but not all drugs, the time of day has been shown to strongly affect the response.

PROBABLE FUTURE ALTERATIONS
OF LIFE PATTERNS BY DRUGS

Indications of the future directions of drug usage already exist in a substantial number of the pharmaceuticals presently available. Some of their effects are currently regarded as side effects, but it is almost an aphorism that today's side effects are tomorrow's therapy. The shortened need for sleep with monoamine oxidase inhibitors, the reduced sexual sensitivity, or even the shortened memory span each have possible therapeutic applications. The real problem in the field of psychopharmaceuticals is not so much the creation of any of the following classes of drugs, but determining who should make the decisions as to when they should be used, on whom, and by whom.

Unquestionably, additional and probably even more startling drug actions will occur as fallout from other research in the field. As newer possibilities occur, and as we gain experience with those already available or possible, there will probably also be a shift in attitude in respect to the most important question of who shall exercise control.

Prolong Childhood and
(Shorten?) Adolescence

The average human life span has been greatly prolonged in the past century, primarily by the reduction in infant mortality and the reduction of deaths from pneumonia in the older age groups. Unfortunately, there is little we can do to reverse or prevent the depredations of aging. Even in the best of health the years beyond "three score years and ten" are not usually one's best.

One of the features that has made human civilization possible is the prolonged childhood of man, since it is then that he is most susceptible to education. This vastly extended period as compared with other animals has been a unique feature of the human venture. Hence it would appear sensible to try to prolong life another few decades by extending the period during which the acquisition of knowledge and skills comes most easily. We are already doing this in a social sense, since the time at which one finishes college is already half a dozen years beyond physical maturity.

Conceivably, if childhood were adequate, the turbulence of adolescence could be short-circuited, with avoidance of many of the problems which thereafter continue to plague people in later life. It would seem sensible to arrange adolescence so that it lasted no more than two hours of some Sunday afternoon.

Reduce Need for Sleep

As previously indicated, a reduction in the need for sleep has already occurred as a side effect of some of the antidepressant drugs. Based on the rigorous training of the Mogul Emperors, as well as current physiological evidence, it appears entirely possible that 3–3½ hours sleep is all that is really required. The habit of sleeping longer quite possibly developed as a survival trait, since it was not safe for a creature such as man with his poor night vision (along with his other inadequacies) to go wandering about at a time of day when he was so little protected.

With the increasing knowledge of the functions of rapid eye movement time and the various stages of sleep, it appears that we may be able to simulate or induce the bioelectric–biochemical activity required and conceivably be able totally to circumvent the need for sleep. Constructive use of these additional billions of man hours every day is indeed a challenge.

Provide Safe Short-Acting Intoxicants

At least under the present rituals and routines in which we live, it seems almost essential that periods of relief be provided. Safe, rapidly acting intoxicants that produce satisfactory dissociation and euphoria would be most valuable. The appeals of alcohol, marijuana, opiates, amphetamines, etc., are at least in part that they do possess some degree of such activity. However, none of them serves the purpose ideally. It is quite likely that if acknowledgment were given of the desirability of such a pharmaceutical, it could be produced within a matter of a few years at most.

Regulate Sexual Responses

Man is one of the few creatures in whom sexual activity is not seasonal. His constant restlessness on this score provides him with both more pleasures and more problems than any other bodily function. Pharmacological regulation of some aspects of this behavior is already available and regulation of others will probably be achieved in the next few years. Banking the fires or stoking them biochemically so that temperature and activity could match more closely the appropriate environmental circumstances would increase the sum total of pleasure and, at the same time, allow man to devote more of his time, intelligence, and energy to more exclusively human activities.

Control Affect and Aggression

There is some evidence that electrolyte balance is related to control of excessive excursions of affect and aggression. Perhaps the skeptical attitudes of Americans toward balneology and mineral water has been mistaken. Chlorination and fluoridation of water have been generally accepted as health measures. Why not lithium in the water supply as well, if it is capable of preventing pathology without circumscribing normal human feelings?

Mediate Nutrition, Metabolism, and Physical Growth

At least as great and possibly greater than psychosomatic effects are the somatopsychic ones. Adequate control of the genetic code or of the messenger functions should enable us, within a few decades, to eliminate most gross physical pathology so that deviations so extreme as to be regarded as ugly will no longer occur. A great deal of the psychopathology that arises because one human regards himself as physically or aesthetically inferior to another could be eliminated. This type of investigation is already under way.

Increase or Decrease Reactivity (Alertness, Relaxation)

Some of the pharmaceuticals available permit us to extend to a small degree the period of reactivity by deferring fatigue. There are others that partially work to permit relaxation when hyperalertnees would only be a nuisance. It is quite possible that appropriate "natural" products (plants, etc.) already exist that would provide the lead toward synthesizing virtually ideal substances for these purposes. Recognition of the need and conscious search would perhaps provide these agents almost at once.

Prolong or Shorten Memory

How much remarkably more rich life would be if we were able to remember whatever we wished. On the other hand, how terribly cruel if we could not forget those things we had seen or done that were unbearable. We are close enough to understanding how memory works to expect that within another decade such agents could become a reality.

Induce or Prevent Learning

There are certain experiences through which one must unavoidably pass that may well scar the organism for an indefinite period. To some degree we do protect ourselves by not incorporating these events into our total psychic organization. In other cases, unfortunately, we do not have such control. Somewhat improved analyses of the biochemical changes that occur during such states should allow us, within the foreseeable future, to have drugs that would prevent fatal flawing.

On the other hand, there are both positive and negative experiences that would greatly enhance performance if the lesson they had to provide could be learned. Tentative beginnings have already been made in the use of drugs that would enhance the learning capacity of the individual so that the "experience" could be achieved vicariously via movies, reading, or oral narration.

The availability of such inducements to learning would probably alter the total educational process so that the time consumed to acquire any one segment would be greatly reduced and the scope greatly broadened to include character education as well.

Produce or Discontinue Transference

The great desire to establish or discontinue transference relationships is overtly evident in primitive societies in which the demand for love philters is a high priority item. In only slightly disguised form the use of chemicals such as deodorants, mouth washes, and perfumes is essentially for the same purpose.

It would undoubtedly be construed as an invasion of privacy to give someone a pharmaceutical without his knowledge or permission. On the other hand, if one could turn off, it would no longer be really necessary in most cases to involve the party of the second part. In theory at least there is no reason why the deconditioning experience should not be greatly augmented through the use of appropriate drugs.

The potential uses in terms of psychotherapy with involved oedipal situations present an almost limitless potential.

Provoke or Relieve Guilt

The biochemical correlates of many of the affective states are being subjected to investigation at the present time. Use of a technique such as that of Delgado[1] should make it possible to evaluate directly not only what such correlates are, but whether the introduction of them will in turn produce the emotional state itself. According to one theory, the whole penal system is directed toward this end. How much simpler life would be if sufficient sense of guilt could be produced relevant to a particular type of situation to prevent its repetition. Punishment would then be truly rehabilitative and practically instantaneous.

At other times an undeserved and unwarranted feeling of guilt can ruin an entire life and even those of others touching it. A substantial part of what a psychiatrist does is to attempt to relieve such unwarranted and destructive guilt feelings. There is already evidence that this can be done pharmacologically with respect to anxiety, which may well be an important component of guilt. Some interesting ethical and legal problems arise if such a drug were perfected; perhaps a board consisting of a judge and a clergyman as well as a psychiatrist would have to agree that such relief of guilt was justifiable before appropriate medication could be given.

Foster or Terminate Mothering Behavior

With mothering behavior so typical of certain animals it appears highly probable that there are "juices" that mediate in the production of this behavior. By enhancing or interfering with their production, it is possible that the extent of such behavior could be controlled. There are cases in which an increase of this function would be in order, but undoubtedly the greatest use would be in terminating such behavior once it had outlived its usefulness. The human female is often involved in difficulties—and in turn involve others in problems—more because of excess inappropriate mothering behavior than because of untoward sexual passion or, for that matter, any other emotion.

Shorten or Extend Experienced Time

Drugs capable of altering our sense of time to some degree at least are already in existence. Jazz musicians credit both marijuana and the opiates with a capacity to extend the experience of time so that both the appreciation and production of music is greatly enhanced. There are various other occupations in which this capacity would be quite important, e.g., magicians, ball players, etc. On the other hand, there are certain experiences which one wishes to have done with as rapidly as possible and any agent that speeded up the passage of experienced time would be useful.

Create Conditions of Famais Vu (Novelty) or Déjà (Familiarity)

Married life would be considerably altered if one could bring to one's mate the feeling of fresh wonder that often characterizes the initial or early experiences. The same would hold true in many business partnerships and other working relationships. On occasion some of the dissociating drugs do produce reactions of this sort, but they are as yet far too crude and unpredictable to be used specifically for this purpose.

It would not do to have all situations or even the majority of them of the "novelty" type. Indeed, it is also important to have available a compound which would rreate a feeling of familiarity, in order to deal more competently with problems that are made more difficult simply because they are new. Some of the euphoriant drugs tend in this direction.

Deepen Our Awareness of Beauty and Our Sense of Awe

By deepening our appreciation of the beauty which surrounds us and allowing us to experience afresh the awe of human existence, we can perhaps better discover—both emotionally and intellectually—the nature of the human venture. It is this type of appeal that has made drugs so familiar an adjunct to religious ecstasies. This usage should be developed with enough improvement in the drugs themselves to insure that the experiences be expansions of reality rather than deceptions into para-universes.

DRUGS AND DESTINY

All of these drug-altered life patterns—and many more to come—are probes into the extension and control of our destinies. There is no more suitable ending than this quotation from Alexander Pope:

Know then thyself, presume not God to scan,
The proper study of mankind is Man.
Placed on this isthmus of a middle state,
A being darkly wise, and rudely great;
With too much knowledge for the sceptic side,
With too much weakness for the stoic's pride,
He hangs between; in doubt to act or rest;
In doubt to deem himself a god, or beast;
In doubt his mind or body to prefer;
Born but to die, and reasoning but to err;
Sole judge of truth, in endless error hurl'd:
The glory, jest and riddle of the world![7]

REFERENCES

1. Delgado, J. Salmon Lecture. Presented to the New York Academy of Medicine, 1969.
2. DiMascio, A., & Rinkel, M. In M. Rinkel (Ed.), *Specific and non-specific factors in psychopharmacology.* New York: Philosophical Library, 1964.
3. Esser, A. H., & Kline, N. S. Routine blood pressure measurement in psychiatric research. *Journal of Clinical Pharmacology,* 1967, *3,* 162–167.
4. Freud, S. *Civilization and its discontents.* London: Hogarth Press, 1951.
5. Furst, P. (Film) *To find our life.* Los Angeles: Latin American Center, University of California, undated.
6. Heninger, D., DiMascio, A., & Klerman, G. L. Personality factors in variability of response to phenothiazines. *American Journal of Psychiatry,* 1965, *121,* 1091–1094.
7. Janke, W. On the dependence of the effect of psychotropic substances on the affective stability. *Medicina Experimentals,* 1960, *2,* 217–223.
8. Janke, W. Uber psychische Wirkungen verschiedener Tranquilizer bei gesunden, emotional labilen Personen. *Psychopharmacologia,* 1966, *8,* 340–374.
9. Klerman, G. L. *Transactions of the Sixth Research Conference on Cooperative Chemotherapy Studies in Psychiatry,* 1961, *6,* 339.
10. Lienert, G. A., & Traxel, W. The effects of meprobamate and alcohol on galvanic skin response. *Journal of Psychology,* 1959, *48,* 329–334.
11. Luoto, K. Personality and placebo effects upon timing behavior. *Journal of Abnormal and Social Psychology,* 1964, *68,* 54–61.
12. McClearn, G. E., & Rodgers, D. A. Genetic factors in alcohol preference of laboratory mice. *Journal of Comparative and Physiological Psychology,* 1961, *54,* 116–119.
13. McPeake, J. D., & DiMascio, A. Drug-personality interaction in the learning of a nonsense syllabic task. *Psychological Reports,* 1964, *15,* 405–406.

14. Munkelt, P., & Othmer, E. Der Einfluss der psychischen Stabilität resp. Labilität und der Körpe-konstitution der Versuchspersonen auf die Wirkung des Psychotonicums 7-[2'- (1''-Methyl-2''phenylaethylamino) aethyl] -theophyllin HCI. *Arzneimittelforschung*, 1965, *15*, 843–849.

15. Nowlis, V., & Nowlis, H. H. The description and analysis of mood. *Annals of the New York Academy of Sciences*, 1956, *65*, 345–355.

16. Office of His Holiness the Dalai Lama. *Tibetans in exile*. New Delhi: Gutenberg Press, 1969.

17. Pope, A. *Essay on Man*. (M. Mack, Ed.), London: Methuen, 1950.

18. Rickels, K. Some comments on non-drug factors in psychiatric drug therapy. *Psychosomatics*, 1965, *8*, 303–309.

19. Shagass, C. In L. Uhr & J. G. Miller (Eds.), *Drugs and behavior*. New York: Wiley, 1960.

20. Sharma, B. P. *Native healers of Nepal*. Unpublished manuscript, undated.

PART FOUR

Consciousness, Self-Awareness, and Human Potentials

Prologue

The transformation of culture leads to strange conversations. As structures loosen and the twilight of uncertainty settles over established habits of thought, old and obdurate questions present themselves more sharply. Central to these questions are concepts of Value and Meaning, of the nature of personal integration and integrity, the place of intention and will in the maintenance of well-being, and the place of the individual in the complex web of social responsibility. These questions become especially poignant in an age when the survival of societies, and of individual man as we know him, can no longer be safely assumed, and when an understanding of the rules governing human conduct becomes a condition for such survival.

Much is being said about the morality of science. While the sciences of man, such as they are, may still be a long way from a science of morality, it seems at least appropriate for psychiatry to examine those areas of knowledge which, by way of religious belief and long nurtured habits of thought and practice, have centered on the moral and spiritual nature of man. The healing element in these disciplines runs through religions, irrespective of particular dogma. Their survival for millenia attests to a certain robust usefulness to homo sapiens. Psychiatry, more than any branch of medicine, mirrors the culture in which it is embedded. The *Malleus Maleficarum* (or, for that matter, King James' *Reflections on Exorcism)* are psychiatric texts of the Middle Ages, albeit with a difference. It took the French Revolution to sanction and support Pinel and couple humane care with the description and taxonomy of mental ·disorder. It took the security of the early Victorian Age to promote the so-called Moral Treatment of patients in groups. It is perhaps significant that the intensive study of consciousness and the behaviorally silent inner world of fantasy and the imagination, at the hands of Carus Titchener, William James, Sigmund Freud, and Carl Jung should have coincided with the emergence of the relativity theory and of quantum physics. James Maxwell published his equations on Faraday's lines of force in the year of Freud's birth. I have elsewhere examined the possible relations between the evolution of physics and the evolution of some key concepts of modern psychiatry, and the part played by language in both.* Here, I am concerned with something more mundane. If one of the central purposes of psychotherapy is the enhancement of self-awareness, self-knowledge, choice, rational intent carried into life, and the furtherance of communication and self-communication, then the usefulness of the purely verbal tools of our trade have to be reexamined. I believe we have gotten into deep trouble in this regard. There has been both word-fallout and word-overkill. In our strident cellophane culture, the word mills grind on, and the word itself has become counterfeit. In the mental health professions, we have all too often become discursive, distancing, remote, and pedantic. Small wonder that there are the so-called "alternatives."

In our day we have youth, the great harbinger of change, developing it's own secret language, strange words, odd syntax, subtle inflections, and absurd inversions, which we "squares" find hard to penetrate. We find dress flamboyant, distinctive, individual,

*Elkes, Joel. Subjective and objective observation in psychiatry: Harvey Lecture, 1962. In *The Harvey Lectures,* (Ser. 57). New York: Academic Press, 1963, pp. 63–92.

yet worn like a uniform; music inventive, strange, atonal, harrowing, world-endish, and loud enough to shut out the outside. In literature and theater there is a sharp shift from structure and plot to chance and unpredictability, from logic to paradox. Indeed, as one looks about, our culture abounds with all manner of strange and profoundly significant experiments and movements to get us out of the word cage in which we dwell. In centers—practically all of them significantly outside formal academia—elaborate methods are being developed to train people to guide and to help them to be themselves in small groups. Again and again common ingredients emerge: the initial resistance to personal exploration; the expression of past feelings, especially past negative feelings in front of others; the honest expression of immediate interpersonal feeling, leading to the cracking of facades; the beginning of self acceptance; the expression of positive feelings and closeness; the encounter with another, the healing capacity of the group, and the changes in the group as a whole. These changes can be profound, though we still do not know how enduring they are. Clearly they have a deep biology of their own, the regularities of which we are only just beginning to describe, let alone understand. Groups are social lenses of high power—refracting, focusing, amplifying interpersonal signals, and greatly enhancing learning by crisis, and learning by lysis. If the small group is the engine of society, it is only just beginning to acquire its systems engineers; and they had better be kindly men.

There is another area that is emerging in parallel. Body language techniques are returning, after being banished to faddism. Breathing, stance, posture, relaxation, the use of one's own weight, and a systematic training of sensory acuity are being developed to enhance the enteroceptive and proprioceptive vocabulary of the individual using his own body. Much inventiveness is going into these new techniques; and many new and strange phenomena will no doubt be discovered as they are used in groups. This field is not new; the East has always regarded the body as a planet worthy of exploration. Hatha Yoga has developed an elaborate system of training for both voluntary and involuntary controls. There is in these exercises great slowness, deliberation, and beauty. It is good, I think, that young people are interested in these things. Some of us even believe that these techniques, including meditation, if taught properly and consistently, could go a long way to satisfy the exploratory drive into drugs and to replace the quick instant "trip" by the good hard work of a "journey." Whatever their use, these approaches obviously represent the obverse of the difficulties to which I have alluded. For against discursiveness and obsessive mechanical rigidity, they put a premium on spontaneity and openness, which indeed may be very unsettling. Against remoteness, there is great emphasis (and great skill) in ensuring personal involvement; against pedantry, and showing off, a much more genuine live-and-let-live kindliness, which makes discoveries quite personal, but lays no claims beyond it. Interestingly, too, there is a shying away from theory, despite a clinical intuition of very high order. There is, in the best attempts, much genuine search, rather than research. Yet, already in the background, a body of theory is forming which may well link up with these practical discoveries. It is concerned with the following considerations: the relation of language to interhemispheric function; the role of body image and the skeletomuscular system in the experience and expression of emotion; the voluntary control of so-called autonomic visceromotor events by means of biofeedback; the place of focused attention—or intentional inattention—in bodily learning; the potential usefulness of active relaxation in clinical research; the power of self-regulation, intent, and will in the maintenance of well-being; and the promise of consciousness-altering drugs in psychotherapy.

It is gratifying to find these questions addressed in the papers which follow in so cogent and timely a way.

JOEL ELKES, M.D.
Distinguished Service Professor
The Johns Hopkins University
Baltimore, Maryland

11. ALTERED STATES OF CONSCIOUSNESS

Beyond Concensus Reality: Psychotherapy, Altered States of Consciousness, and the Cultivation of Awareness

Charles T. Tart, Ph.D.

I would hazard a guess that every one considers himself or herself to be quite "realistic." Indeed, I suspect we are all rather attached to this idea, and it would be quite insulting if I personally told you that you were not realistic. Realistic means that we are in good contact with "reality." But what is this reality that we passionately believe we are in good contact with?

The argument I shall make is that the predominant reality we are in contact with is *consensus reality,* a socially shared reality created by our ancestors and parents, and actively maintained, with slight modifications, by each of us personally and all of us collectively. I believe this idea is firmly supported by much scientific evidence, even though it is not popular.

CONSENSUS REALITY

Figure 11-1 illustrates what psychologists talk about as "the naive view of perception." It assumes that there is a world outside of us that is faithfully captured by our sense organs and reproduced in our minds. Thus, if a cat is in front of us, we see a cat. In addition to accuracy, passivity is

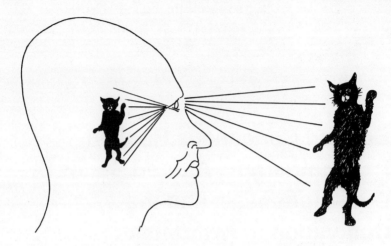

Fig. 11-1.   Naive view of consciousness perception.

implicit in this process: the real objects of the real world control our perceptions. Modern psychological and psychiatric knowledge makes it clear that, to the contrary, our perception of the world (and of ourselves) is a very active and complex process. We *construct* the percepts we perceive through active processes that we had to learn in infancy but which, in adulthood, have become so efficient and automatized that the active nature of the process is no longer apparent to our consciousness. Figure 11-2 is a more adequate representation of the nature of perception. Here I have

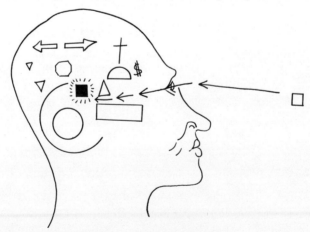

Fig. 11-2.   Consensus reality—fit.

fancifully shown various figures existing inside our heads to represent learned perceptual categories that have a readiness to respond to sensory input that is reasonably close to the prelearned categories. When the appropriate sensory pattern comes along, the prelearned perceptual category is activated and we "perceive." In many ways it would be more accurate to say that we perceive our learned categories rather than the objects stimulating them.

In many circumstances this is a desirable and efficient operation: if I want to buy a loaf of rye bread at the store it is generally sufficient for me to find an oblong object, brownish in color, with the words "rye bread" written on it. I don't really need to be aware of the innumerable small ways in which this particular loaf of rye bread is absolutely unique and differs from my prelearned conceptions of "rye bread." Indeed, if I took time to minutely examine the uniqueness of this particular loaf of rye bread, it might take me hours to get out of the store! Living in any particular culture requires rapid, efficient, automated recognition of important objects and social actions in the culture.

What happens, however, when we are confronted by something that we have no prelearned perceptual category for? Quite often we simply don't perceive the object, unless it forces itself on us quite strongly; or we may perceive it in a highly distorted way, automatically organizing our perception of it on the basis of a few of its characteristics we do have prelearned perceptual categories for, and thus creating a very distorted perception of it. Figure 11-3 illustrates this phenomenon: in the situation depicted there, an orthodox Christian angel, complete with wings and halo, walks across the room. Since we "know" that angels as such do not exist, we have a prelearned rejection of this possibility; we may either not perceive it at all, in spite of the fact that physical stimuli have reached us and stimulated our sense organs, or we may seize upon some *familiar* feature, such as the candle held in the angel's hands in this case, and perceive only that. Or we may see an "actor" wearing a white robe. If anyone did perceive it as an angel, it would be best for his reputation if he kept quiet about it. It may be safer to "see" the emperor's new clothes.

I think we fail to realize the incredible extent of the semi-arbitrary construction of perceptual categories in the course of becoming enculturated, the almost total automatization of them, and the degree to which they are tied into the system of rewards from others and our internalization of such reward systems in our own self-image, so that the resulting consensus reality has enormous power over us. Although I have focused on perception, our thinking and action also become automatically

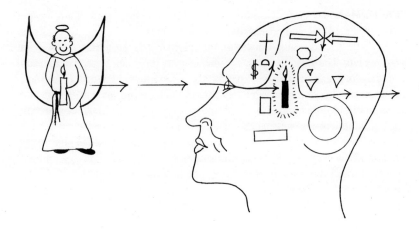

Fig. 11-3.   Consensus reality—nonfit, distortion.

influenced and controlled by the categories of consensus reality. A brief
Sufi teaching story illustrates the power of our social conditioning:

> One day a man approached Bayazid, the great mystic of the ninth century,
> saying that he had fasted and prayed for thirty years but had not found the joy which
> Bayazid described. Bayazid told him that he might continue for three hundred years
> and still not find it.
>   "How is that?" asked the would-be illuminate.
>   "Because your vanity is a barrier to you."
>   "Tell me the remedy."
>   "The remedy is one which you cannot take."
>   "Tell me, nevertheless."
>   Bayazid said: "You must go to the barber and have your (respectable) beard
> shaved. Remove all your clothes and put on a girdle around yourself. Fill a nosebag
> with walnuts and suspend it from your neck. Go the the marketplace and call out:
> 'A walnut will I give to any boy who will strike me on the back of the neck.' Then
> continue on to the justices' session so that they may see you!"
>   "But I cannot do that; please tell me something else that you do as well."
>   "This is the first move, and the only one," said Bayazid, "but I had already
> told you that you would not do it; so you cannot be cured."[1]

We are, then, simultaneously the *beneficiaries* of our culture's
richness and the *victims* of its narrowness.

THE HUMAN SITUATION

I have tried to sum up the situation in which we find ourselves in Figure 11-4. The turning circle or wheel in the left-hand corner represents an individual, and the various little symbols represent, in a simplified way, the perceptual, cognitive, and behavioral categories (most of which are quite implicit) with which we confront the world. The lines connecting various identical and similar categories represent the fact that we have a personality structure, drawing upon our energy and emotions, that gives each of us a certain degree of coherency.

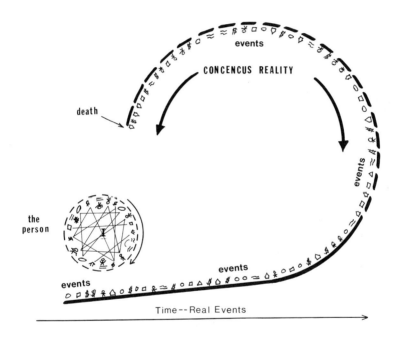

Fig. 11-4.   Idealized, simplified consensus reality.

The wheel of our self rolls on through time, through events. In many ways, however, the wheel of our self does not roll on through "real" events in any general sense, but through events as structured by a consensus reality. We very seldom deal with general reality per se; we deal, for example, with buildings that almost universally have right angles; we deal with people who speak one language and wear certain kinds of clothes, with people who can generally be expected to act within certain expected patterns. I have shown an idealized, simplified consensus reality in Figure 11-4, in which almost the only events happening in the consensus reality are events for which there are prelearned categories in the person. I have shown a very occasional event, represented by little triangles, for which there is not a prelearned category, but these events are minor compared with the events for which we are prepared. This match between personality and a simplified consensus reality constitutes what people would think of as a utopia, or what people imagine the "good old days" were like, when life was safe and predictable, when people could be counted on to behave properly, and the like.

Note also that I have represented consensus reality as not following real time linearly, but moving back on itself in a circle. This circling represents the fact that our social systems try to stop the flow of change—try to set up a closed system in which we'll always be safe, in which life will always be predictable. There are some exceptions, of course, but this is a general trend of culture. In what we think of as the "good old days" the wheel of a person's life ran smoothly through a consensus reality highly adapted to it, until it was terminated by death.

I suspect that some readers have been agitated looking at these figures because I have broken a rule of our particular consensus reality: I have deliberately spelled consensus incorrectly in the figure in order to make you uneasy! You don't expect a professor to misspell major words, or editors to overlook such mistakes. It is exactly this uneasiness resulting from something happening that differs from your expectations that illustrates an aspect of the power consensus reality exerts over us.

Most of us know, of course, that reality is much more complex, hence in Figure 11-5 I have shown the same person dealing with a much more complex consensus reality. There are many things in this consensus reality for which our particular person does not have prelearned, implicit categories. Thus, the kinds of events represented by the little plus signs, the three ring signs, etc., tend to be overlooked by this person or perceived in a distorted manner because they are not part of his enculturation, his internalized reality. Perhaps they belong to a subculture within the culture that he is not familiar with or is uncomfortable in dealing with; perhaps they are things he is simply not interested in and so pays little attention to them. You will notice also that in the wheel representing the person some of the little figures appear with double bars blocking them from the periphery: this represents what we know about suppression and repression. We simply don't want to see certain things, and we generally don't in ordinary circumstances. The culture may or may not collaborate in attempting to suppress such events within its consensus reality. We don't like to think about poor people, so we set up zoning standards in suburbs so that no one who is obviously poor will be able to live there, thus protecting our subcultural consensus reality.

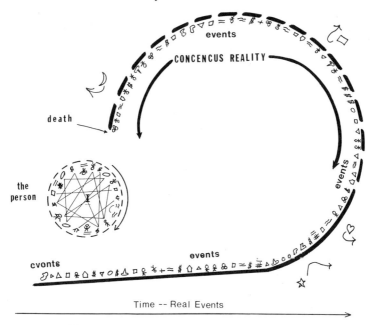

Fig. 11-5.   Idealized, complex consensus reality.

Our person's wheel of life rolls through this consensus reality with occasional bumps and punctures; everyone encounters events for which he is not preprogrammed. If a person is very open, he may be able to expand his personality structure as a result of being faced with events that he's not preprogrammed to perceive and react to in certain ways, or he may have sufficient defenses not to notice particularly the bumps and punctures of life.

Note also that a variety of events are shown trying to enter consensus reality from outside, but they are deflected from it. A culture is, in many ways, a conspiracy not to allow certain kinds of events to happen. On a positive level, the experience of starvation is now generally warded off for most people in our culture. The other side of the coin is that if a "real angel" walked into your room, you might not recognize it for what it was.

As we know, many people do not fit very well into our particular consensus reality. Figure 11-6 represents a person who, with reference to our first person (Fig. 11-4) is liable to be labeled either a rebel or a psychotic. The prelearned categories for perception, cognition, and behavior include several of the categories that were either left out of our first person's personality or were actively repressed. While our second person may have a rougher or smoother course of life than the first, depending on the particular structure of the consensus reality, he is a most disturbing person to the first. He may be the rebel who keeps pointing out the unpleasant fact that people do go hungry in the United States, or he may be the psychotic who, while perhaps "crazy" and out of touch with consensus reality in some sense, is very much in touch with certain aspects of the consensus reality around us that we personally don't want to notice. We deal with him by labeling him "crazy" so we don't have to take him seriously.

Note well, however, that our second person is just as much the simultaneous beneficiary and victim of the consensus reality of his culture

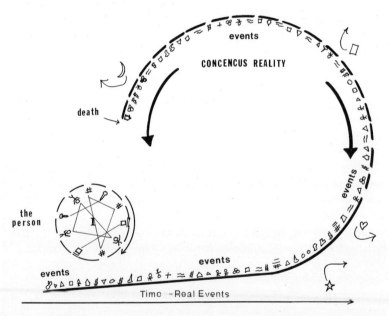

Fig. 11-6. Consensus reality—"rebel," psychotic.

as the first: he is reacting to life through automatized, prelearned categories and hence is very much controlled by his culture's consensus reality.

Now, as indicated by the title of this chapter, I want to talk about going beyond consensus reality. By local cultural standards, one of the persons in the last two figures might be considered "normal" or "mature," while the other might be considered "bad" or "crazy," and yet both are *products of* and *controlled* by the consensus reality of their culture. Regardless of their individual degree of happiness, regardless of the amount of reward they get from others who are also stuck within that particular consensus reality, neither of them is free from his earlier enculturation; neither has gone beyond his particular consensus reality.

There are three major ways that an individual may alter his particular relationship to consensus reality and, in some ways, go beyond it. The three basic means of going beyond consensus reality are psychotherapy, experiencing and working in altered states of consciousness, and the cultivation of awareness. The first is well known in our culture; the other two are not. Although each can be used in isolation, I believe that the future will see a synthesis of these three ways, to our lasting benefit.

PSYCHOTHERAPY

In my understanding of what states of consciousness are, I work from the basic concepts, that of structure and that of awareness, with awareness also constituting a kind of psychic energy. Psychotherapy, as a means of changing one's personality, can be seen as primarily a way of altering particular structures so that their operation is not in conflict with other structures within the personality or with the external, commonly shared structures that constitute our consensus reality. Thus psychotherapy aims at discovering explicit and implicit structures that underlie a person's unhappiness and changing their operation. This can be done by unlearning—dismantling such structures entirely—or by isolating them from other structures—disconnecting them to eliminate various secondary gains that serve to reinforce them.

Psychotherapy is a unique contribution of our Western culture, and I believe, something relatively new in our world. While the other two ways of going beyond consensus reality that I shall discuss have much to recommend them, I suspect psychotherapy is often essential at certain points. The structures that form our personality and determine our ordinary state of consciousness (which is our tool for coping with consensus reality) are often so *implicit,* so interconnected with reward and punishment systems, that we have no way of realizing how much they control and influence us without the specialized probings and workings of psychotherapy. Since we are all familiar with Western psychotherapy, I shall not discuss it further.

ALTERED STATES OF CONSCIOUSNESS

The second major means of going beyond consensus reality is experiencing and *working with* altered states of consciousness. I emphasize working with, for I have come to doubt the truth of the old adage "He who tastes knows." I think it is more on the order of "He who tastes has an *opportunity* to know," but if we don't work with our experiences there is no guarantee that we will learn from them. Again, space limitations prevent me from adequately describing what altered states of consciousness are, or, in the scientific terminology I am trying to introduce, what *discrete* altered states of consciousness are, so I shall just briefly say that an altered state of consciousness represents a radical, gestalt reorganization of the functioning of the mind. Some faculties may be possessed both in the ordinary state and in a particular altered state: e.g., marijuana smokers continue to speak English, but the overall style of their consciousness is quite different. This change often means that certain human potentialities are manifested in an altered state that do not manifest in the ordinary state.

I am deliberately avoiding using a term like a "higher" state of consciousness, since that would lead to a discussion distorted by implicit value judgments as to what we value in consciousness. No altered state of consciousness that we have much scientific information about is unequivocally better than any other state; each one has certain advantages for certain kinds of tasks, and certain disadvantages for other kinds of tasks. The important thing for our present discussion is that an altered state of consciousness represents a radical reorganization of the functioning of the consciousness. Stage 1, rapid eye movement dreaming, is a radically different organization of consciousness than nondreaming sleep, and both are different from our ordinary waking state; all three are different from being intoxicated with a psychedelic drug.

Our ordinary state of consciousness is our means of coping with consensus reality. It is a *tool,* which means it possesses interrelated characteristics that fit it to consensus reality. If you drastically change the pattern of your consciousness by entering an altered state, your relationship to consensus reality may change drastically. I originally described Figure 11-6 as representing a person whose ordinary state of consciousness was differently organized than someone else's, but we can conceptualize it also as a possible way of reorganizing the first person's state of consciousness, as an altered state of consciousness. The perceptual-cognitive-behavioral categories are now organized quite differently, and they respond to different aspects of consensus reality. In this example, the person is picking up certain aspects of consensus reality that were repressed in his ordinary state of consciousness.

Note well, however, that even though the person's experience may be radically different, and he may value it more than his ordinary state of consciousness, he is still in a state of consciousness that is automatically reacting to certain aspects of consensus reality and not others. While the relationship to consensus reality has changed drastically, consciousness is still very much dominated by consensus reality. Various kinds of events that have been rejected by consensus reality as a whole, the ones shown as being deflected from the circle of consensus reality, are still not available to the person. To illustrate this point with a practical example, getting drunk may sensitize one to quite different aspects of consensus reality than ordinarily, but few people report totally novel experiences or a transcendent experience when drunk.

What happens to a person who experiences an extremely unusual altered state of consciousness? Figure 11-7 may help to illustrate. In this altered state of consciousness, the person has a number of perceptual—cognitive—behavioral categories that have no counterparts at all in his consensus reality, symbolized by the hearts and the cork-shaped symbols, but which correspond to real events that are not structured into consensus reality. This claim is made by many experiencers of altered states, that their perception of reality somehow becomes superior to that in their ordinary state. This claim has never been adequately tested scientifically, but I have seen enough evidence to make me give partial credence to it.

Here the necessity of *working* with altered states of consciousness enters. If you are dissatisfied with your ordinary existence, your ordinary state of consciousness, the contrast of being in a novel, radically reorganized altered state may be very pleasing. It may indeed give you new understanding of aspects of consensus reality and/or your personality structure, and possibly put you in better contact with aspects of reality not included in consensus reality in some instances. However, what are you going to do with such experiences? There are many instances of people

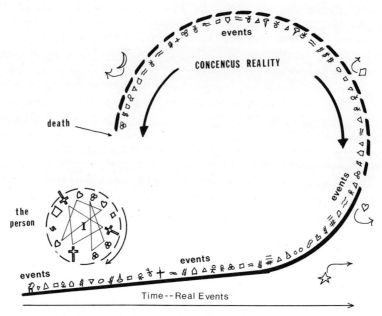

Fig. 11-7.   Consensus reality—altered state of consciousness.

who reached altered states and then simply bored us with enthusiastic preaching about the superiority of this state or that state, when clearly they are just as neurotic as they have always been; their neuroses are just centered around a different set of contents. Experience per se does not necessarily lead to maturity.

I think two major kinds of growth can come from experiencing altered states of consciousness. First, by having a powerful experience of a radical reorganization of your consciousness, you can begin to question the ultimate validity of your ordinary state. That is, the assumption that our ordinary state is natural and best is so powerful that it takes a direct experience of a radically reorganized way of functioning to make us realize that our ordinary state is a construction, and that there are many other ways it could be constructed. Second, if you are already engaged in personal growth work or in psychotherapy, the altered perspective on consensus reality, your personality, and things beyond consensus reality may provide valuable insights and motivations that can feed into your ordinary state of consciousness work, insights that might be difficult to gain otherwise. While altered states of consciousness do not necessarily lead to maturity or going beyond consensus reality, they provide some unique opportunities for doing so *if* they are worked with properly.

THE CULTIVATION OF AWARENESS

I will generally call the third major route the cultivation of awareness. In my understanding of the nature of discrete states of consciousness, I mentioned that the two basic working categories are structures and awareness, the latter also acting as a kind of energy to activate the structures. My observations have convinced me that ordinarily our capacity to simply be aware or pay attention to things is extremely limited because the structures that have been built up in our minds in the course of enculturation tend to automatically capture our attention and direct it in habitual ways, rather than allow us to perceive things freshly and different from our usual way.

The meditative traditions, primarily associated with the East, have been very aware of this automatization of our perception, cognition, and action, and have seen it as a major source of bondage to previous conditionings. In terms of the earlier examples, consensus reality may be created and reinforced by our peers and by ourselves in our actions, but in many ways we carry consensus reality around in our heads. Our ordinary state of consciousness is awareness automatically captured and directed by the structures that constitute consensus reality. If we could learn to use our natural capacity for awareness without it being *automatically* directed by these structures, we could gain a great deal of freedom; that is, we could largely leave the structures intact if we could use them *at will,* rather than automatically having our awareness use them.

How is this new awareness accomplished? Let me give you one brief example, a type of meditative practice known as *vipassana,* or mindfulness, in the Buddhist tradition. The basic instructions for this meditation are simple: sit quietly, observe whatever happens to you, whether it is sensation or thought or feeling, with impartiality. Do not welcome any sensation or experience as being more desirable than any other, and do not reject any experiences as being undesirable. Simply pay attention to *whatever* is.

These instructions are quite simple, but if you try the exercise you will find that they are extremely difficult to follow. In our ordinary consciousness we welcome experiences that please us (even apparently painful experiences that have secondary gains), and we reject experiences that displease us. Since much of what pleases and displeases us has been conditioned in us by our enculturation, consensus reality is upheld: we have been conditioned to like it and defend it. In Eastern terms, we are *attached* to certain experiences, and *attached* to avoiding certain other kinds of experiences; thus we channel our awareness and psychological energies in order to keep our current system going.

The cultivation of full awareness of *whatever* is, whether it pleases us or not, is, I suspect, the technique of ultimate generality in learning to go beyond consensus reality. It is learning to pay attention to what is, which may mean paying attention to many unpleasant things, but it also means learning to notice many things that may turn out to be quite rewarding in the long run but have not been available to us because our culture has not trained us to look for them. It is a thoroughly scientific attitude, for it says we must accurately observe the data in spite of our favored theories.

CONCLUSION

Space prohibits me from discussing the interactions of these three ways.

This chapter has consisted of a quick and very intellectual discussion of the way we are conditioned by consensus reality, and of ways of going beyond it. Let me summarize our situation by quoting someone more lyrical and effective than myself, the poet Wordsworth, in *Ode on Intimations of Immortality:*

> There was a time when meadow, grove, and stream,
> The earth and every common sight,
>   To me did seem
> Apparelled in celestial light,
> The glory and the freshness of a dream . . .

Contrasting this experience with his ordinary state of consciousness perception, he said:

> It is not now as it hath been of yore;
>   Turn whereso'er I may,
>   By night or day,
> The things which I have seen I now can see no more.

We are indeed the beneficiaries of a rich culture, but, as Wordsworth so well conveys, we have paid a high price for the automatic investment of our awareness in the machinery of our consensus reality.

Psychotherapy must, I believe, enlarge its scope beyond that of the present, beyond simply adjusting people to function more effectively and more happily within a given consensus reality. It must combine the traditional techniques of Western psychotherapy with the use of altered states of consciousness and the many ways of cultivating awareness to foster human growth to its full potentialities. Whether this will happen or not depends partly on our own vision and efforts, but also in many ways on cultural forces that are beyond our control. I hope we shall grow into a fuller understanding of what it is to be a human being, for no matter how rich any one particular culture is, it is still a selective, parochial view that inherently is in opposition to other cultures, other consensus realities.

REFERENCE

1.   Shah, I. *Tales of the Dervishes*. New York: Dutton, 1970.

12. COMPLEMENTARITY OF CONSCIOUSNESS

Man's Two Cerebral Hemispheres and Their Implications for Psychotherapy

John C. Rhead, Ph.D.
Roland Fischer, Ph.D.

Over the years philosophers, theologians, and behavioral scientists have speculated at length about the uniqueness of man. It has been suggested that man is unique because of his erect posture and bipedal gait, his logic and language, and his capacities for artistic creation and unifying religious experience. Recent experimentation in the behavioral sciences indicates, however, that the most unique feature of our species may in fact be our "bicameral mind"[20] with its two distinctive cognitive modes largely lateralized in the right and left cerebral hemispheres. The left, the "major," dominant, or "Aristotelian," the Apollonian hemisphere, is involved in analytical, digital, field-articulating, sequence-perceiving processes such as speech, language, writing, logical reasoning, and related functions,[12] all of which subserve rational decision making for survival. The cognitive mode of the right, the "minor," nondominant, or "Platonic," the Dionysian hemisphere, on the other hand, is analogical, synthesis oriented, and nonverbal. It is a scanning mode of visuospatial gestalts and fields involved in symbolic and metaphoric signification, an intuitive, image-making, and musical mode.[5]

In this paper we shall review and elaborate the following propositions: a genetically given structural and functional difference between the right and left cerebral hemispheres allows man to interpret the same stimulus configurations in at least two distinct ways; the two cerebral hemispheres mature at different rates during the development of the normal individual; the functional development of each hemisphere is contingent upon optimal hemisphere-specific stimulation and training during relatively fixed developmental periods; and the scientific and technological *Weltanschauung* of our time contains a strong bias toward the rational thought processes characteristic of the Aristotelian or left hemisphere. This bias in favor of left hemispheric ideation, we further posit, has resulted in the neglect of such Platonic or right hemispheric processes as intuitive–holistic thinking, whether it is exemplified by truly imaginative artistic–scientific creativity or mystical–religious experience. Moreover, this imbalance favoring the left cerebral hemisphere is probably reinforced by the fact that, at a neurological level, hemisphere-specific information processing is contralaterally inhibitory. Finally, the implications of all of the above factors for the future of psychotherapy will be explored.

THE ONTOGENY OF HEMISPHERIC SPECIALIZATION

Recent electrophysiological studies favor the view that hemisphere-specific responsiveness can be observed in infants less than one year old. Crowell et al.[10] were among the first to demonstrate differential hemispheric activity in infants. Studying normal human newborns, these authors found different electroencephalographic patterns in the two hemispheres in response to photic stimulation. Gardiner et al.,[16] in the pilot phase of an ongoing study, reported lateralization of electroencephalographic response to speech and music. Using spectral analysis to calculate a laterality index involving the ratio of power in the alpha band from the left to right hemispheres, they found a greater preponderance of alpha activity in the left hemisphere when a six-month-old infant was exposed to the sounds of a music box, and a reverse of this pattern when exposed to speech. Since alpha activity is presumed to indicate the absence of information processing, such data may be interpreted as reflecting lateralization of speech and music in the left and right hemispheres, respectively, within the first six months of life. This conclusion appears to be borne out by Molfese,[28] who has published evidence of lateralization through evoked potential studies in babies younger than ten months of age.

The data of Crowell et al.,[10] Gardiner et al.,[16] and Molfese[28] are consistent with the fact that either hemisphere may subserve language functions during approximately the first five years of life. According to Kinsbourne[24] and Zangwill[40], left hemisphere dominance for language is progressively established through a genetically preprogrammed displacement of right hemispheric connections from the speech output control neurons. Kinsbourne concludes that

. . . cerebral dominance is not merely the result of more advanced specialization of one hemisphere than the other but involves active competition between hemispheres, which the left hemisphere (the 'rational' hemisphere, evidently in the interest of survival) is genetically destined to win.[24]

The data discussed above[10, 16, 28] can be construed as support for Kinsbourne's theory[24] and is neurophysiological manifestations of the ontogeny of hemispheric specialization.

COGNITIVE BALANCE AND INTEGRATION

There are a number of lines of evidence that seem to converge on the conclusion that some balance in the training and use of the two cerebral hemispheres is necessary for optimal cognitive functioning, mental health, self-actualization, and personal growth.

What is meant by "optimal cognitive functioning?" Is it not in some sense a balance between internal success, or peace of mind, and external success, or productive and creative activity in the world? Let us explore why an interhemispherically balanced education is vital for optimal functioning.

Many authors have emphasized the involvement of the symbolic mode of cognition in creative endeavor.[3, 25] The intuitive symbolic type of cognition seems dependent upon the participation of the right hemisphere. However, if creativity is to be communicable, then it must integrate right hemispheric imagination with left hemispheric expressive abilities. Stated in the negative by Bogen and Bogen:

If transcallosal inhibition is indeed a prominent aspect of cerebral function, we can see a physiological basis for the fact that failure to develop fresh insights (in the sense of new understanding of the outside world) is closely related to a failure to gain further sight into one's other self.[4]

The issue of interhemispheric balance and integration also bears upon the broader areas of mental or emotional health, self-actualization, and personal growth. Let us define the emotionally healthy individual as one who manifests a certain degree of social competence, a spontaneity in the giving and receiving of affection under appropriate circumstances, a sensitivity to the sacred without necessarily subscribing to a formal religious code, and an all-embracing intuitive appreciation of the nature of the universe and his place in it. This sense of being a meaningful part of the whole could be described as intuitive philosophical maturity, wisdom, acceptance, or understanding. Roszak hints at the role of symbols in achieving this state:

> . . . symbols have a sacred, religious quality. . . . The symbol means the experience. Experience and symbol taken together are what we might call a *root meaning:* an irreducible sense of significance, a foundation the mind rests and builds upon. Root meanings cannot be explained or analyzed; rather they are what we use among ourselves to explain—to give meaning to—lesser levels of experience. They are the diamond that cuts all else.[35]

How does one contact the kind of symbols that seem capable of conferring such a sense of meaning? The model of Fischer[13] and the supporting data of Goldstein and his colleagues[17, 18] indicate that a shift from left to right hemispheric information processing can be induced by levels of subcortical arousal that are above (hyper) or below (hypo) the levels of arousal associated with routine daily activities. Increasing levels of subcortical arousal (hyperarousal) are interpreted, at least within our Western culture, as creative, hyperphrenic, cataleptic, and ecstatic experiences. Decreasing levels (hypoarousal), however, result in experiences of relaxation, deepening meditative states (as produced by certain Eastern practices), and ultimately samādhi.[13] However, irrespective of the direction of the change in subcortical arousal (i.e., whether hyper or hypo), any deviation in the level of such arousal from the middle range associated with daily routine tends to result in a decreasing availability of left hemispheric cortical interpretations and a corresponding increasing reliance on the right cerebral hemisphere.[17]

EVIDENCE OF IMBALANCE

There is a growing recognition in the technologically advanced nations of the world today that the products (and by-products) of technology are not necessarily desirable. The United States provides a prime example of a country filled with alienated individuals who find themselves submerged in pollutions of air, water, and noise of apocalyptic proportions. The machines man has created in his own image are not only failing to bring him the promised "good life," but are rendering him increasingly incapable of leading a satisfying existence. Moreover, we seem to be entrapped in a vicious circle within which ever more technology is being used in vain attempts to halt the spread of ecological disasters brought about by technology in the first place. These second-order "technological fixes" ultimately merely aggravate the original symptoms as well as the underlying disease.

The problem lies in the implicit belief that the rational and unlimited technological conquest of nature will necessarily lead to a better life for mankind. A corollary to this belief is that any nontechnological approach to the pursuit of happiness is "reactionary, irrational, and primitive."[39] The danger of this belief system is that it simultaneously perpetuates itself while blinding us to alternatives, or, as Thompson has stated: "As long as we fail to step back and call into question our most basic assumptions, there is no other way to go but deeper and deeper into the trap. . . ."[39]

We submit that this technological, scientific, rational belief system has resulted in an overemphasis on the logical–analytical cognitive mode of the left hemisphere, which in turn has resulted in a rebound effect, characterized by a dramatic overcompensatory swing toward the cognitive mode of the right hemisphere. The symptoms of this rebound include a declining interest and participation in organized, prestructured science and religion and a corresponding upsurge in experiential religious pursuits such as those offered by Eastern meditation, hallucinogenic drug use, and revivalistic, emotional–ecstatic, participatory rites (e.g., Sufi dancing). This change reflects the view that God never died; He has been alive and well in the right hemisphere all the time. Other symptoms include increasing interest and involvement in the "esoteric sciences"[31] and, more generally, all things magic and miraculous, such as astrology, numerology, palmistry, parapsychology, Tarot card and I-Ching readings, witchcraft, alchemy, and astral projection "out of the body."

This rebound effect may be interpreted as a response to a long history of right hemispheric deprivation. It is as if the person were aware of his deprivation-induced uneasiness but unaware of its precise source. He correctly diagnoses right hemispheric deprivation as part of the problem but simultaneously comes to the incorrect conclusion that all left hemispheric cognition is harmful. The conspicuous denial of all left hemispheric values may be an overcompensation resulting from such faulty reasoning.

It has been suggested that mankind tends to cluster according to preferred cognitive mode into two separate types of people.[27] The scientific–technological–industrial revolution fostered the Aristotelian type with a functionally overdeveloped left hemisphere and a correspondingly atrophied right—while the cognitive backlash of this progression has created the Platonic hippie type of the counter culture with a functionally overdeveloped right hemisphere and an atrophied left. Thompson paints this picture poetically:

> One part of mankind wishes to take us into rockets, computers, and a cultural unity that comes from computerized medicine, computerized music, poetry and film, and cybernetic organisms in which the education of the mind is achieved by hooking up the cells of the brain directly to teaching machines. If one has *pratyahara* (yogic control of the senses), he has no need of drugs; if one has *kriya* (control of the central nervous system), he has no need of computers; if one has *samādhi* (Cosmic consciousness), he has no need of moon rockets; for it is the characteristic of an infinite space that all the points are equidistant from one another, and so one does not have to *get* anywhere if he is at his own center.[39]

IMPLICATIONS FOR EDUCATION

Much of the agony of society and its individual members may be attributed to the failure to integrate the talents and values associated with right and left hemispheric cognitive modes, at both the individual and organizational levels. This lack of integration represents itself as a schism, and as this schism in society and in the cerebral cortices of its members deepens, things can only be expected to get worse.

If things are not to worsen, then things must change. Where does one begin to change a disintegrating social system and its dysfunctional values? A modest beginning might be attempted in the field of education by changing the input to students. The necessary change would be in the direction of a more hemispherically balanced and integrated curriculum.

One of the central concepts of traditional education is the intelligence quotient, or IQ. This measure purports to be a ratio of intellectual to chronological age, but in fact, as "intelligence" has come to be defined increasingly in terms of left hemispheric capacities, the IQ has come to be essentially a ratio of left to right hemispheric capacity, corrected for age.

Children in most educational systems are selected for advancement on the basis of (left hemispherically biased) IQ tests. They are then placed in learning situations in which they are exposed to left hemispheric stimulation and they are differentially reinforced for making responses that reflect the utilization of the left hemisphere over the right, in order to graduate into a society in which they are expected to function almost as if they did not have right hemispheres.

Those children who do not achieve high scores on traditional IQ tests may have a general (i.e., bilateral) lack of cerebral capacity to process information, or they may only be deficient in the left hemisphere while their right may still function adequately. In either case their educational exposure is likely to be curtailed on the basis of their test results. Those who do well on IQ tests but subsequently display a penchant for right hemispheric cognition may find themselves feeling like round pegs in square educational holes and drop out altogether.

The net result of this unnatural selection is a waste of human resources and a diminished fulfillment in the lives of individuals.[36] In the language of the day, it brings about a failure to actualize fully the human potential. Squibb has made the point that definitions of intelligence "always have social, cultural, ideological and political assumptions behind them."[38] Those who are able to meet the criteria of "intelligence" at a given time in a given culture are then the very same persons who are given maximum exposure to educational opportunities. In this way, educationally speaking, the rich get richer and the poor get poorer.

Nowhere is the issue of progressive discrepancy of educational opportunity more critical than in the current controversy surrounding the question of apparently genetic involvement in the reported differences of IQ between races.[21, 22] It has been hypothesized, on the one hand, that black children have lower IQs than white ones, even when adequate controls for environmental factors have been provided. On the other hand, it has been argued by Bohannan[9] that there is no possibility of measuring intelligence without cultural bias, and he therefore poses the question: "Why do serious students of human behavior fool around with a dated idea like 'intelligence'?" Taking an intermediate position, we submit that recognition of the distinctive cognitive modes of the two cerebral hemispheres and their competitive development calls for a reformulation of the nature–nurture controversy.

Recall at this point Kinsbourne's[24] argument that interhemispheric competition for dominance in verbal ability is a natural developmental sequence, and that the left hemisphere is "genetically destined to win" this competition. During the course of this development there are critical periods for the acquisition of certain skills (analogous to the well-known critical period for "imprinting"), and after these periods have passed such skills will be learned with difficulty, if at all. For example, consider the plight of the person attempting to learn to speak a second language without a foreign accent after he has been exposed only to his native tongue for the first 20 years of his life. Since he has already passed the critical period during which the right hemisphere was able to participate in the acquisition of language, he will probably learn only a "left hemispheric" version of his second tongue, one which is devoid of the "musical" (right hemispheric) qualities of the native accent.

The general implications for education are obvious, though successful implementation of specific needed changes in educational systems of course will be difficult. An education is required that provides a balanced exposure to stimuli appropriate to each of the cognitive modes, as well as an adequate opportunity to develop the ability of expression through each. Such trends are already visible at the college level, where there is an increasing emphasis on "experiential" learning. Although such an emphasis may be seen as part of a compensatory or rebound effect as a response to right hemispheric deprivation, it nevertheless represents a homeostatic shift toward a balanced approach to the use of one's nervous tissue.

RECENT APPLICATIONS TO PSYCHOTHERAPY

One may conceptualize psychotherapy as a collection of practices intended to overcome or ameliorate some of the difficulties that people encounter in their attempts to optimize their existence. Such difficulties can be the result of environmental and/or genetic influences, with the term "environmental influences" being synonymous with the word "education" when the latter is broadly construed. An optimum existence implies that one maintains a relative freedom from psychological distress such as anxiety and depression as well as a sense of fulfillment, purpose, or meaning in life—all without denying or grossly distorting reality. This definition is not meant to imply that one should not feel fear in the presence of danger, or grief at the loss of a loved one, nor does it imply stasis; life is a process of change and even the most self-actualized, mentally healthy, and spiritually developed among us are expected to go through periods when we must adjust our perceptions, beliefs, and values to new inputs. These adjustment periods may involve difficulties ranging from mild conflict over choices to be made all the way up to the "dark night of the soul." However, for the person who is maintaining the optimal existence herein defined as the goal of psychotherapy, such adjustments are made without undue hesitation, so that he or she is able to maintain, for the most part, a sense of meaning and freedom from distress. For such a person, periods of anomie are the exception rather than the rule.

Research into the differences between the two cerebral hemispheres in terms of their types of functioning or cognitive modes may well have broad implications for the theory and practice of psychotherapy. Some of these implications have already been explored by Galin,[15] who suggests that the relative independence of functioning, as well as the difference in the cognitive mode employed by the two hemispheres, may account for many of the dissociative phenomena seen in psychiatric patients, with the right hemisphere serving as the anatomical locus for what psychoanalysts refer to as the unconscious. He goes on to speculate that increasing sophistication in our knowledge of the differences between the cognitive modes of the two hemispheres may allow the development of procedures that can provide more direct access to unconscious mental processes, and he suggests that the results of unilateral versus bilateral electroconvulsive shock treatment may reflect changes in the balance of functioning between the two hemispheres.

Most traditional psychotherapy has utilized procedures that would seem to emphasize the capacities of the left hemisphere in achieving its goals, rather than those of the right. Although the utilization of dream material may be considered an exception to this rule, in that dreams may well be the product of the right hemisphere (as Galin[15] has suggested), the focus has been largely on verbal transactions and logical reasoning. There are a number of newer developments on the psychotherapeutic scene that seem to reflect a trend toward incorporating the unique capabilities of the right hemisphere in order to achieve the goals that have always been achieved with only marginal success when this hemisphere has been largely ignored.

Many of these newer developments have sprung up first in the growth centers and similar institutions that have become so popular, where they are employed with persons who have not been designated as "patients" in need of "psychotherapy," but rather "normals" who are seeking personal growth, self-actualization, or spiritual development. (In terms of the optimum existence model described above, the difference is merely one of degree—the initial degree of departure from optimum.) As these new procedures begin to show promise in the settings in which they are spawned, they gradually seep into the mainstream of traditional psychotherapeutic practice. Here they are sometimes further refined, though at other times it seems they are merely standardized to the point of orthodoxy and hence become far less effective due to the rigid manner in which they are employed.

Some of the new practices that seem to reflect an awareness of the previous overemphasis on the cognitive mode of the left cerebral hemisphere in psychotherapy are discussed below.

Gestalt Therapy, developed by Perls,[32] uses a good deal of visual imagery and puts almost complete emphasis on the immediate experience associated with such imagery. Not only does the Gestalt therapist fail to suggest that the patient attempt to logically analyze his experience, but in fact a rather unique and amusing vocabulary has been developed to discourage, by means of ridicule, any such attempts.

The late Italian psychiatrist, Assagioli, developed a school that he called Psychosynthesis.[2] The very name of the school is an obvious clue as to its goal: the integration of the various aspects of the human personality. Although developed before there was any great interest in the difference between the cognitive modes of the two cerebral hemispheres, the procedures employed in Psychosynthesis can be seen to draw very clearly on the unique capacities of both hemispheres in an attempt to integrate them.

There are several newer techniques with noticeable somatic emphases. A number of these imply, either explicitly or implicitly, that certain forms of experience are available through body movement, awareness, and/or manipulation. These experiences in turn are usually described in terms that are consistent with our model of right hemisphere cognition—holistic, intuitive, and the like. Hence, the practice of Structural Integration[34] attempts to realign the posture of the body by a deep massage-like procedure that actually tears the connective tissue in areas where it has developed abnormally. Part of the theory behind this procedure is that certain experiences may be controlled and even repressed altogether by chronic muscle tension or abnormal postures. Interestingly enough, some people who undergo this treatment report sudden recovery of previously repressed material, often in a rather instantaneous, nonsequential manner. Such experiences sound as if they might be mediated by the right hemisphere. It may even be that, by means of some kind of central nervous system feedback loop, the chronic muscle tension responsible for postural abnormalities acts in some fashion as a transcallosal inhibitory mechanism, keeping memory traces in the right hemisphere from crossing the corpus callosum to the left.

Other techniques emphasizing the body include biofeedback, meditation, dance and movement exercises, and sentic cycles. Budzynski and Peffer report that subjects trained with biofeedback to produce electroencephalographic theta have experiences that are highly intuitive and "integrative."[8] The latter term is used to refer to the quality of the experience that is in some way healing, constructive, and capable of synthesizing previously conflictual or problematic feelings, impulses, or beliefs. Such a synthesis often seems to require the transcendence of one's usual (left hemisphere) logic in order to reconcile otherwise paradoxical material.

A number of meditative techniques have recently become very popular in the West, some of them imported from their native lands in the East, and some of them apparently representing more local innovations.[29] Within this mass of diverse techniques, a thread common to many of them is that of physical relaxation achieved without a loss of alertness. Such a state is often pursued by means of sitting still in an erect posture. By practicing one of these techniques, it may be that one brings into play the mechanism mentioned above with regard to Structural Integration; that is, by relaxing the body while remaining alert, it may be possible to facilitate the transfer of experience or information between the cerebral hemispheres, a transfer that is usually inhibited by a feedback mechanism associated with muscle tension. In any case, the kinds of intuitive understanding of the nature of life and the universe usually assumed to be the object of meditative practices is, once again, very much akin to the kind of understanding that we attribute to the right hemisphere. It is as if, perhaps, such understanding is inherent within the cognitive capacities of the right hemisphere, and meditation allows some kind of transfer to the left. In such a way one's left hemisphere might come to "know," and perhaps try to communicate, what one's right hemisphere "knew" all the time. Such communication, of course, may have to use the language of the right, speaking through poetry, music, painting, dance, or the like.

Dance and practices involving free-flowing bodily movement in general have found little recognition in psychotherapy journals to date.[1] However, they are quite common in the offerings of growth centers, promising to put one more in tune with the natural rythms of one's body and of the universe, in a very intuitive—i.e., right hemispheric—manner.

The use of sentic cycles involves much less gross bodily movements than does dance, but according to Clynes[9] it can nevertheless result in the evocation of powerful emotional experiences that have therapeutic potential. Such therapeutic potential does not seem to derive from any kind of logical explanation or analysis of the experiences. The person is merely asked to express each of several basic emotions a number of times. The mode of expression is the pressing of a button with the finger, with the total movement being only a fraction of an inch. Plotting the pressure applied to such a button as a function of time generates curves that are distinctive in form for each of a number of basic emotions and are replicable within individuals, across individuals, and across cultures. Once again it seems that some fundamental experience or knowledge that is inherent in the human nervous system is being brought more clearly into consciousness, and once again the model of transfer from right to left hemisphere is potentially applicable.

Several techniques utilize imagery, a modality of experience and expression associated with the right hemisphere. One of these is Gestalt Therapy, which was described above. Another is art therapy, hardly a new technique, but one that has recently become more popular, especially with some of the newer innovations in the field. One of these innovations is the use of mandalas as a therapeutic and diagnostic tool.[23] Mandalas have traditionally been regarded as manifestations of, and triggers for the experience of the inherent order and harmony of the universe. However, only recently has it been discovered that anyone can generate mandalas, given drawing or painting materials and some slight constraints toward centeredness and symmetry. Moreover, the generation of such mandalas seems to be capable of promoting movement toward the experience of such harmony and order, as well as giving some indications as to the areas in one's life in which such a sense of harmony, order, or unity is lacking.

Imagery can be used without overt physical expression. Leuner's technique of Guided Affective Imagery (GAI),[26] which is both diagnostic and therapeutic, calls on the reclining and relaxed subject to report spontaneous imagery, with broad directions from the therapist or guide. A modification and extension of GAI is found in Guided Imagery with Music (GIM).[7] Here the use of musical selections as background to the experiences allows a more subtle form of guidance and also appears to evoke more affectively potent experiences more quickly. With both GAI and GIM there is an emphasis on allowing the spontaneous occurrence or experiences that might be considered to have their origin in the subconscious, but such experiences are also consistent with an interpretation that invokes the right hemisphere in lieu of the subconscious, especially when music is employed[19].

One very promising form of therapy that also seems to promote the occurrence of such experiences is psychedelic psychotherapy, which utilizes LSD and similar drugs. One particularly interesting application of this therapeutic modality is in the area of death and dying. The resolution of the emotional distress and conflict that often accompanies the approach of death is usually beyond the logic of the left hemisphere. However, some of the symbolic experiences encountered when LSD and similar drugs are given, which seem to be mediated by the right hemisphere, appear to be helpful in the resolution of such difficulties. In fact, Richards and his colleagues[33] have demonstrated statistically significant reductions in anxiety, depression, and fear of death in terminally ill cancer patients in response to LSD-assisted psychotherapy. In speculating about the way in which their treatment induces such dramatic effects in their patients, these authors suggest that

> The encounter with elements of the deep unconscious in the form of transpersonal experiences (such as the Jungian archetypes, racial and collective memories, experience of the cosmic drama, divine and demonic appearances, etc.) enabled them to relate in a very tangible and convincing manner to psychic realities that were far beyond their individual framework. It seems that it was this opening of the transpersonal and cosmic panorama that provided a background and referential system against which the fact of individual destruction appeared to be relatively unimportant.[33]

IMPLICATIONS FOR THE FUTURE
OF PSYCHOTHERAPY

Dean[11] has coined the term "ultraconsciousness" to refer to "a suprasensory, suprarational level of mental activity that transcends all other human experience and creates a sense of oneness with the universe," and which has in the past been referred to as cosmic consciousness, nirvana, satori, samādhi, kairos, unio mystica, etc. If one assumes that the right hemisphere is the seat of the ultraconscious, then future practices, training, and research in the field now known as psychotherapy can be expected to devote substantial resources to the pursuit of the royal road to this form of consciousness. It seems unlikely that any one universal psychic highway will be discovered or constructed, but rather that the development will involve multiple pathways, each being optimal only for certain individuals under specific circumstances.

The possible changes in the practice of psychotherapy range all the way from innovations in the field of biological psychiatry to the incorporation of techniques heretofore considered the province of the clergy. Let us first explore some of the possible biological implications of cerebral hemisphere specialization. New forms of psychosurgery may evolve that would seek to manipulate the interrelationship between the two hemispheres. Complete severing of the corpus callosum has already shown promise in the control of epilepsy.[37] Lesser lesions, in this area as well as other anatomical sites in the central nervous system, may prove to have salutary effects on the integration of the capacities of the two sides of the brain in certain cases. The opposite approach might also be taken. That is, a surgical technique might be developed that would produce an augmentation of the neurological connections between the two hemispheres. Such a technique might involve the transplantation of living nervous tissue from some other part of the body (or from a deceased donor). It could even employ nonbiological materials to construct an external shunt or splice that would conduct impulses. Such a "rewiring" would be somewhat analogous to the procedures sometimes used with acupuncture, in which electrical circuits are established external to the body in order to bypass or balance functions of the nervous system. One obvious advantage to such an approach is that it would allow the imposition of all manner of devices to control, amplify, and regulate the flow of impulses through the circuit.

Other interventions that are basically biological in format might attempt to temporarily suppress the activity of one hemisphere (probably the left) in order to allow the other to be more active or dominant. Once such a temporary disruption in the usual balance has been effected, then diagnostic and/or therapeutic interventions might be applied. The GAI and GIM techniques described above would be candidates for such interventions, as would sentic cycles and almost any technique using imagery. Certain forms of meditation might also be aided by a temporary suppression of the left hemisphere. Ornstein is fond of describing the practice of meditation on *koans* (logically unsolvable riddles) in terms of "making an end run around the left hemisphere."[30] However, if it were possible to biologically suppress the left hemisphere for a short time the quarterback could presumably go right through the center of the line.

At least two methods already exist that might be used to temporarily suppress the functions of a cerebral hemisphere. One of these, unilateral electroconvulsive therapy, is used as a therapeutic measure. However, it is not usually combined with any of the techniques mentioned above. The other, unilateral injection of sodium amobarbital into one of the carotid arteries, has found its primary application as a diagnostic tool in medicine. However, its effect is that of quite dramatic suppression of the activities of the side of the brain corresponding to the laterality of the injection. Although in this procedure the effect is probably too brief to allow significant therapeutic application of GIM or the like, and the risk is too great to permit routine application, it could be of diagnostic value in selected cases.

No doubt other methods for altering interhemispheric dominance or balance that are primarily biological or physical in nature will be developed. Biofeedback is already being explored in this regard, with positive feedback contingent upon making appropriate changes in the interhemispheric ratio of voltage output within a given frequency range, rather than upon changes in absolute values of voltage and/or frequency at a particular site on the skull. Other procedures, such as subjecting the head to powerful electromagnetic fields that differ on certain parameters for the two sides of the head, may evolve in the foreseeable future. There is also the possibility of the development of new chemical compounds that, when introduced into the body, will differentially affect the activity of the two cerebral hemispheres.

The future of psychotherapy will probably also see the development of new procedures for utilizing right hemisphere cognition without direct manipulation of the physical body. Elaborations, extensions, and innovations in procedures such as GAI, GIM, meditation, and sentic cycles can be expected. Although it is acknowledged that all these procedures probably have some specifiable effect on the physical body, and three of them impose physical stimuli (auditory) on the body, they are not seen as primarily biological or physical interventions. Innovations in these nonbiological areas could involve combinations of already existing techniques, as well as the development of entirely new ones.

The innovations that come about in the practice of psychotherapy will no doubt have implications for the training of therapists and the research paradigms and strategies that come to be popular in exploring new horizons. With regard to training, therapists, especially those without medical backgrounds, will face the prospect of having to learn to use the apparatus associated with biofeedback or whatever other physical interventions they may care (and are allowed by law) to attempt.

However, there is a much larger issue looming on the horizon for the training of psychotherapists. As new forms of therapy with greater emphasis on the cognitive mode of the right hemisphere evolve, it will become increasingly important that the therapist have access to that mode in his own cognitive repertoire. He will have to "speak the (nonverbal) language," as it were. Such an ability seems most likely to result from the therapist having direct experience in the techniques and practices he proposes to apply to others. This experience has already been suggested by many as a requirement for any therapist who wishes to administer psychedelic drugs to others. Going a step further, Frager[14] has offered a proposal for a graduate program in transpersonal psychology. As the name implies, "transpersonal psychology" has to do with concepts, experiences, and activities that transcend the individual person. Such experiences are probably for the most part mediated by the right hemisphere, and hence his proposed model for graduate training finds direct application to the subject matter of this paper. For training at the M.A. level he suggests, under the heading of "Spiritual Work," that the student make "at least some commitment to a personal discipline and regular practice" of a "path" that would be designed to actualize his ideals. Pursuit of the Master's degree would also require weekly group meditation and "students would have the opportunity to practice chanting, periods of silence, and other methods of contacting their inner spiritual nature." For the doctoral candidate the requirements would be a bit stiffer:

> Students would be encouraged to engage in a period of intensive field work as a part of their program. For example, those particularly interested in Zen or Yoga might live in a Zen monastery or Yoga ashram in the United States or travel to Japan or India, or both.[14]

The implications of cerebral specialization for research in psychotherapy follow quite directly from the above discussion of training. The researcher, like the clinician of the future, may have to learn the languages of the right hemisphere before he can even theorize to himself about the phenomena under investigation, to say nothing of communicating his theories and data to his colleagues. Since the right hemisphere is nonverbal, it is intriguing to contemplate what new forms of communication may evolve to replace the word, which may have been "in the beginning," but may one day be superseded.

REFERENCES

1. Alperson, E. D. Carrying experiencing forward through authentic body movement. *Psychotherapy: Theory, Research and Practice,* 1974, *11,* 211–214.
2. Assagioli, R. *Psychosynthesis.* New York: Viking Press, 1965.
3. Barron, F. *Creativity and personal freedom.* Princeton, N.J.: Van Nostram, 1968.
4. Bogen, J. E., & Bogen, G. M. The other side of the brain III: The corpus callosum and creativity. *Bulletin of the Los Angeles Neurological Society,* 1969, *34,* 191–220.

5. Bogen, J. E., & Gordon, H. W. Musical tests for functional lateralization with intracarotid amobarbital. *Nature*, 1971, *230*, 524–525.

6. Bohannan, P. Heritability of intelligence. *Science*, 1973, *182*, 115.

7. Bonny, H. & Savary, L. M. *Music and your mind: Listening with a new consciousness*. New York: Harper & Row, 1973.

8. Budzynski, T., & Peffer, K. *Twilight-state learning: A biofeedback approach to creativity and attitude change*. Paper presented at Transformations of Consciousness Conference sponsored by the R. M. Bucke Memorial Society and the Department of Psychiatry, McGill University, Montreal, October 24–26, 1973.

9. Clynes, M. Sentography: Dynamic forms of communication of emotion and qualities. *Computers in Biology and Medicine*, 1973, *3*, 119–130.

10. Crowell, D. H., Jones, R. H., Kapuniai, L. E., & Nakagawa, J. K. Unilateral cortical activity in newborn humans: An early index of cerebral dominance? *Science*, 1973, *180*, 205.

11. Dean, S. Metapsychiatry: The interface between psychiatry and mysticism. *American Journal of Psychotherapy*, 1973, *130*, 1036–1038.

12. Eccles, J. C. Brain, speech and consciousness. *Naturwissenschaften*, 1973, *60*, 167–176.

13. Fischer, R. A cartography of the ecstatic and meditative states. *Science*, 1971, *174*, 897–904.

14. Frager, R. A proposed model for a graduate program in transpersonal psychology. *Journal of Transpersonal Psychology*, 1973, *6*, 163–166.

15. Galin, D. Implications for psychiatry of left and right cerebral specialization: A neurophysiological context for unconscious processes. *Archives of General Psychiatry*, 1974, *31*, 572–583.

16. Gardiner, M., Schulman-Galambos, C., & Walter, D. O. *Faculative asymetries in infants and adults*. Paper presented at the UCLA January Conference on Cerebral Dominance, UCLA Neuropsychiatric Institute, Los Angeles, Calif., 1973.

17. Goldstein, L. & Stoltzfus, N. W. Psychoactive drug-induced changes in interhemispheric EEG amplitude relationships. *Agents and Actions*, 1973, *3*, 124–132.

18. Goldstein, L. Stoltzfus, N. W., & Gardocki, J. F. Changes in interhemispheric amplitude relationships in the EEG during sleep. *Physiology and Behavior*, 1972, *8*, 811–815.

19. Gordon, H. W., & Bogen, J. E. Hemispheric lateralization of singing after intracarotid sodium amylobarbitone. *Journal of Neurology, Neurosurgery, and Psychiatry*, 1974, *37*, 727–738.

20. Jaynes, J. *The evolution of consciousness and bicameral mind*. Paper presented at Transformations of Consciousness Conference sponsored by the R. M. Bucke Memorial Society and the Department of Psychiatry, McGill University, Montreal, October 24–26, 1973.

21. Jensen, A. R. How much can we boost IQ and scholastic achievement? *Harvard Educational Review*, 1969, *39*, 1–123.

22. Kaufman, A. S. Comparison of the performance of matched groups of black children and white children on the Wechsler Preschool and Primary Scale of Intelligence. *Journal of Consulting and Clinical Psychology*, 1973, *41*, 186–191.

23. Kellogg, J. The interpretations of colors and shapes in mandalas. Unpublished manuscript, 1977.

24. Kinsbourne, M. *Hemispheric collaboration and competition*. Paper presented at Transformations of Consciousness Conference sponsored by the R. M. Bucke Memorial Society and the Department of Psychiatry McGill University, Montreal, October 24–26, 1973.
25. Krippner, S., & Hughes, W. Dreams and human potential. *Journal of Humanistic Psychology,* 1970, *19,* 1–20.
26. Leuner, H. Guided affective imagery (GAI): A method of intensive psychotherapy. *American Journal of Psychotherapy,* 1969, *23,* 4–22.
27. MacKinnon, D. The nature and nurture of creative talent. In Semeonf, B. (Ed.), *Personality assessment.* Baltimore, Md.: Penguin Books, 1966.
28. Molfese, D. L. Auditory evoked responses to speech and music stimuli. *Journal of the Accoustical Society of America,* 1973, *53,* 363.
29. Naranjo, C., & Ornstein, R. E. *On the psychology of meditation.* New York: Viking Press, 1971.
30. Ornstein, R. *Graduate seminar on altered states of consciousness.* Psychology Department, Stanford, University, Stanford, Calif., Fall, 1970.
31. Ornstein, R. *The psychology of consciousness.* San Francisco: W. H. Freeman, 1972.
32. Perls, F. S. *Gestalt therapy verbatim.* Lafayette, Calif.: Real People Press, 1969.
33. Richards, W. A., Grof, S., Goodman, L. R., & Kurland, A. A. LSD-assisted psychotherapy and the human encounter with death. *Journal of Transpersonal Psychology,* 1972, *4,* 121–150.
34. Rolf, I. P. Structural integration. *Confinia Psychiatrica,* 1973, *16,* 69–79.
35. Roszak, T. *Where the wasteland ends.* New York: Doubleday, 1972.
36. Smith, I. M. *Spatial ability.* London: University of London Press, 1964.
37. Sperry, R. W., Gazzaniga, M. S., & Bogen, J. E. Interhemispheric relationships: The neocortical commissures: Syndromes of hemisphere disconnection. In P. J. Vinken & G. S. Bruyn (Eds.), *Handbook of clinical neurology* (Vol. 4). Amsterdam: North Holland, 1969.
38. Squibb, P. The concept of intelligence—A sociological perspective. *The Sociological Review,* 1973, *21,* 57–75.
39. Thompson, W. I. *At the edge of history.* New York: Harper & Row, 1971.
40. Zangwill, O. L. *Cerebral dominance and its relation to psychological function.* Edinburgh: Oliver & Boyd, 1960.

13. HYPNOTHERAPY

Hypnotic Imagery in Learning and Healing

Gerald G. Jampolsky, M.D.

At the Center for Attitudinal Healing in Tiburon, Calif., we have been involved in utilizing hypnosis to bring about an altered state of consciousness as a method of modifying behavior in such a way as to enhance learning and healing.

In the field of medicine, there has been a tremendous increase in the past five years in the utilization of hypnosis in the areas of psychosomatic medicine, pain relief, relaxation, and the stimulation of imagination and imagery. Most of this interest has been expressed by physicians who are not psychiatrists but who have learned to utilize hypnosis after graduating from medical school. In Europe and Canada there has been an increased interest in autogenic training, which is a structured process in which the patient learns how to relax and to hypnotize himself.

At the same time that medical specialists are becoming more involved in the use of imagery, nonmedical groups are becoming interested in the same process. Groups like Silva Mind Control, Erhard Seminar Training, and Mind Dynamics make use of imagery and the hypnotic process, but they call it just a "process" or "a guided fantasy."

We have been involved in stimulating and encouraging the positive use of imagination and imagery in all forms. We have used images in an attempt to deemphasize sequential, logical thinking, which traditionally has been relied upon as the main way of achieving more self-awareness, or of solving one's own problems.

Our initial interest in hypnosis has led to our involvement in similar processes that lead to an altered state of consciousness. Some of these processes are meditation, yoga, the imagery used in the biofeedback experience, and the imagery used in clairvoyance, telepathy, and disassociative or out-of-body experiences.

Two of the most important advantages of utilizing suggestion in the form of imagery are that it allows the patient to change his belief system, and it allows him to extend his awareness of the present so that he no longer has to be affected by the linear time of past, present, and future. This means that the subject is helped to let go of his emotional and anxiety type of attachment to the past and future, resulting in free energy for learning in the present.

We have found that the positive use of imagery can increase the rate of learning. There is also evidence that use of imagery in an altered state of consciousness can positively affect mental health.

EMOTIONS OF CHILDREN WITH LEARNING DISABILITIES

My personal interest in learning disabilities began some 44 years ago when I was in the first grade and was unable to learn to read. I had reversal problems and frequently read "dog" for "god." I was unable to learn the alphabet by rote, and, in effect, had almost no rote memory, so I was not able to remember my phone number and address. My coordination was poor; my attention span was minimal. In those days they did not use the term "hyperkinesis," but I was frequently told that I had "ants in my pants," and it is clear to those of you who know me now that I today fit the syndrome of a "hyperkinetic adult." I remember being told I wasn't trying hard enough in school and was not working up to my capacity.

Matters were complicated by the fact that I came from a Jewish home that put great stress on academic achievement. In addition, I had two older brothers who breezed through school with excellent grades. I had many of the same teachers they had had. It seemed almost inevitable that each new teacher I had would say, "Oh, I remember your brothers well." This statement tended to cause gastrointestinal spasms—a reaction to my inference that what the teacher was really saying was, "I'll approve and accept you only if you perform like your brothers."

Since I continued to do poorly academically, I apparently decided unconsciously to get my strokes either from negative attention by becoming the class clown, or by attempting to be the popularity kid and running for every school election. These maneuvers did not hide from my "inner knowing self" that I was dumb and stupid and that I was painfully shy inside my outer facade. I became excellent at deceiving others as well as myself.

I later found that one of my best learning routes was tactile. In medical school I was excellent at anatomy and clinical medicine, in which touching was allowed. Histology and neuroanatomy, which require spacial orientation at which I was so poor, caused me the greatest ofand I barely passed those courses.

I trust I have made it clear that I was sort of a mixed-up boy with perceptual problems, as well as secondary and primary emotional problems. I suspect that these factors played an important role in motivating me to go into the field of adult and child psychiatry so that I might find out what makes me tick, and hopefully, find harmony and peace within myself.

Many of the factors touched upon by this personal vignette are just as prevalent today among children that I see as they were among children in the early 1930s.

DIAGNOSTIC CATEGORIES

While we have become much more sophisticated in diagnosing and labeling, there has not been a great deal of progress made, in my opinion, in assisting these children. Most authorities seem to agree that these children fall into a continuum. They fall in the range of having, from the etiological standpoint, primary emotional problems to that of having organic or perceptual problems. The broad diagnostic category that is most in vogue today is "learning disability." The term "dyslexia" seems to be less popular today, and one more often hears the term "cerebral dysfunction." The stress around academic competition frequently causes secondary emotional reactions in the child who has a primary organic–perceptual problem. Most authorities tend to agree that about 15 percent of the school population are afflicted with this disorder.

In a study done in a high school in Marin County, Calif., about 2 percent of the seniors are still reading on a second or third grade level. Many of these students have had exhaustive multiple educational–medical workups and have been subjected to a variety of treatment modalities, running from psychiatric treatment to the most current fad in remediation—but often to no avail.

Before describing some of the hypnotic techniques we have been developing at the Center for Attitudinal Healing, I would like to share with you some of my personal beliefs about our educational structure that I hope will enable us to see more clearly the relevance of using hypnotic imagery with these children.

EDUCATIONAL SYSTEMS' APPROACH TO LEARNING PROBLEMS

In general, our educational system seems to me to be oriented in such a way as to reward those students who are competent in rote and sequential memory both from a visual and auditory standpoint; it awards those whose best facility is to process information that they see and hear. It additionally rewards those who can take that information, integrate it in the brain visually and spacially, and then use it in the form of writing. The system rewards those who are conforming and whose minds tend to work in a rational, logical, sequential manner.

In effect, then, our educational system tends to reward those who learn best by making use of their left brain functions. This system punishes the child who may be bright but can't memorize, can't remember a sequence of directions, can't distinguish his right from his left or up from down, or can't visualize symbols in the form of letters and integrate them in his brain so that they become words with meaning, so that he may then read with understanding. In addition, the educational system puts these children into a competitive environment in which they are constantly being tested, evaluated, and in which the emphasis is often on their errors and what they have done wrong.

DYNAMICS THAT HYPNOSIS AFFECTS

Most of the methods, then, only repeat what they have already done, with the feeble hope that the child will eventually learn by repetition. The aversive experiences for these children in most schools is monumental. The most important emotional factor generated by this system is fear, which is frequently accompanied by frustration. The children fear that their past experience will predict and predicate the present and future—which means more failure and more fear and more guilt. From fear come feelings of helplessness, hopelessness, futility, guilt, and then more frustration and anger and hostility—sometimes direct and sometimes indirect. The learning process becomes more painful for the students and their self-esteem diminishes. These children are frequnelty in an educational environment that is 80 percent doomed to fail. My contention is that for learning to occur, there has to be an 80 percent chance of success. It is equally important, if students are to learn to their fullest capacities, that learning be pleasurable.

It behooves us, then, to develop methods that help the child, the parents, the teacher, and even the physician to disassociate themselves from painful past learning experiences in order to stop the negative reinforcement. The majority of educational processes emphasize teaching the student parts of what he is to learn. Only when he has mastered bits and parts is he presented the whole picture. To function best, many children need to be presented the total picture first, and then the parts. It is with regard to the latter factors that hypnotic imagery has its relevance.

HYPNOSIS WITH CHILDREN WHO HAVE HAD
PERCEPTUAL READING PROBLEMS

The first example is a group of children in Marin County, Calif., who were studied in 1973. They were in the third and fourth grades and were having difficulty learning to read. In the first and second grades these particular children had been thought to have some degree of cerebral dysfunction, in that they all demonstrated some types of perceptual problems that were thought to play a part in their difficulty in learning to read.

At the time of our study, these children had been reevaluated by the school psychologist, and it was found that they no longer had demonstrable perceptual problems but were still having major trouble learning to read. At the point we entered, the educators thought the prime problem to learning was a secondary emotional one from their previous past, painful learning experience.

We had small experimental and control groups. We found all the children to have low self-esteem and low self-concepts. Dr. Stanley Coopersmith of the University of California at Davis was our consultant, and we used his tests for self-esteem.

A good many of the children were under pressure from their parents to learn to read, and some were forced to read each night at home. We found that the teachers of these students were quite frustrated and had some feelings of incompetency due to the students' lack of progress in learning to read. There seemed to be a negative feedback system in which the child, teacher, and parent were each creating more frustration, fear, anger, and guilt in each other.

In our project, all procedures were recorded with video taping. We worked for three 45-minute sessions with each of three groups: the children, the parents, and the teachers. The procedure used for the parents and teachers was almost identical to that used with the children. In the school setting, we used the words "suggestive techniques" and "autosuggestive techniques," rather than the word "hypnosis" because those terms seemed more acceptable to everyone in the school setting.

SPECIFIC HYPNOTIC IMAGERY TECHNIQUES

Our task as we saw it was first to help these children learn how to relax and to use images other than visual ones; then to give them a method by which they could get over the fears and emotional turmoil that had resulted from their past experiences; and finally, to give them a new way of learning by teaching them to fuse or identify with a new, hypnotically developed total self-image. In this new self-image, the children were taught to see themselves reading fluently, accurately, and with pleasure.

Many of these children had poor visual memory, manifested by poor recall of dreams or by looking at an object such as a pen and not being able to visualize the pen in the minds eye with the eyes closed. We, therefore, did not use the usual visualization induction technique for children, but used kinesthetic techniques such as feeling a fur on the face, feeling a weight pull their arm down, and feeling a gas balloon pull their arm up. This procedure turned out to be fun for them, and their easy successes at these new experiences in which they felt they were increasing their use of imagination served to increase their cooperativeness.

In Step 2 we suggested that they put themselves someplace they would enjoy being, and where they would be relaxed, such as on the beach, on a raft, in the mountains, etc. Attention to rhythmic breathing was also emphasized.

Step 3 was designed to assist in disposing of, and making disappear, old memories that had been painful in the process of learning. The suggestion given in this step was for the children to put their hands on their head, go through their skull, and gently lift out their brain and put it on the ground in front of them. They then took a hose in their hand and began to wash out their brain to get rid of all the black stuff, dirt and grime that made up those old painful memories of having difficulty learning to read. They then put their brains back in their heads, feeling their brains much lighter and freer.

In this process they were encouraged to get rid of their old belief system and establish a new belief system in which anything was possible and nothing was impossible. They were encouraged to wash away such words as "but," "I'll try," "it's difficult," "if only." It was pointed out that these words tended only to create negative picture images that made the past repeat i5self. This is a method we have found successful in stopping the internal dialogue that Carlos Castaneda has so eloquently written about in his books, particularly in *Tales of Power*.

In Step 4 we had the children pick their favorite subject and imagine themselves writing a small book about this subject.

In Step 5 we had them use tactile, auditory, and visual imagery so that they could see and feel themselves reading from their books—fluently, successfully, confidently, and joyfully, with a smile on their faces. They then pictured themselves on a motion picture screen. In using this image, they were observed spontaneously flipping the imaginary pages of the book, and eye movement tracking was also noted.

In Step 6 it was suggested that they begin to see a door on the screen; they opened it and then climbed into their own body on the screen. This process makes use of a fusion process that allows for incorporation as part of learning. (By climbing into the person on the screen, they become that person.) Most educational processes go on the assumption that learning will take place by identification. (Here the child remains separate from the teacher, but tries to take on the characteristics of the teacher.)

They need to fuse or get inside their teacher, or fuse and get inside their own image of themselves. This is a process whereby the teacher and student become one. This procedure allows the child to learn through his active imagination and to experience the whole process as a total experience. It makes use of imagery and deemphasizes "thinking" and intellectualization and the attempt to put together the pieces and fragments into a total picture. To these children, that conventional process of learning by concentrating on the pieces is like throwing a jigsaw puzzle up into the air and asking the child to put it together while it is in the air.

In Step 7 it is suggested that the child take the mental picture of himself and put in it his blood cells—which then goes to all the tissues in his body: his brain, muscles, and skin; and then this mental picture of himself beromes one.

In a sense, an illusion that the child has created becomes a new true reality for himself, and therefore is no longer an illusion. Another aspect of this technique is that it allows for a sense of timelessness to develop and tends to get rid of the hangups most of us develop when we are stuck to linear time. It particularly allows us to let go of our emotional attachments to the past that interfere with our perceiving the present as an ever fresh, new moment. This process also emphasizes right brain functioning and gets away from left brain traps of measuring sticks, evaluating, and making judgments. The fun is letting the image flow and simply becoming the person in the image, and letting the action take place without effort and without thinking about it.

In Step 8, an autohypnotic, or, if you prefer, an autosuggestive technique was taught the child, using the same steps outlined previously. The child was instructed to utilize this process five to ten minutes before going to school. Incidentally, in later studies we modified this procedure by having the child tape himself, giving himself suggestions and then listening to his tape in the twilight state and after he or she was asleep.

GROUP HYPNOTIC TECHNIQUES WITH TEACHERS AND PARENTS

In the procedure for parents and teachers, emphasis was placed on developing positive pictures of seeing the children read successfully and without effort. Parents were encouraged not to be involved in their children's reading program and not to try to get them to read. The teachers were encouraged to develop positive mental pictures of their children reading more fluently and with pleasure, and to feel a lightness and fluidity in their relationship with the child and to stop all critical statements.

RESULTS

Wide-Range Achievement Tests and the Durrell Reading Tests for Speed, Accuracy, and Comprehension showed that students in the experimental group increased reading skills one and one-half years in a period of two months, as compared to an average increase of one month in the control group.

The Coopersmith Simple Self-Esteem Test showed a tremendous increase in the experimental group's self-esteem. Parents reported they felt much closer and easier and less tense and driven with their children. The teachers not only reported a difference in the children in this project, but they also reported that they felt more relaxed and less tense with their other students. They all reported more energy and less fatigue at the end of the school day.

The students were tested one year later and were continuing to make excellent progress compared to the control group. A noteworthy side reaction at the end of the year was that the children and parents of the control group contacted me and wished to be involved in the suggestive and autosuggestive process, and this program was carried out. Some aspects of this work have been published elsewhere.[3]

HYPNOSIS IN REVERSAL PROBLEMS

A second example of the use of hypnosis in learning disabilities is in reference to assisting children who have reversal problems. These are children who write 2's, 3's, 5's, 6's, 7's, and 9's backward. They also tend to confuse u's and n's, b's and d's.

In one study,[2] we found a very successful method for using hypnotic techniques as a way of sensitizing the child to muscle and vibratory memory so that he could learn to correct perceptual errors. I have found that due to their visual perceptual problems some of these children seem to learn better when viewed as if they were blind; then, to begin with, techniques are used that would be used with the blind.

In this particular project, I developed a vibratory pencil that I made out of an electric toothbrush. With the child in a light trance state, we found that he could utilize touch, vibratory, and muscle memory as a way of perceiving numbers and executing them correctly, whereas he was persistently inaccurate when he used visual cues. For example, the vibratory pencil made a 7 on the child's back and it was thought that the number 7 was processed into the brain by vibratory pathways.

We found that the vibratory pencil could also assist in handwriting, in that it was large enough that the child could not squeeze it to death, it had a weight that gave him a feedback that he had a pencil in his hand, and, because it vibrated, it glided along and writing became fun rather than painful and boring.

HYPNOSIS IN TEACHING GRAMMAR

A third example of the use of hypnosis in learning is the teaching of grammar, another area that is frequently considered by the student to be dull, boring, and difficult. Initially, children were given relaxation and autosuggestive techniques, and the suggestion was given that they were going to learn their grammar by an easy, fun way—by feeling and touching, not by seeing. It was thought that hypnotic techniques might emphasize the experience and help make learning by touching more sensitive and powerful. Each student was given a stick about 1½ feet long that had indentations on i5, and other small sticks were attached by hinges to the longer stick. The student then identified, while blindfolded, the noun, verb, adjective, etc., by feeling the smaller sticks come off the main stick. It was felt that this method was not only pleasurable, but that it enhanced the learning process.

We have also used these hypnotic techniques with hyperactive children and with children who are chronically absent from school. Two brief examples of children in the latter category may be of interest, since it is not an uncommon problem.

HYPNOSIS WITH CHILDREN'S PSYCHOSOMATIC PROBLEMS

The first example is a child whom we will call Harry. Harry was eight years old, was at the bottom of his class in the third grade, and for the previous year and a half had not been to school more than two full days in a row. He had very severe asthma, was hospitalized frequently, and was rarely in school because of his continued asthma attacks. His pediatrician, who had heard of our work in hypnosis, referred him to us recently.

One need not be a psychiatrist to have been impressed with all the secondary gain Harry was getting with his symptoms. He was "King of His Land." My approach with him was not to suggest that through hypnosis his symptoms would disappear. (This would have been too threatening for him.) On the contrary, I suggested that we could work out a process together whereby he could learn, if he wished, to bring on even more severe asthma attacks, so that he could scare and control his parents all the more. This intrigued him. It was also pointed out to him that if he wished, he could learn to get rid of an asthma attack and that he could learn not to have them.

This approach really got his interest and enthusiasm going, because he could see it as a gain for him with even more control over people. We made a lung out of clay and drew some crude pictures of a lung. He agreed to taperecord the session, and he was able to bring on an excellent asthma attack by visualizing and feeling his bronchi constricting. I might add that his face turned quite blue, which is guaranteed to scare most parents—and sometimes even physicians.

With equal agility he was able to get rid of his asthma attack by feeling and visualizing his bronchi widening and relaxing. He was most impressed by hearing the replay of the tape, and the rales and the heavy breathing and the noise the lungs could make—as well as the control his lungs had to be quiet and calm when he so chose. He was bubbling over with excitement about playing the tape to show off to his parents his latest accomplishments. Together we wrote a script; we became coproducer and codirector and put our "movie" on tape, utilizing autosuggestions that he listened to every night. I saw him three more times, after which he began to go to school each day and his total school attendance and performance began to change.

Needless to say, I also worked with the parents and went to the school and worked with the school personnel. Both were able to understand the child's defenses against his fear, which resulted in his manipulation. They began to be firm and they stopped giving him secondary gain for his symptoms.

The second child was also eight years of age. He also was missing many days of school. His problem was that he had never been able to have a bowel movement in a toilet and didn't want to go to school. (Neither did his classmates want him there, as he frequently would have a bowel movement in his pants.) He had been in treatment with a well-known child psychiatrist in California before I saw him. I therefore wasn't sure what approach to take. I found out that his chief interest was rocket ships, fire engines, astronauts, and the moon. In the hypnotic session I decided to combine all of these ingredients.

The first session took place in the bathroom of my office. The bathroom became a spaceship that had a fire engine in it with a special toilet on the fire engine. The taste of flory that we put in the script was that David would become the first child to defecate on the moon. As David and I approached the moon, he asked me to take over the space-craft while he got on his toilet seat and his imaginary fire engine in our imaginary space-craft. As soon as we landed, we both heard the "plop plop" sounds of success. It was a most joyous occasion. However, during the week that followed he continued to have bowel movements in his pants. During the second week he began to have bowel movements in the toilet in his home, and I saw him only two more occasions.

To this day, I fondly remember David as the first boy in history to defecate on the moon. You see, it was a very real experience for both of us—I think we were truly inside each other.

HYPNOSIS COMBINED WITH BIOFEEDBACK
TRAINING

We have also been using hypnotic techniques in conjunction with our work in biofeedback with children. I became interested in and involved with biofeedback research because I was particularly curious about the images that might be used or developed by biofeedback.

Biofeedback technology is a method whereby an individual can learn to control the autonomic systems in his body and thereby learn to modify such modalities as brain waves, temperature, muscle, and skin resistance. There is visual and auditory feedback to these systems. Some people seem to need a concrete measurement in the form of a needle on a gauge, or a sound, into develop imagery; the majority of people seem to be able to modify these internal processes through other methods such as hypnosis and meditation. We have found that by utilizing a combination of our own techniques, Jacobson's technique,[1] and autogenic techniques, we could facilitate the biofeedback process.

In June 1975, we completed a small pilot project with hyperactive children and controls, using muscle biofeedback. The results were not significant except for an increase in the self-esteem, self-concept area.

Another project we did in Spring 1975 was a collaboration with Tamalpais High School (Mill Valley, Calif.) in the teaching of psychophysiology in a psychology course for juniors. A number of people volunteered their time for this project, including Joanne Kamiya of the Langley Porter Institute and Maryellen Haight, now affiliated with Sonoma State College.

This became an exciting learning experience for students and staff combined. Joanne Kamiya gave some initial remarks about the principles of biofeedback, and all the students had an opportunity to have some experience on at least one biofeedback instrument. Six students volunteered for a three-week involvement three times a week.

The students found that learning about psychophysiology by learning to modify their own modalities was exciting and rewarding. Records were kept of their imagery states in beta, alpha, and theta. Most of the students said they experienced an increase in self-esteem from the knowledge that in learning to control their internal environment they could lose the fear of being swallowed up by their external environment, and that they had learned a meaningful way of relaxing.

SUMMARY

In summary, an attempt has been made to point out some of the problems children with learning disabilities have when they face an educational environment that is geared to analyzing the world into separate bits and pieces. It has been emphasized that most of our present educational system seems geared to rewarding analytical, logical, rational, and sequential thought processes.

Our general approach has been initially to assist these children in learning and problem solving by giving them a variety of techniques to help them "stop thinking." We then provide techniques with which they can learn the art of relaxing and eventually learn in states of consciousness other than our so-called "alert awake state." Next, we have emphasized the giving up of linear time concepts of past, present, and future, and establishing timelessness of the moment.

It is our belief that by assisting these children to use hypnotic imagery we have stimulated their use of right brain functioning and brought about a better right brain and left brain balance. The child then developssense of unity with his internal and external worlds by using holistic imagery. It has been stated that the positive use of imagination can bring about that harmonious balance of feeling at one with oneself and the world. The net result of using positive imagination is that the child no longer feels that he is trapped by his environment.

I will end on a speculative note: as further research is completed in this area, we will find the dynamics of learning and healing to be one and the same.

REFERENCES

1. Jacobson, E. *Progressive relaxation*. Chicago: University of Chicago Press, 1938.
2. Jampolsky, G. Combined use of hypnosis and sensory and motor stimulation in assisting children with developmental learning problems. *Journal of Learning Disabilities*, November 1970, *3*, 11.
3. Jampolsky, G., & Haight, M. A special suggestive and auto-suggestive technique used in helping certain children with reading problems. *Academic Therapy*, Winter 1974.

14. LSD PSYCHOTHERAPY

The Use of LSD-Type Drugs in Psychotherapy: Progress and Promise

O. Lee McCabe, Ph.D.
Thomas E. Hanlon, Ph.D.

Throughout time and across cultures, man has used a variety of consciousness altering techniques for social, religious, and therapeutic purposes. The use of psychoactive chemicals to effect personality change represents one of the most persistent of these practices. Although there have been numerous compounds enlisted in the service of this goal, the present report focuses on those agents classified variously as hallucinogenics, phantasticants, psychotomimetics, utopiates, psychedelics, etc. Differing from those psychotropic drugs that have a predominantly stimulating or depressing action, psychedelic drugs induce profound transformations in the experiencing of self and of the external environment, i.e., in the perception of time, space, and subject–object relationships.

The number of substances that can alter the sphere of human consciousness is large. One survey identified 174 species or varieties of higher (seed) plants, representing 116 genera and 50 families, as having such psychoactive potential.[33] Additionally, there are numerous fungi with psychotomimetic or euphoriant properties, as well as a growing pharmacopia of man-made psychedelic compounds. The most well known of the synthetic substances, lysergic acid diethylamide (LSD), is the prototype of the drugs to be discussed in this report. In addition to LSD, some of the other psychedelic drugs that have been considered to be of potential psychotherapeutic importance have been psilocybin, mescaline, and a series of short-acting psychedelic amphetamines, e.g., dipropyltryptamine (DPT) and methylenedioxyamphetamine (MDA).

Although LSD-type drugs have yet to receive an imprimatur as scientifically approved adjuvants to psychotherapy, the persistent use of these substances for a variety of apparently adaptive purposes suggests that no compendium of psychotherapeutic techniques can be regarded as complete without considering the role these agents play in facilitating the therapeutic enterprise. The present report is therefore concerned with the application of these drugs to the treatment of psychiatric disorders, beginning with the pioneer studies of the 1950s and continuing through the investigations funded by the National Institute of Mental Health over the past decade. From these investigative experiences, an appraisal is made of the drugs' clinical efficacy and safety, and conclusions are drawn regarding their possible inclusion in the psychiatric armamentarium of the future.

EARLY HISTORY OF THE CLINICAL USE
OF LSD-TYPE DRUGS

Although the effects of peyote (mescaline) attracted some early investigational interest, including studies by Ellis, [30, 31] Klüver, [51] and Mitchell[70], and later studies by Denber[27], Huxley[42], and MacLay and Guttman[63], it was not until the discovery of LSD that research into drug-induced altered states of consciousness received real impetus. First synthesized by Stoll and Hofman in 1938, its psychological effects serendipitously discovered by the latter in 1943,[40] LSD has been the focus of more than 2000 scientific reports. Most of these studies date from the 1950s, when systematic clinical experimentation was initiated.

In doses as miniscule as 50 millionths of a gram (i.e., 50 μg), LSD can produce profound alterations in perceiving, thinking, and feeling. The potency of LSD is even more impressive when one considers that in spite of profound reactivity, only 10 percent of the total dose can be found in the central nervous system at any one time. Early studies in mice demonstrated that radioactively labeled LSD disappeared from the brain and blood within one hour. Later spectrophotofluorometric measurements on samples of human plasma resulted in a calculated half-life in man of 175 minutes.[23] These findings have led to the conceptualization of LSD as a chemical catalyst that triggers a sequence of latent neuropsychological potentials taking either phenomenologically positive or negative form. Due to the occasional schizophrenic-like behavior (due in large measure to nonspecific influences) of the LSD recipient, LSD and similar compounds were seen as causing drug-induced psychoses, and, therefore, were assigned the pejorative label "psychotomimetics." The model psychosis hypothesis subsequently instigated feverish, but essentially futile, efforts to solve the enigma of naturally occurring psychosis.

The first reported therapeutic application of LSD was within a chemotherapeutic framework, i.e., administration of the drug without concomitant psychotherapeutic intervention. In his original work, Condrau used LSD as a specific antidepressant because of its putative euphorigenic properties.[24] Although he found that some depressed patients showed improvement, mood tended to return to baseline levels following LSD treatment. A similar study was carried out by Savage with essentially the same results; however, he speculated that the drug might be useful in facilitating psychotherapy.[82] Subsequent attempts to define the role of LSD in psychotherapy may be classified into two basic approaches, the "psycholytic" and the "psychedelic."

Psycholytic Psychotherapy: LSD-Type Drugs and Psychodynamics

BASIC THEORY AND PROCEDURAL VARIATIONS

Psycholytic psychotherapy may be described as a combination of a psychedelic drug and psychoanalytically oriented technique. Typically, this method involves using relatively small doses (25–100 μg) of LSD in weekly or biweekly sessions to expedite the development and employment of traditional phenomena of psychoanalysis such as abreaction, catharsis, activation of the unconscious, recall of repressed memories, induction and interpretation of symbolic images, etc. Within the psycholytic model there are numerous variations in technique. Some practitioners use the drug on an occasional basis as an adjunct to analysis. The drug is given only after a considerable period of psychotherapy when, as Buckman puts it, ". . . the patient is beyond the state of insisting on a magical and quick cure, and after he has begun to be able to tolerate a considerable degree of frustration or anxiety."[15] In this approach, the therapist is present during a major part of the session, using a short period for direct interpretation. Scheduling of successive sessions is determined individually, usually after the material evoked during previous sessions is integrated. Other psycholytic analysts consider the content elicited under LSD as the most relevant material with which to deal in psychotherapy, superordinate to even the analysis of the transference.

The writings of psycholytic investigators also reveal differences in theoretical orientation within the psychoanalytic framework, each school of thought tending to find its concepts confirmed in the drug sessions. For example, Sandison et al., of the Jungian school, frequently saw in their therapeutic experiments with LSD, "archaic, impersonal images," as well as "great archetypes of the collective unconscious."[80] Similarly, Grof, a Rankian, inevitably observed a reliving of the birth trauma in patients undergoing LSD therapy.[36] Indeed, Grof considers treatment to be incomplete until the birth experience is relived. His position is well depicted in the following description:

> After a greater number (15—60) of sessions, all (subjects) . . . tended to a . . . uniform symptomatology in LSD sessions and . . . free intervals. This included: overwhelming, free-floating anxiety, deep depression, . . . guilt feelings, explosive aggression, . . . etc. The clinical condition of the patient was usually . . . precarious. . . . When LSD therapy was continued, the symptoms directly overgrew into the birth experience—relived in a brutal biological way. Unpleasant phenomena . . . were interspersed with ecstatic episodes and finally after fully overcoming the birth trauma, the transcendental character successively dominated the picture and a far-reaching improvement and reconstruction of personality occurred.[36]

Another variation in the psycholytic approach has been in the choice of drug. Psilocybin has been used psycholytically in Germany,[55, 57] Sweden,[46] Holland,[8, 9, 104] and Belgium.[4, 5] LSD has been used in Denmark and Norway,[7] Czechoslovakia,[36] and Great Britain.[59, 65, 80] In the United States, LSD psycholysis, or modifications thereof, were used predominantly by Abramson,[1] Chandler and Hartman,[17] and Eisner and Cohen.[29]

Some psycholytic therapists have also used additional pharmacological aids such as Ritalin, Librium, Dramamine, and various amphetamines to expedite psycholytic treatment. Ling and Buckman[59] felt that Ritalin (20–40 mg), administered one-half hour after LSD, attenuated the anxiety caused by the release of repressed material and recommended its regular use. This procedure was also recommended by Chandler and Hartman[17] and Eisner and Cohen.[29] Leuner used Ritalin and amphetamines experimentally and found them to be "useful in certain ways" but did not recommend their regular application.[56]

REPRESENTATIVE STUDIES

The first report in the literature of an LSD-type drug used as an aid to psychotherapy is that of Busch and Johnson[16] in 1950 describing the results of the psycholytic treatment of eight causes of "psychoneurosis." All patients reportedly had experiences that positively influenced the course of their illness. The revivification of childhood experiences was particularly noted. Two patients reportedly improved sufficiently for treatment to be discontinued. Unfortunately, no information was given of the specific techniques used, frequency of administration, or number of treatments.

In Hamburg, in 1955, Frederking found LSD to be an aid in the psychotherapy of 25 patients considered refractory to anlaysis.[35] In the same year, Katzenelbogan and Fang used LSD for narcosynthesis in 20 psychotic patients, most of whom were considered schizophrenic.[48] From Powich Hospital in England, Sandison published the results of his first 36 cases treated with LSD.[80] A two-year follow-up of 30 of these patients reported 19 improved. The next year Davies and Davies used LSD with 16 mental defectives.[26] Although the authors felt that LSD was useful in psychotherapy, they reported the drug to have no "lasting" effect. In 1957, Feld et al. reported a 100 percent improvement rate ($N = 18$) for all patients treated except those with chronic brain damage.[34] In the same year, at a psychiatric day hospital, Martin found improvement in 45 of 50 chronic neurotics, 9 of whom relapsed after two years.[65] Sandison and Whitelaw reported on 94 patients receiving psychotherapy with LSD.[81] Forty-three had either completely recovered or were greatly improved; a total of 66 percent allegedly had received some benefit. Lewis and Sloane, summarizing their experiences with LSD at Maudsley Hospital, concluded that the drug was a definite aid in psychotherapy and made note of its helpfulness with obsessional patients.[58] Whitelaw presented a detailed case of fetishism treated successfully with LSD and psychotherapy.[106]

In succeeding years, thousands of patients were treated with LSD. The early studies of psycholytic therapy (as well as those of psychedelic therapy) indicated sufficient psychotherapeutic potential for LSD-type drugs to generate international conferences on the topic. These meetings were held in New York City in 1959,[1] in London in 1961,[25] on Long Island in 1965,[2] and in Washington, D.C. in 1966.[73] As an indication of the extent of the practice of psycholytic therapy, the participants in one of these conferences had treated a total of 1099 patients. At this particular conference, Peck reported on his series of 218 patients wherein "excellent" results were obtained in 140 (64 percent) and at least "good" results in 183 (84 percent).[76]

In 1967, Mascher published a comprehensive review of psycholytic therapy in which studies from 1953 to 1965 were summarized.[66] The survey was based on 42 papers from all over the world and involved a total population of 1603 patients. The diverse reports were compared by compiling treatment results in terms of Sandison and Whitelaw's[81] formulations of "very much improved," "slightly improved," or "not improved." Of the 1603 cases reported, 68 percent were listed as "particularly severe" or "chronic" cases; the remaining 32 percent were considered "severe." The mean size of the LSD dosages administered by the various teams was 52 μg. Three-quarters of the 28 teams reporting kept their average doses below 250 μg. The data indicated that treatment "success" was most frequently (62.5 percent of cases) associated with multiply psycholytic sessions (both individual and group). There were equivalent success rates (56 percent) in those cases($N=788$) treated either with a single psycholytic session after intensive presession therapy or with multiple psycholytic therapy conducted within individual sessions. The least effective (40 percent success) psycholytic procedure was a group-sessions-only format. The data also indicated that anxiety neurotics were most responsive (up to a 70 percent success rate) and alcoholics and drug addicts were most refractory (31 percent) to this form of treatment. Although an evaluation study such as this is limited by interinvestigator variations in treatment approaches and criterion standards, the study does convey the scope of the clinical research conducted up to that time. For a variety of social and political reasons, research on psycholytic therapy (and on LSD-type drugs, in general) has waned, currently being conducted by only a few investigators, e.g., Arendson-Hein and Bastiaans in Belgium and Leuner in Germany.

Psychedelic Psychotherapy: LSD-Type Drugs and the "Peak" Experience

BASIC THEORY AND PROCEDURAL VARIATIONS

Theory development within the psychedelic model has been sketchy. Basically, it is an empirically derived approach anchored in the assumption that LSD-type drugs, administered in a specific context and in sufficiently high dosages, can produce a profound, emotional, ego-transcendent, and presumably "corrective" experience in an individual properly prepared for the drug reaction. Psychedelic theory does not eschew the therapeutic relevance of the varied psychodynamic material which is the predominant focus of psycholytic drug sessions. However, the psychedelic model considers the transcendental experience to be the major fulcrum for permanent behavioral redirection. In nondrug contexts, this phenomenon has been referred to as a "peak,"[67] "immediate,"[101] "kairos,"[49] "cosmic,"[14] or "conversion"[43] experience. Frequently, the experience has been couched in religious terms (cf. "unio mystico," "samádhi," "moksha"), due largely to the fact that the insights derived therefrom often are perceived as noetic and ultimate, as answers to the fundamental questions of life with which the religions of the world have dealt. With the attainment of this state, the ego (the "I" or "me" who observes and experientially participates in the world of conventional reality) ceases to exist in its ordinary condition of separateness and selfhood. Instead, there is an experience of undifferentiated participation in a unified field which is perceived as the very ground of one's being and universe, beyond finite and temporal reality. The experience transcends the personal and mundane, thereby effecting a different perspective on old perceptions, attitudes, difficulties, etc. Human problems subsequently seem of low priority, or as totally illusory. The coping behaviors and reverberating emotions that were generated and maintained in the service of resolving personal difficulties are viewed as superfluous and are thereby rendered inoperative. The universe is viewed as if through a new medium. One becomes more aware of his relationship to the family of man, and all life forms are looked upon as participants in a collective journey of unfathomable but immense importance. Apparently, as a result of the unitive experience, even inanimate objects in the environment are regarded with a new affinity, for the individual may feel he has "participated with" these objects at a molecular, atomic, or otherwise common denominative level.

The question of the ultimate validity of such perceptions is best left to philosophers. The fact remains that for thousands of years, people have reported similar experiences—induced spontaneously or with various agents and maneuvers, e.g., plants, chemicals, fasting, breath control, meditation, prayer, etc.—and that in the wake of such experiences, dramatic changes in behavior have been observed to occur. In attempts to maximize the probability of positive changes resulting from the altered states of consciousness produced by LSD-type drugs, the psychedelic model of treatment evolved. Rather than being solely a function of drug effects, this model of treatment considers therapeutic behavioral change to be the reliable consequence of a spectrum of extradrug variables, including the personalities of the patient and the therapist, the quality of preparation, and the emotional and physical atmosphere and surroundings—generally termed "set and setting." The concept of "set and setting," particularly as it engenders in the patient a sense of trust in his therapist and in the procedure, is viewed as the most crucial ingredient of successful therapeutic outcome.

In the more generally accepted paradigm, a phase of conventional psychotherapy precedes the drug session that is expressly focused on the patient's strengths and resources as well as on his conflicts, defenses, and dynamics. The preparatory sessions are aimed at creating a confident receptivity to the impending drug experience. Given a positive working relationship between therapist and patient, the drug-induced peak experience hopefully consolidates whatever therapeutic gains have been achieved and provides the foundation for altered perceptions of self and others.

REPRESENTATIVE STUDIES

One of the first clinical investigations to suggest that therapeutic benefit might attend ego-loss experiences was Hoffer and Osmond's LSD work with alcoholics in 1961,[39] which also marked the emergence of psychedelic therapy as a distinct treatment modality. Most of the early work with the psychedelic procedure focused on alcoholic patients, based on the idea that the experience might prove helpful in producing a condition resembling delirium tremens that would allow the patient to "hit bottom" earlier than he might do otherwise. However, the large doses of LSD used (200 gamma or more), pushed many of the subjects beyond the psychotomimetic experience into a conversion-like experience. Outcome data suggested that it was the ego-transcending experience, rather than the hypothesized aversive activity of LSD, that was subsequently associated with rehabilitation.

Hubbard, one of the pioneers of psychedelic therapy on this continent, treated a number of chronic alcoholics with a single large dose of LSD. All of the recipients seemed to benefit to some extent, a number to a degree that they themselves considered "miraculous."[75] Although quantified results are not available on Hubbard's large series of subjects, it is reported that he found the treatment to be so outstandingly successful that there was no question regarding its efficacy.[12] Subsequent research by the Canadians and others[19, 44, 64, 74, 94, 95] consisted of open trials in which the psychedelic use of LSD with alcoholics was found to be both safe and effective.

The first published account of the effects of the high-dose procedure with nonalcoholic patients was that of MacLean and co-workers.[64] These investigators claimed that in a series of 33 patients (diagnoses were personality trait disturbance and anxiety neurosis), over 90 percent were "much improved" or "improved" after a median follow-up period of nine months. Ball and Armstrong described high-dose LSD treatment of a small series of sexual deviates. In some of the cases, they reported "remarkable, long lasting remedial effects."[10] Claims of unusual therapeutic improvement following high-dosage LSD exposures in psychoneurotic patients have also come from the Mental Research Institute in Palo Alto, Calif.,[89] and the Carrier Clinic in New Jersey.[90]

Over several years, investigation of high-dose LSD therapy was pursued at the International Foundation for Advanced Study in Menlo Park, Calif. In a series of publications, consistently impressive results were claimed with patients diagnosed as psychoneurotic anxiety reaction, psychoneurotic depresssive reaction, immature personality, and adjustment reaction.[71, 84, 87, 88, 91]

Exemplary of the results of the psychedelic approach were those of Sherwood et al. involving 25 patients.[91] Some degree of "improvement" (objective criteria not specified) was observed in 84 percent of the cases, with total resolution of the presenting problem being effected in nearly half (12) of the cases. In general, changes were characterized as follows:

Movement away from resistiveness and defensiveness toward an increasing sensitivity and openness to all experience, increasing awareness of . . . deeper needs, developing confidence in . . . [one's] own inner reactions as a trustworthy guide to behavior, and increasing ability to form new relationships. The most pronounced changes typically occur when the subject is able to move into the . . . psychedelic experience.[91]

Savage and co-workers reported on 77 cases who were given psychedelic therapy in an outpatient setting.[83] The single high-dose technique was employed, including intensive preparation and follow-up. Therapeutic effectiveness was determined by examining the results of psychological tests, clinical evaluations similar to those employed in studies of conventional psychotherapy, and a Behavior Change Interview. All measures indicated a "shift toward more 'ego-syntonic' behavior for most subjects."[83]

As with the psycholytic literature, there are only a few controlled studies on the effectiveness of the psychedelic approach, and all but one of these involved the treatment of alcoholics with LSD. The psychedelic aspect of these studies generally consisted of high-dose administration; none involved the administration of LSD within the context of individual psychotherapy that included fairly intensive session preparation and subsequent integration of insight. Although for the most part evaluations were systematic and carefully implemented, it appears that the perfunctory procedures used by such studies often worked against the occurrence of those drug-related experiences considered to have the most beneficial impact in the course of an ongoing therapeutic process. In view of this limitation, it is not surprising that the bulk of the evidence reported was negative. [13, 18, 19, 32, 41, 93, 103]

One of the most systematic controlled studies yielding negative results was that of Ludwig and Levine, who found no post-treatment or follow-up differences between three LSD-treated groups of alcoholics and one group receiving milieu therapy alone. [62] Initially involving the random assignment of a total of 176 chronic alcoholic patients to "hypnodelic" therapy (LSD plus hypnosis and psychotherapy), "psychedelic" therapy (LSD plus psychotherapy), LSD alone, and routine milieu therapy, the study noted improvement in the majority of patients in all four treatment categories. In effect, LSD patients fared well according to psychometric and behavioral criteria, but so did milieu therapy patients—Ludwig and Levine rightfully considering this result illustrative of the need for controlled evaluations in assessing LSD effects. Furthermore, no relationship was found between profoundness of LSD reaction (as measured by alteration in consciousness) and final outcome. Although they saw little promise for the use of LSD in the treatment of chronic alcoholics on the basis of their results, the authors conceded that their use of LSD with psychotherapy did not fully reflect the psychedelic model as propounded by other investigators.

Three controlled studies involving alcoholics yielded what appeared to be short-term positive effects. Comparing a group of 28 LSD-treated alcoholics with a group of 34 receiving routine care in the same hospital setting, Cheek et al. found greater improvement at three months in the LSD group on measures of sobriety, work, and family adjustment. [18] There were no significant differences between the two groups, however, at 6- and 12-month follow-up. Essentially the same results were found by Hollister et al., who reported a significant difference between 29 LSD- and 23 dextroamphetamine-treated patients at two-month follow-up on a locally devised scale of drinking behavior. [41] Again, no significant difference between experimentals and controls was discernible at six months.

The third study was that of Bowen et al., who administered high-dose LSD (500 μg) in the context of a Human Relations Training Laboratory involving the teaching and practice of interpersonal skills in group settings.[13] Although finding no significant outcome differences at 12 months among their three groups (63 high-dose LSD patients, 22 low-dose patients, and 55 controls), the authors refer to earlier observed positive changes in many high-dose LSD patients. Psychometric pre- and post-testing of 41 of the LSD cases (mean interval 21 days) and 41 controls (mean interval 38 days) revealed significant differences in 4 of 36 measures favoring the LSD group.[97] Compared to controls,

> The lysergide treated group showed greater emotional stability, ego strength and ability to face reality in a calm, mature manner ($p < .01$), experienced a reduction in tension and frustration ($p < .05$), tended to describe themselves as more confident and outgoing in social relationships ($p < .05$), and endorsed fewer atypical MMPI statements (F scale; $p < .01$).[97]

In an extensive review of LSD treatment in alcoholism published in 1971, Abuzzahab and Anderson listed 5 controlled and 13 uncontrolled studies of variations of the psychedelic approach.[3] The only controlled psychedelic study in the literature on other than alcoholic patients was that of Ludwig and Levine,[61] who assigned 70 narcotic drug addicts to five brief treatment techniques variously employing LSD, psychotherapy, and hypnosis. An early version of the Psychiatric Evaluation Profile, a self-administered questionnaire measuring therapeutic change, served as the major evaluation instrument. Results at both two weeks and two months favored "hypnodelic" therapy, a unique combination of all three forms of treatment, over each form used individually and over the utilization of LSD plus psychotherapy.

Compared to the psycholytic approach, the psychedelic use of LSD-type compounds had certain methodological advantages that allowed it to meet stringent regulatory and evaluative criteria. Since only a single dose was employed and since it was essentially a time-limited procedure, it was ideal for controlled evaluative studies. The fact that a single treatment of LSD was employed was also a safety factor that enhanced its attractiveness. However, as we have indicated above, the controlled studies that were undertaken utilized a variety of treatment techniques that invariably did not adhere to what might be regarded as the ideal psychedelic therapy paradigm. Hollister et al.,[41] Johnson,[45] and Smart et al.,[93] for example, utilized a treatment method best described as psychedelic chemotherapy, in which the major emphasis was on the administration of the drug itself. The amount of psychotherapy in the preparation and post-treatment phases was minimal. Adding hypnotic induction to the process, Ludwig and Levine also utilized a limited preparation period and abbreviated drug sessions.[62]

RECENT PROGRESS IN THE CLINICAL USE OF LSD-TYPE DRUGS

The LSD Studies Funded by the National Institute of Mental Health

In an attempt to remedy some of the shortcomings of previous investigations, the systematic exploration of psychedelic therapy has been underway at Spring Grove Hospital since 1963, and more recently at the Maryland Psychiatric Research Center in Baltimore, Md. These studies have been funded by grants from the National Institute of Mental Health, Department of Health, Education, and Welfare. The therapeutic procedures used in this research were distilled over many years from the cumulative experience of the various staff members involved. The basic treatment process consisted of three interrelated phases: (1) a series of drug-free interviews in which rapport was established and the subject was prepared for the psychedelic drug session; (2) the psychedelic drug session itself; and (3) several subsequent interviews for the integration of the drug session experiences.

The preparation usually lasted an average of 12 hours, extended over a period of three to four weeks. The drug session was undertaken only after the therapist had gained intimate knowledge of the patient's developmental history, dynamics, defenses, and difficulties, close rapport had been established, and the patient had been specifically and comprehensively prepared for the procedure. The objective of the high-dose session was the production of a peak, or transcendental, experience. The underlying process was regarded as corrective and remedial. It was designed to program and guide the evolving episodes of experience so as to achieve meaningful catharsis, inhibition of anxiety, conflict resolution, emotionally validated insight, attitude redirection, elevated self-esteem, and deepened philosophical perspective.

The experimental drug sessions themselves were carried out in a special treatment suite furnished as a comfortable living room, with sofa, easy chair, rugs, drapes, pictures, flowers, and high-fidelity music equipment. The patient's therapist and a psychiatric nurse were in constant attendance throughout the period of drug action. For most of the session, the patient reclined on the sofa and wore eyeshades and stereophonic earphones, alternately listening to carefully selected classical music and interacting with the therapist.

Initially, the program of psychedelic research involved the use of LSD exclusively. Successive patient samples in a series of LSD studies covering a five-year period were comprised of alcoholics, neurotics, terminal cancer patients, and narcotic addicts. More recent research has employed other psychedelic compounds with essentially the same type of subjects as those administered LSD. Except for one controlled study of the use of DPT with hospitalized alcoholics, these have been open clinical assessments involving smaller size samples. Summarized descriptive information and outcome results of these and the earlier LSD studies are presented in Table 14-1.

LSD THERAPY OF ALCOHOLISM

The first Spring Grove LSD project was initiated in 1963. In this pilot research, 69 hospitalized alcoholics were treated with dosages of 200–900 μg in open clinical trials replicating the psychedelic method utilized by the Canadian investigators. Pre- and post-treatment Minnesota Multiphasic Personality Inventory (MMPI)[38] results revealed more immediate changes to include marked reductions in the Depression (D) and Psychasthenia (Pt) scales, the latter a measure of rumination or preoccupation with unproductive distraught thought content. At a six-month follow-up point, 23 (exactly one-third) of the patients had maintained complete abstinence from alcohol during the intervening period.[53]

Following the pilot work, which indicated that LSD was safe and at least as effective as previous interventions, a double-blind controlled study of the effectiveness of LSD in the treatment of hospitalized alcoholics was undertaken at Spring Grove.[52] In this study, 135 patients were randomly assigned to either high-dose (450 μg) or low-dose (50 μg) LSD treatment. A comprehensive psychological test battery was administered prior to acceptance into the program and one week after the LSD session. Follow-up assessments were obtained at 6, 12, and 18 months.

Psychological tests administered one week following the drug session indicated a significant improvement in both treatment groups of the study. Ratings of adjustment made by an independent team of social workers on follow-up samples revealed that 44 percent of the high-dose group were considered "essentially rehabilitated" at six months, as opposed to 25

TABLE 14-1

Summary of Spring Grove Hospital, Md. Psychiatric Research Center Studies of Psychedelic Psychotherapy

Investigators	Treatment	Year	Sample Size	Population	Dosage Range (μg)	Frequency of Drug Sessions	Evaluation Point (mo)	Improvement* (%)
Kurland et al.[52]	Low-dose LSD	1971	40	Alcoholics	50	Once	6	25
	High-dose LSD		64		450	Once	6	44
Richards et al.[78]	High-dose LSD	1972	31	Terminal cancer patients	200–500	Once	Post-treatment	71
Savage & McCabe[85]	High-dose LSD	1973	37	Heroin addicts	200–500	Once	12	33 abstinent
	Routine care		37		Control	None	12	5 abstinent
Savage et al.[86]	Low-dose LSD	1973	31	Neurotics	50	Once	6	45
	High-dose LSD		31		350	Once	6	52
	Psychotherapy		27		Control	None	6	26
Grof et al.[37]	H/L-dose DPT	1973	47	Alcoholics	15–150	Multiple†	6	47
Richards et al.[79]	High-dose DPT	1976	30	Terminal cancer patients	75–127.5	Once	Post-treatment	‡
Rhead et al.[77]	H/L-dose DPT	1976	32	Alcoholics	15–165	Multiple†	6	44
	Psychotherapy		26		Control	None	6	50
	Routine care		29		Control	None	6	38

*For alcoholic populations, percentages given are for those considered "essentially rehabilitated."
†Including one high-dose session, i.e., the administration of at least 60 mg of DPT.
‡Global improvement data unavailable.

percent of the low-dose group. Rehabilitation rates in terms of drinking behavior for this time period were found to be 53 percent versus 33 percent, respectively, a difference significant at the .05 level. No differential treatment effects were found for the remaining follow-up periods.

The fact that the low-dose group did as well as it did was considered reflective of both the intensive preparation and the actual administration of LSD. Many of the 50-μg sessions involved "considerable abreaction and catharsis of psychodynamically charged material."[52] It was also noted that at the 18-month assessment, psychedelic psychotherapy had been successful in helping over half of the alcoholics treated in the program (including both high- and low-dose patients), as opposed to a 12 percent improvement rate for a comparable group of alcoholics previously treated with conventional methods in the same facility.

LSD THERAPY OF PSYCHONEUROSIS AND BORDERLINE CONDITIONS

The overall rate of recovery for the sample of alcoholics in the ongoing controlled study was considered sufficiently encouraging to prompt exploration of the value of psychedelic psychotherapy in the treatment of the hospitalized neurotic patient.[68, 69, 86] In this double-blind controlled study, 96 patients, most of whom were diagnosed psychoneurotic disorder, depressive reaction, were randomly assigned to high-dose LSD ($N-31$), low-dose LSD ($N=32$), and conventional treatment ($N=33$). A battery of tests, including measures of intelligence and organicity, personality and behavioral inventories, and projective techniques, were administered prior to treatment and approximately seven weeks later, which was generally one week after the LSD session. As before, follow-up assessments of adjustment were conducted at 6, 12, and 18 months.

Analysis of short-term effects revealed that all three patient subgroups showed significant improvement immediately after treatment on most of the criterion measures employed.[69] Differential treatment effects in terms of means occurred in 19 of 50 instances, all of which indicated the superiority of high-dose LSD over conventional treatment. Although usually of lower magnitude, low-dose LSD was found to be superior to conventional treatment in 11 instances. The comparative improvement noted was not only indicative of a greater reduction in overall symptomatology, but also of a greater increase in "self-actualized" functioning.

At the six-month follow-up point, all groups showed significant improvement across a number of test variables, representing a general reduction of pathology rather than a specific pattern of symptom change. Contrary to post-treatment findings, statistical analyses at this point revealed no significant differential effects. The meaningfulness of results on a few measures at 12 months favoring high-dose LSD over conventional treatment was considered attenuated by the possible unrepresentativeness of the follow-up sample, and results at 18 months were uniformly nondifferentiating.

LSD THERAPY OF PHYSICAL AND PSYCHOLOGICAL DISTRESS SECONDARY TO TERMINAL ILLNESS (CANCER)

In view of preliminary findings by Cohen[21] and Kast[47] on the promising use of LSD in cases of terminal cancer and successful experiences with a few pilot LSD-treated cases, LSD cancer research was initiated at the Spring Grove Research Department and continued at the Maryland Psychiatric Research Center, incorporating essentially the same investigative staff. The original work of what has now become an extended research program involved the treatment of 31 terminally ill cancer patients with LSD.[78] Consistent with the psychedelic approach, psychotherapeutic procedures included a high-dose, therapeutically guided LSD session within the context of short-term psychotherapy, and entailed intensive preparation and follow-up care. Patients were referred for treatment by the Oncology Service of the Sinai Hospital, Baltimore, Md. Selection criteria included the presence of anxiety, depression, and uncontrollable pain. In each case, pre- and post- (three days) LSD session ratings of physical–emotional status were made by physicians, nurses, family, LSD therapist, and an independent rater. Observations were also made of pre- and postsession narcotic drug use for the alleviation of pain.

Results of the study indicated that on a global measure of overall improvement incorporating the observations of multiple raters 9 patients (29 percent) showed "dramatic" improvement following psychedelic therapy, 13 patients (42 percent) were moderately improved, and 9 patients (29 percent) were essentially unchanged. For the entire sample of 31 patients, the mean daily dose of narcotic medication decreased, though not significantly.

LSD THERAPY OF NARCOTIC ADDICTION AND SOCIOPATHY

The results of the controlled study with hospitalized alcoholics led to an investigation of the efficacy of brief residential psychedelic therapy for chronic narcotic addicts.[85] In addition to daily urine monitoring for narcotics, the treatment model incorporated a high-dose (200–500 μg) LSD administration at the completion of several weeks of preparatory psychotherapy. The effects of this treatment were compared with those of a concurrent procedure involving daily urine surveillance and weekly group therapy in an outpatient abstinence program.

In this partially controlled study, 73 volunteer addict inmates from Maryland correctional institutions were randomly assigned to treatment (LSD) and control (outpatient clinic) conditions. Members of the treatment group were admitted to the outpatient clinic immediately following psychedelic therapy. In effect, all of the subjects were treated identically except for the initial six-week period of residential treatment incorporating individual psychotherapy that included a high-dose LSD session. In addition, both groups were equivalent on all pretreatment demographic and psychometric variables, including severity of psychopathology and prognosis. Major outcome criteria were based on evaluative assessments of the treatment and control groups at selected points during the 12 months following discharge from the correctional institutions to the community-based program.

Comparative abstinence data throughout the year were found to be significantly in favor of the group treated with psychedelic therapy. Results indicated that 9 (25 percent) of 36 subjects in the treatment (experimental) group maintained total abstinence from narcotic drugs for at least one year versus 2 (5 percent) of 37 in the control group. After relapsing briefly, three additional LSD patients subsequently remained abstinent for the remainder of the year, bringing the number of those LSD-treated patients essentially abstinent during the period of one year to 12 (33 percent). Although there was a trend in favor of the treatment group, there were no statistically significant differences between the groups on global community adjustment measures.

THE SAFETY OF LSD THERAPY

The safety record established by the Baltimore LSD research team was exemplary. Of nearly 400 treated cases, only 2 patients experienced an adverse behavioral reaction: one in the alcoholic study and one in the psychoneurotic study. Both recovered uneventfully after conventional psychotherapy and neuroleptic medication. Although 15–20 percent of the patients treated in the local LSD program over the years fell within a "borderline psychotic" category, which at times posed special problems for the therapist, the majority nevertheless underwent the procedure successfully.

Although the specter of chromosomal damage due to LSD was raised several years ago,[22] subsequent investigations were either equivocal or contradictory.[11, 28, 60] A double-blind collaborative investigation involving Spring Grove and the cytogenetics laboratory at the National Institutes of Health, yielded negative results, no difference being found in the rate of chromosomal aberrations before and after administration of LSD to 37 individuals participating in the alcoholic and neurotic studies. A detailed report of this research has been published elsewhere.[100]

The relative safety with which LSD can be administered in a controlled, supervised medical setting was also illustrated in the results of a survey reported by Cohen.[20] In this report, Cohen presented the findings of a side effects and complications questionnaire completed by 44 investigators who had administered LSD to 5000 individuals on 25,000 occasions. The relative incidence of suicide was found to be .4 per 1000 for LSD patients versus a zero incidence for controls. Regarding psychotic reactions lasting more than 48 hours, respective incidences were 1.8 per 1000 LSD patients and .8 per 1000 controls. Considering the iatrogenic record of most therapeutic interventions in psychiatry, including placebos, these reported incidences were surprisingly low.

In the psychedelic drug sessions conducted by the Baltimore group, psychosomatic reactions such as headaches, tremors, nausea, palpitations, breathing difficulties, etc., were frequently encountered. They usually occurred early in the sessions and appeared to be related to emerging traumatic unconscious material and the consequent mobilization of defenses and resistance. In sessions involving cancer patients, there were, of course, additional physical problems relating to the patient's basic disease. Of 50 such patients, all but one tolerated the psychedelic drug sessions well in spite of physical debilitation caused by malignancy. One patient who was acutely terminal at the time of LSD administration lapsed into coma as the drug effects abated and died later that evening.

The DPT and MDA Studies

As the LSD research program progressed at the Maryland Psychiatric Research Center, some of the disadvantages of LSD as an adjunct to psychotherapy became increasingly apparent. The principal drawback was its long duration of action (8–12 hours), which made its use an expensive and often arduous undertaking. In addition, because LSD was active orally, the abuse potential of the drug was correspondingly high. Sensationalistic reports of the abuse that had occurred among the general public were so widely publicized that potential patients often had preconceived notions regarding the drug that seriously hampered subject recruitment and treatment acceptance.

For the above reasons, local attention centered in 1970 on a new psychedelic compound, DPT, first investigated by Vourlekis et al.[105] The potential advantages of DPT were many. Although it produced the same range of altered states of consciousness found with LSD, this new agent had a substantially briefer duration of action (1½–2 hours in low dosage and 4–6 hours in high dosage), and, as opposed to the protracted undulating action of LSD, its effects terminated abruptly and completely. Another promising characteristic of DPT was that it was inactive orally, a fact that considerably diminished its abuse potential.

DPT THERAPY OF ALCOHOLISM: A PILOT STUDY

Szara's preliminary observations of the subjective effects of DPT[99] were encouraging enough to prompt pilot work with hospitalized alcoholics.[37] In this research, 51 patients were treated with a modified psychedelic therapy approach in which DPT was administered on multiple occasions in dosages ranging from 15 to 150 mg, with each case receiving at least one high dose (60 mg and above). Short-term DPT effects were determined by examining pre- and post-treatment scores on a comprehensive psychological test battery. Social history and global adjustment assessments were obtained on 47 (92 percent) of the patients at six-month follow-up.

As with LSD, results indicated "dramatic" short-term effects, with positive changes observed in a variety of measures of psychopathology and self-actualization. At six months, pretreatment to follow-up differences on the scales of interpersonal adjustment, abstinence, and global adjustment reached a high level of statistical significance. The number of patients considered "essentially rehabilitated" was 22 (47 percent) with regard to global adjustment and 25 (53 percent) with regard to abstinence. Eighteen patients (38 percent) had maintained complete abstinence for the entire follow-up period.

Undertaken at approximately the same time, a controlled study of the process effects of low-dose (15–30 mg) DPT versus placebo indicated that 1½–2-hour therapy sessions were differentially facilitated by the active drug.[98] On the basis of blind observations, DPT sessions were rated significantly higher than placebo sessions on recall of memories and experiences, emotional expressiveness, depth of self-exploration, psychodynamic resolution, and productivity.

DPT THERAPY OF PHYSICAL AND
PSYCHOLOGICAL DISTRESS SECONDARY TO
TERMINAL ILLNESS (CANCER)

The next application of DPT in the research program was the treatment of the terminally ill cancer patient.[79] Using essentially the same treatment approach as that with LSD, 30 patients were administered a single high dose (75–127.5 mg) of DPT in the context of psychedelic psychotherapy. Obtained pre- and post-treatment, criterion measures included the Mini-Mult[50] (a shortened version of the MMPI),[38] the Personality Orientation Inventory (POI); an index of self-actualization, or psychological maturity),[92] and independent ratings of "emotional conditions."

Results of the study indicated significant improvement in six of eight Mini-Mult clinical scales and in two primary scales and three of ten subscales of the POI. Significant improvement was also found in clinical ratings of depression and anxiety. Subsequent analysis of the data on the same sample plus four additional patients revealed a positive relationship between the experiencing of a peak reaction with DPT and favorable outcome.

DPT THERAPY OF ALCOHOLISM:
A CONTROLLED STUDY

The most recent in the series of DPT studies was a controlled investigation of the comparative effectiveness of DPT-assisted psychedelic therapy, conventional psychotherapy, and routine hospital care in the treatment of chronic alcoholics.[77] Although pilot research conducted elsewhere by Faillace et al.[32] involving 12 chronic alcoholics had not been encouraging, local experiences were promising enough to prompt controlled investigation. The design of the study called for the administration of DPT in what was regarded as a modified psychedelic psychotherapy model, i.e., up to 35 hours of individual psychotherapy involving a maximum of six drug administrations, one of which consisted of a high dose (75–165 mg). Conventional treatment involved up to 35 hours of individual psychotherapy, during which guided affective imagery was occasionally employed. Criteria of effectiveness were derived from a comprehensive psychological test battery, yielding 41 measures of either positive or negative functioning, which was administered pre- and post-treatment. A social history questionnaire was completed initially and at 6- and 12-month follow-up points.

During the course of the study, 175 patients were assigned to the three treatment groups, and of these 103 completed treatment. Of the criterion measures examined pre- and post-treatment, analysis of covariance results for only two measures favored DPT treatment over routine hospital care (the Self Regard scale of the POI and the Hypochondriasis (Hs) scale of the MMPI). There were no significant differences between DPT and conventional treatment for this time period. Significant follow-up results obtained at the 12-month point favoring conventional treatment over DPT-assisted psychotherapy and routine hospital care were considered equivocal because of differential compositions of the follow-up samples. It was, nevertheless, demonstrably clear that there were no detectable advantages in the use of DPT in terms of the follow-up data that were available.

MDA ADMINISTRATION TO PROFESSIONALS

Another agent that was considered as a possible alternative to LSD in drug-assisted psychotherapy was an analogue of mescaline, MDA. Evaluating MDA as a possible adjunct to psychotherapy, Naranjo and his associates[72] had administered the drug to volunteers in dosages ranging from 40 to 150 mg. Effects of the drug reached peak intensity within two hours and continued for approximately eight hours. Psychotropic effects reported by the subjects were intensification of feeling, a facilitation of insight, and heightened empathy.

The initial investigative probe at the Maryland Psychiatric Research Center consisted of the administration of 75 mg of MDA to professionals who had had previous experience with LSD.[102] Results indicated minimal loss in ability to attend, concentrate, and perform complex visual–motor tasks. Subjects had little difficulty communicating or shifting from exploring inner content to responding to external environment. Psychotropic effects were essentially the same as those reported by Naranjo et al., except that drug effects seemed to last longer, vis., 10–12 hours. The emotional states experienced were relaxation, calmness, and serenity. Although not overwhelming, less pleasing emotional states were at times reported by a few of the subjects, indicating a variability in response that was regarded as meriting future investigative attention. Generally, a state of enhanced well-being was reported. The state of consciousness facilitated by MDA appeared to make the acquisition of new insights an easier process. In addition, at the dosage level employed, MDA seemed to invite inner exploration.

MDA THERAPY OF OUTPATIENT
PSYCHONEUROTICS

Positive experiences with the preliminary use of MDA led to the study
of the use of this agent in the context of drug-assisted psychotherapy.
Accordingly, an open clinical investigation was conducted of the response
of ten neurotic outpatients (five male and five female) to the adjunctive
use of MDA in an individual psychotherapy regimen lasting two to six
months, depending on need, and including a maximum contact of 75
hours.[107] Two to four MDA sessions per patient were conducted,
averaging eight hours in duration, with escalated doses ranging from 75 to
200 mg. Standardized psychiatric assessment devices were administered
pre- and post-treatment and at six-month follow-up.

The clinical impressions obtained from the study were that MDA
appeared to facilitate the improvement of patients involved in the
psychotherapeutic program. Significant pre- versus post-treatment and
pretreatment versus six-month reductions were noted in measures of
depression, anxiety, and obsessive-compulsive traits. Notable positive
changes were also made in self-actualization and in a sense of well-being.
Mean global improvement at follow-up was found to be significant at the
.01 level. Although no patient was judged to be worse, some responded
better than others. MDA was well tolerated; no serious side effects or
complications occurred.

Findings from the study indicated that patients could be gently
introduced to altered states of consciousness by progressively increasing
dosages of MDA, the approach being particularly helpful in allaying fears
of loss of control. Use of the drug was found especially helpful in
expediting the recovery of inner material usually excluded from awareness.
On the basis of both process and outcome measures, the conclusion was
drawn that MDA was uniquely suited to the facilitation of therapeutic
insight without producing disruptive effects.

THE SAFETY OF DPT AND MDA THERAPIES

As with LSD administered in medically supervised sessions, the
safety record of DPT was impressive. In both pilot and controlled studies,
DPT has been locally administered to approximately 200 individuals on
numerous occasions, including at least one high-dose administration, and
serious sequelae at post-treatment evaluation or follow-up have yet to be
encountered. The occasional occurrence of transient subjective discomfort
during DPT sessions, related to the rapid onset of the drug, has been the
only untoward reaction of note.

Regarding the safety of MDA, no contraindicating toxic reactions were reported when over 500 patients were administered daily dosages of MDA ranging from 10 to 300 mg for the treatment of depression and/or anorexia in numerous clinical trials conducted between 1949 and 1957.[96] In a series of self-experiments, Alles[6] noted an increase in blood pressure and pupillary dilation. Results of the Maryland Psychiatric Research Center staff study indicated an initial drop in systolic blood pressure followed by a significant rise over the pretreatment mean level accompanied by a slight but nonsignificant increase in pulse rate. As indicated above, the subsequent clinical trial involving 10 subjects and 35 MDA administrations ranging from 75 to 200 mg was conducted without incident.

PRESENT STATUS AND FUTURE DIRECTIONS OF LSD-TYPE DRUGS IN PSYCHOTHERAPY

The State of the Art

Administered in the context of psychotherapy, LSD-type drugs serve as catalysts to self-exploration and therapeutic interaction. They appear to be of particular benefit in the process of treating individuals resistant to more conventional psychotherapeutic approaches such as chronic neurotics, borderline psychotics, and character disorders, including alcoholics and narcotic addicts.

Although frequently accompanied by reactions that are unremarkable to the casual observer, experiences produced by LSD-type drugs are overwhelming to the recipient, often affecting the psyche in such compelling ways that subsequent perceptions and functioning are irrevocably altered. The therapeutic impact of the experience, however, tends to vary from individual to individual. Less variable is the influence of adequate preparation and sensitive session management, which appear to spell the difference between a tumult of kaleidoscopic sensations and a pregnantly meaningful, ameliorative experience.

Although such immediate effects as symptom alleviation and constructive changes in motivation and self-perception are easily recognized and validated, in most individuals long-term effects are more difficult to discern. Part of the problem lies in the unavailability of significant portions of treatment populations for follow-up study. Another weakness in final assessment of efficacy is the inadequacy of criterion measures in documenting changes that are often existential in nature and, as such, not always reflected in situational adjustment or psychiatric status. Barring an exceptionally curative procedure, however, it is generally problematic to measure behavioral change in groups of individuals over extended periods and to attempt to relate results to a specific intervention. For a myriad of reasons, changes in behavioral patterns and life circumstances occur that tend to obfuscate the effects of any time-limited sequence of events, however dramatic or meaningful.

Extensive, systematic investigation at Spring Grove Hospital and the Maryland Psychiatric Research Center of the potential utility of psychedelic drugs in psychotherapy has demonstrated that these compounds have decided usefulness in expediting, facilitating, and enriching the process of psychotherapy in individuals with serious life adjustment problems. The limitations of the high-dose approach to psychedelic psychotherapy that relies on the reintegration powers of a single peak experience have become increasingly apparent. Findings to date indicate that such an experience, albeit conversion-like on occasion, is not the sine qua non of personality reintegration, nor does it ensure freedom from symptoms or permanence of behavioral change. Accordingly, the direction in which locally conceived psychedelic drug-assisted psychotherapy is moving is toward an integration of the psycholytic and psychedelic approaches, more recently termed, "extended psychedelic therapy." Positive drug experiences, which usually are undervalued in psycholysis (and psychoanalysis), are being elicited in this new approach with multiple high-dose (and, at times, low-dose) drug sessions, encompassing areas of traditional psychodynamics as well as perinatal and peak experiences and substantially contributing to the unfolding of meaningful phenomena in the therapeutic process. The controversial assumption of the psychedelic paradigm that enduring personality change can occur despite the bypassing of signficant psychodynamic conflict becomes a moot point with this approach. Recognizing the therapeutic potential of the peak experience (while at the same time relinquishing the near magical goal of the one-session model), this new therapeutic hybrid at once incorporates the strengths and eliminates the weaknesses of its respective components.

Psychotherapy utilizing psychedelic drug administration does not appear to have substantial public health import, mainly because it is a highly specialized technique requiring intensive training and implementation that precludes its use on a mass basis. Although it appears that LSD-type drugs increase an individual's receptivity to skillful therapeutic intervention, they render one especially vulnerable to the hazards of poor therapy. If psychedelic drugs are to be meaningful adjuncts to psychotherapy, they will be so only insofar as therapists possess the necessary skills to use them.

Recommended Priorities for Future Research

The optimal use of LSD-type drugs in a clinical setting requires that future research address the following critical issues.

VARIABILITY OF RESPONSE

It is obvious that psychedelic therapy produces unique effects within each individual. Equally obvious is the considerable investigative effort that must be directed toward ascertaining the correlates of variations in response. From studies conducted so far, it appears that the benefits derived from the use of psychedelic agents depend to a large extent on the degree of trust in the therapeutic relationship and on the personality characteristics, receptivity, and current conflicts of the patient. The extent and permanence of observable behavior change appear at least partially dependent upon the reinforcement of new attitudes that is provided by both ongoing therapy and social interaction.

PREDICTION OF RESPONSE

Another avenue of research worth pursuing relates to the prediction of therapeutic outcome. Since psychedelic treatment represents a considerable investment of both time and resources, it is especially important to attempt to increase the probability of a favorable response through more selective screening procedures. With an accumulation of approximately 600 psychedelically treated cases (400 involving LSD and 200 DPT), investigators and therapists at the Maryland Psychiatric Research Center are presently in a position to isolate predispositional characteristics within diagnostic categories and apply these to the selection of future cases. Hopefully, this discrimination will result in an increase in future recovery rates.

SPECIFIC VERSUS NONSPECIFIC DRUG EFFECTS

Evaluating the effectiveness of psychedelic psychotherapy requires that the specific contribution of the psychedelic drugs per se be isolated and quantified. One of the principal problems faced by investigators in this endeavor is the difficulty in teasing out the effects of the agents themselves from among the myriad of therapeutic influences operative in the psychedelic procedure. Two such influences are the intensity and fairly prolonged duration of the therapist–patient interaction—presumably remedial—involved in the approach. Another is the sympathetic attention of study evaluation teams, which are frequently made up of social workers and other health care professionals disposed to be of service to those in need. "Flight into health" also works against the differentially positive appraisal of any long-term therapeutic venture since the crises and intensities of reaction experienced by both drug- and placebo-treated cases tend to diminish with the passage of time. The unavailability of a suitable placebo that is neither transparent (if inactive) nor uniquely ameliorative (if active) is still another obstacle in the implementation of objective evaluation procedures.

EGO TRANSCENDENCE VERSUS OTHER DRUG EFFECTS

Future research efforts relating to psychedelic psychotherapy should involve assessment of the specific prognostic value of ego transcendence in relation to other therapeutically relevant variables. Although retrospective assessments of psychedelic reactivity appeared positively related to outcome in almost all of the studies in the presently reported program, there was by no means a one-to-one relationship between predictor and criterion. The post hoc nature of the observations permitted only tentative interpretations of the meaningfulness of the relationships that were found.

COMPARATIVE EFFICACY OF DRUGS

Future research should also be directed at determining the comparative effectiveness of the various psychedelic drugs that are presently available. MDA, for example, appears to have the advantage of facilitating psychotherapy at both low- and high-dose levels, allowing a more smoothly integrated psycholytic–psychedelic approach than has heretofore been possible. Psilocybin appears to be one of the more promising therapeutic agents among the psychedelics.[54] Both it and MDA need to be examined objectively, employing more familiar agents as points of reference. Following the lead of the psychopharmacology of antipsychotics, controlled comparative studies involving random assignment to one of several concurrently administered psychedelic agents should be undertaken in any comprehensive evaluation program.

PERMANENCE OF CHANGE

Provision for extended follow-up in LSD-type drug research is imperative. A healthy skepticism is revealed in the work of Bowen et al,[13] who observed "very real and dramatic" personality changes over the short term with the single-dose approach, but questioned whether these changes could be maintained without additional help in their integration and application to the problems of daily living. In effect, the likelihood of any single experience producing a radical, enduring modification in the personality functioning of most individuals with serious life adjustment problems is understandably remote. The evolution of the extended psychedelic therapy model, the utility of which requires further evaluation with respect to long-term follow-up, may be viewed as the experiential recognition of the limitations of the earlier psychedelic paradigm.

Obstacles to Future Research

In the United States, limitations in systematically assessing the role of LSD-type drugs in psychotherapy arise principally from shortages of research funds and specifically trained personnel at most local levels due to the lack of State and Federal support of programs and the general disinterest displayed by the pharmaceutical industry. In spite of recognition of the potential of LSD-type drugs by many individuals involved in clinical treatment and research in psychiatry, there is an obvious reluctance on the part of established investigators to become immersed in LSD-type drug research that is largely a reaction to societal misgivings and widespread public abuse of such drugs. For this and other similar reasons, including early ill-advised investigational programs having little or no mental health import, the more conservative behavioral scientists have tended to avoid what is generally regarded as a sensitive area of research. Mention has already been made of the limitations of the psycholytic and psychedelic procedures in terms of cost-effectiveness. Unfortunately, the prospect of narrow application of a procedure precludes both extensive systematic evaluation and broad-based support.

Many investigators concerned with assessing the impact of psychedelic drugs have been caught up in the phenomenological aspects of the overall drug experience and others have been primarily concerned with clinical effectiveness. The psychedelic procedure still remains a treatment in search of a theory. Although it is presently a procedure of demonstrated, if limited, effectiveness and applicability, its underlying principles and mechanisms of action have yet to be elucidated in a way that will assure the more uniform attainment of maximum clinical benefit.

REFERENCES

1. Abramson, H. A. (Ed.). *The use of LSD in psychotherapy.* New York: Josiah Macy, Jr., 1960.
2. Abramson, H. A. (Ed.). *The use of LSD in psychotherapy and alcoholism.* New York: Bobbs-Merrill, 1967.
3. Abuzzahab, F. S., & Anderson, B. J. A review of LSD treatment in alcoholism. *International Pharmacopsychiatry,* 1971, *6,* 223–235.
4. Aguilar, M. T. La psilocybine: Perspectives d'utilisation en psychiatric clinique. *Acta Neuralogica et Psychiatrica Belgica,* 1963, *63,* 114.
5. Alhadeff, B. W. Aspects cliniques de l'emploi du delysid et de l'indocybine en psychiatrie. *Journal Semaine de Pharmacie,* 1963, *245,* 296.
6. Alles, G. A. *Neuropharmacology Transactions 4th Conference.* New York: Josiah Macey, Jr., 1957.
7. Alnaes, R., & Skang, O. E. Klinishe og psykopatologishe fenomener under psykoterapi ved hjelp an LSD kanelert med bickjemishe funn. *Tidskrift far Den Norske Laegeforening,* 1963, *23,* 1721.
8. Arendsen-Hein, G. W. LSD in the treatment of criminal psychopaths. In R. Crocket, R. Sandison, & A. Walk (Eds.), *Hallucinogenic drugs and their psychotherapeutic use.* Springfield, Ill.: Charles C Thomas, 1963, p. 101.
9. Arendsen-Hein, G. W. Treatment of the neurotic patient, resistant to the usual techniques of psychotherapy with special references to LSD. *Topic Problems of Psychotherapy,* 1963, *4,* 50–57.
10. Ball, J. R., & Armstrong, J. J. The use of LSD in the treatment of the sexual perversions. *Canadian Psychiatric Association Journal,* 1961, *6,* 231.
11. Bender, L. & Sanker, D. V. S. Chromosomal damage not found in leukocytes of children treated with LSD-25. *Science,* 1968, *160,* 1343–1344.
12. Blewett, D. B., & Chwelos, N. *Handbook for the therapeutic use of lysergic acid diethylamide-25, individual and group procedures.* Unpublished manuscript, 1958.
13. Bowen, W. T., Soskin, R. A., & Chotlos, J. W. Lysergic acid diethylamide as a variable in the hospital treatment of alcoholism. *Journal of Nervous and Mental Diseases,* 1970, *150,* 111–118.
14. Bucke, R. M. *Cosmic consciousness: A study of the evolution of the human mind.* New York: University Books, 1961. (Original copyright, 1901 by Innes and Sons.)
15. Buckman, J. Theoretical aspects of LSD therapy. In H. A. Abramson (Ed.), *The use of LSD in psychotherapy and alcoholism.* New York: Bobbs-Merrill, 1967, pp. 87–97.
16. Busch, A. K., & Johnson, W. C. LSD as an aid in psychotherapy. *Diseases of the Nervous System,* 1950, *11,* 241.
17. Chandler, A. L., & Hartman, M. A. LSD-25 as a facilitating agent in psychotherapy. *Archives of General Psychiatry,* 1960, *2,* 286.
18. Cheek, F. E., Osmond, H., Sarett, M., & Albahary, R. S. Observations regarding the

use of LSD-25 in the treatment of alcoholism. *Journal of Psychopharmacology*, 1966, *1*, 56–74.

19. Chwelos, N., Blewett, D. B., Smith, D., & Hoffer, A. The use of LSD-25 in the treatment of chronic alcoholism. *Quarterly Journal of Studies on Alcohol*, 1959, *20*, 577–590.

20. Cohen, S. Lysergic acid diethylamide: Side effects and complications. *Journal of Nervous and Mental Diseases*, 1960, *130*, 30–40.

21. Cohen, S. LSD and the anguish of dying. *Harper's Magazine*, 1965, *231*, 69–88.

22. Cohen, S. Psychotherapy with LSD: Pro and con. In H. A. Abramson (Ed.), *The use of LSD in psychotherapy and alcoholism*. New York: Bobbs-Merrill, 1967.

23. Cohen, S. The hallucinogens. In W. G. Clark & J. del Guidice (Eds.), *Principles of psychopharmacology*. New York: Academic Press, 1970.

24. Condrau, G. Klinische Erfahrungen an Geisteskranken Mit Lysergsaure diathylamid. *Acta Psychiatria et Neurologia*, 1949, *24*, 9–32.

25. Crocket, R., Sandison, R. A., & Walk, A. (Eds.). *Hallucinogenic drugs and their psychotherapeutic use*. Springfield, Ill.: Charles C Thomas, 1963.

26. Davies, M. E. B., & Davies, T. S. Lysergic acid in mental deficiency *Lancet*, 1955, *269*, 1090.

27. Denber, H. C. B. Studies on mescaline, VII: The role of anxiety in the mescaline-induced state and its influence on the therapeutic results. *Journal of Nervous and Mental Diseases*, 1956, *124*, 74–77.

28. Egozcue, J., Irvin, S., & Maruffo, C. A. Chromosomal damage in LSD users. *Journal of the American Medical Association*, 1968, *204*, 214–218.

29. Eisner, B. G., & Cohen, S. Psychotherapy with lysergic acid diethylamide. *Journal of Nervous and Mental Diseases*, 1958, *127*, 528.

30. Ellis, H. Mescal, a new artificial paradise. *Annual Report of the Smithsonian Institution*, 1898, 437–548.

31. Ellis, H. Mescal, a study of a divine plant. *Popular Science Monthly*, 1902, *41*, 52–71.

32. Faillace, L. A., Vourlekis, A., & Szara, S. Hallucinogenic drugs in the treatment of alcoholism: A two-year follow-up. *Comprehensive Psychiatry*, 1970, *11*, 51–56.

33. Farnsworth, N. R. Psychotomimetic and related higher plants. *Journal of Psychedelic Drugs*, 1972, *5*, 67–74.

34. Feld, M., Goodman, J. R., & Guido, J. A. Clinical and laboratory observations on LSD-25. *Journal of Nervous and Mental Diseases*, 1958, *126*, 176–183.

35. Frederking, W. Intoxicant drugs (mescaline and lysergic acid diethylamide) in psychotherapy. *Journal of Nervous and Mental Diseases*, 1955, *121*, 263–2)6.

36. Grof, S. *Tentative theoretical framework for understanding dynamics of LSD psychotherapy*. Paper presented at the Psychotherapeutic Congress, Chicago, Ill., June 1966.

37. Grof, S., Soskin, R. A., Richards, W. A., & Kurland, A. A. DPT as an adjunct to psychotherapy of alcoholics. *International Pharmacopsychiatry*, 1973, *8*, 104–115.

38. Hathaway, S. R., & McKinley, J. C. *Minnesota Multiphasic Personality Inventory manual* (Rev. ed.). New York: Psychological Corporation, 1951.

39. Hoffer, A., & Osmond, H. A card sorting test helpful in making psychiatric diagnosis. *Journal of Neuropsychiatry*, 1961, *2*, 306–330.

40. Hofmann, A. Discovery of d-lysergic acid diethylamide—LSD. *Sandoz Excerpta*, 1955, *1*, 1.

41. Hollister, L. E., Shelton, J., & Krieger, G. A controlled comparison of lysergic acid diethylamide (LSD) and dextroamphetamine in alcoholics. *American Journal of Psychiatry*, 1969, *125*, 1352–1357.
42. Huxley, A. *The doors of perception*. New York: Harper Brothers, 1954.
43. James, W. *The varieties of religious experience*. Toronto: Random House, 1902.
44. Jensen, S. E. Treatment program for alcoholics in a mental hospital. *Quarterly Journal of Studies on Alcohol*, 1962, *23*, 315–320.
45. Johnson, F. G. LSD in the treatment of alcoholism. *American Journal of Psychiatry*, 1969, *126*, 481–487.
46. Kaij, L. LSD—behandlung an Neuroses. *Sartryck un Suenska Lakartidningen*, 1963, *60*, 60.
47. Kast, E. LSD and the dying patient. *Chicago Medical School Quarterly*, 1966, *26*, 80–87.
48. Katzenelbogen, S., & Fang, A. I. D. Narcosynthesis effects of sodium amytol, methedrine and LSD-25. *Diseases of the Nervous System*, 1953, *14*, 85.
49. Kelman, H. "Kairos" and the therapeutic process. *Journal of Existentialism*, 1960, *1*, 233–269.
50, Kincannon, J. C. Prediction of the standard MMPI scale scores from 71 items. *Journal of Consulting and Clinical Psychology*, 1968, *32*, 319–325.
51. Klüver, H. *Mescal: The "divine" plant and its psychological effects*. London: Paul, Trench, Trubner, 1928.
52. Kurland, A. A., Savage, C., Pahnke, W. N., Grof, S., & Olsson, J. E. LSD in the treatment of alcoholics. *Pharmakopsychiatrie NeuroPsychopharmakologie*, 1971, *4*, 83–94.
53. Kurland, A. A., Unger, S., Shaffer, J. W., & Savage, C. Psychedelic therapy utilizing LSD in the treatment of the alcoholic patient: A preliminary report. *American Journal of Psychiatry*, 1967, *123*, 1202–1209.
54. Leary, T., Metzner, R., Presnell, M., Weil, G., Schwitzgebel, R., & Kinne, S. A new behavior change program using psilocybin. *Psychotherapy: Theory, Research and Practice*, 1965, *2*, 2.
55. Leuner, H. *Die experimentelle Psychose*. Berlin: Springer-Verlag, 1962.
56. Leuner, H. Present state of psycholytic therapy and its possibilities. In Abramson, H. A. (Ed.), *The use of LSD in psychotherapy and alcoholism*. New York: Bobbs-Merrill, 1967, p. 108.
57. Leuner, H., & Halfeld, H. Psychotherapy under the influence of hallucinogens. *The Physician's Panorama*, 1964, *2*, 13–16.
58. Lewis, D. J., & Sloane, R. B. Therapy with lysergic acid diethylamide. *Journal of Clinical and Experimental Psychopathy*, 1958, *19*, 19–31.
59. Ling, T. M., & Buckman, J. *Lysergic acid (LSD-25) and Ritalin in the treatment of neurosis*. London: Lombarde Press, 1963.
60. Loughman, W. D., Sargent, T. W., & Israelstam, D. M. Leukocytes of humans exposed to lysergic acid diethylamide: Lack of chromosomal damage. *Science*, 1967, *158*, 508–510.
61. Ludwig, A. M., & Levine, J. A controlled comparison of five brief treatment techniques employing LSD, hypnosis and psychotherapy. *American Journal of Psychotherapy*, 1965, *19*, 417–435.
62. Ludwig, A. M., & Levine, J. *LSD and alcoholism*. Springfield, Ill.: Charles C Thomas, 1970.

63. Maclay, W. A., & Guttman, E. Mescaline hallucinations in artists. *Archives of Neurological Psychiatry*, 1945, *45*, 130–137.

64. MacLean, J. R., MacDonald, D. C., Byrne, U. P., & Hubbard, A. M. The use of LSD-25 in the treatment of alcoholism and other psychiatric problems. *Quarterly Journal of Studies on Alcohol*, 1961, *22*, 34–45.

65. Martin, J. H. LSD (lysergic acid diethylamide) treatment of chronic psychoneurotic patients under day-hospital conditions. *International Journal of Social Psychiatry*, 1957, *3*, 188–195.

66. Mascher, E. Psycholytic therapy: Statistics and indications. In H. Brill, J. O. Cole, P. Deniker, H. Hippius, & Bradley, P.B. (Eds.), *Neuro-Psychopharmacology*. Amsterdam: Excerpta Medica, 1967, pp. 441–444.

67. Maslow, A. H. Cognition of being in the peak experience. *Journal of Genetic Psychology*, 1959, *94*, 43–66.

68. McCabe, O. L. Psychedelic (LSD) psychotherapy: A case report. *Psychotherapy: Theory, Research and Practice*, 1974, *11*, 2–10.

69. McCabe, O. L., Savage, C., Kurland, A. A., & Unger, S. Psychedelic (LSD) therapy of neurotic disorders: Short term effects. *Journal of Psychedelic Drugs*, 1972, *5*, 18–28.

70. Mitchell, S. W. The effects of Anhalonium Lewinii (the mescal button). *British Medical Journal*, 1896, *2*, 1625–1629.

71. Mogar, R., Fadiman, J., & Savage, C. Personality change associated with psychedelic (LSD) therapy; a preliminary report. *Psychotherapy: Theory, Research and Practice*, 1964, *1*, 154–162.

72. Naranjo, C., Shulgin, A. T., & Sargent, T. Evaluation of 3, 4-methyl-enedioxy-amphetamine (MDA) as an adjunct to psychotherapy. *Medicina et Pharmacologia Experimentalis*, 1967, *17*, 359–364.

73. *Neuro-Psycho-Pharmacology, Proceedings of the Fifth International Congress of the Collegium Internationale Neuro-Psycho-Pharmacologium*. New York: Excerpta Medica (International Congress Series No. 129), 1967, p. 1114.

74. O'Reilly, P. O., & Reich, J. Lysergic acid and the alcoholic. *Diseases of the Nervous System*, 1962, *23*, 331–334.

75. Osmond, H. Psychopharmacology: The manipulation of the mind. In D. Solomon (Ed.), *LSD: The consciousness-expanding drug*. New York: G. B. Putnam's Sons, 1964, pp. 31–48.

76. Peck, T. T. J. The use of LSD in psychotherapy. In H. A. Abramson (Ed.), *The use of LSD in psychotherapy and alcoholism*. New York: Bobbs-Merrill, 1967.

77. Rhead, J. C., Soskin, R. A., Turek, I., Richards, W. A., Yensen, R., Kurland, A. A., & Ota, K. Y. Psychedelic drug (DPT)-assisted psychotherapy with alcoholics: A controlled study. *Quarterly Journal of Studies on Alcohol*. In press.

78. Richards, W. A., Grof, S., Goodman, L. E., & Kurland, A. A. LSD-assisted psychotherapy and the human encounter with death. *Journal of Transpersonal Psychiatry*, 1972, *4*, 121–150.

79. Richards, W. A., Rhead, J. C., Grof, S., Goodman, L. E., DiLeo, F., & Kurland, A. A. Dipropyltryptamine (DPT) as an adjunct in the counseling of cancer patients. In A. H. Kutscher, et al. (Eds.), *Psychopharmacologic and narcotic analgesic drugs in the care of the dying patient and the bereaved*. New York: Columbia University Press. In press.

80. Sandison, R. A., Spencer, A. M., & Whitelaw, J. D. A. The therapeutic value of

lysergic acid diethylamide in mental illness. *Journal of Mental Science,* 1954, *100,* 491–507.

81. Sandison, R. A., & Whitelaw, J. D. A. Further studies in the therapeutic value of lysergic acid diethylamide in mental illness. *Journal of Mental Science,* 1957, *103,* 332–343.

82. Savage, C. *Lysergic acid diethylamide* (Research Report, Project NM 001.056.06.02). Bethesda, Md.: Naval Medical Research Institute, NNMC, September 1951.

83. Savage, C., Fadiman, J., Mogar, R., & Allen, M. H. The effects of psychedelic (LSD) therapy on values, personality, and behavior. *International Journal of Neuropsychiatry,* 1966, *2,* 241–254.

84. Savage, C., Hughes, M. A., & Mogar, R. The effectiveness of psychedelic (LSD) therapy: A preliminary report. *The British Journal of Social Psychiatry,* 1967, *2,* 59–66.

85. Savage, C., & McCabe, O. L. Residential psychedelic (LSD) therapy for the narcotic addict: A controlled study. *Archives of General Psychiatry,* 1973, *28,* 808–814.

86. Savage, C., McCabe, O. L., Kurland, A. A., & Hanlon, T. E. LSD-assisted psychotherapy in the treatment of severe chronic neurosis. *Journal of Altered States of Consciousness,* 1973, *1,* 31–47.

87. Savage, C., Stolaroff, M. H., Harman, W., & Fadiman, J. Caveat! The psychedelic experience. *Journal of Neuropsychiatry,* 1963, *4,* 4–5.

88. Savage, C., Stolaroff, M. H., Savage, E., & Fadiman, J. Therapeutic effects of the LSD experience. *Psychological Reports,* 1964, *14,* 111–120.

89. Savage, C., Terrill, J., & Jackson, D. D. LSD, transcendence and the new beginning. *Journal of Nervous and Mental Disease,* 1962, *135,* 425–439.

90. Schmiege, G. R. The current status of LSD as a therapeutic tool. *Journal of the Medical Society of New Jersey,* 1963, *60,* 203–207.

91. Sherwood, J. N., Stolaroff, M. J., & Harman, W. W. The psychedelic experience: A new concept in psychotherapy. *Journal of Neuropsychiatry,* 1962, *4,* 69–80.

92. Shostrom, E. L. *Personal orientation inventory.* San Diego: Educational and Industrial Testing Service, 1963.

93. Smart, R. C., Storm, T., Baker, E. F., & Solursh, L. *Lysergic acid diethylamide (LSD) in the treatment of alcoholism.* Toronto: University of Toronto Press, 1969.

94. Smith, C. M. A new adjunct to the treatment of alcoholism: The hallucinogenic drugs. *Quarterly Journal of Studies on Alcohol,* 1958, *19,* 406–417.

95. Smith, C. M. Some reflections on the possible therapeutic effects of the hallucinogens. *Quarterly Journal of Studies on Alcohol,* 1959, *20,* 292–301.

96. Smith, Kline and French Laboratories. *Report on clinical evaluation of SKF #5 (amphedoxamine).* Philadelphia, 1957.

97. Soskin, R. A. Personality and attitude change after two alcoholism programs: Comparative contributions of lysergide and human relations training. *Quarterly Journal of Studies on Alcohol,* 1970, *31,* 920–931.

98. Soskin, R. A., Grof, S., & Richards, W. A. Low doses of dipropyltryptamine in psychotherapy. *Archives of General Psychiatry,* 1973, *28,* 817–821.

99. Szara, S. *Background information on the pharmacological and clinical data of N, N-dialkyltryptamine derivatives.* Unpublished manuscript, 1965.

100. Tjio, J., Puhnkc, W. N., & Kurland, A. A. LSD and chromosomes: A controlled experiment. *Journal of the American Medical Association,* 1969, *210,* 849–856.

101. Touber, E. S. The role of immediate experience for dynamic psychiatry. In S. Arieti (Ed.), *American handbook of psychiatry.* New York: Basic Books, 1959.

102. Turek, I. S., Soskin, R. A., & Kurland, A. A. Methylenedioxyamphetamine (MDA) subjective states. *Journal of Psychedelic Drugs*, 1974, *6*, 7–14.

103. Van Dusen, W., Wilson, W., Miners, W., & Hook, H. Treatment of alcoholism with lysergide. *Quarterly Journal of Studies on Alcohol*, 1967, *28*, 295–304.

104. Van Rhijn, C. H. Significant hallucinations. In R. Crocket, R. Sandison, & A. Walk (Eds.), *Hallucinogenic drugs and their psychotherapeutic use*. Springfield, Ill.: Charles C Thomas, 1963, p. 137.

105. Vourlekis, A., Faillace, L., & Szara, S. Psychotherapy combined with psychodysleptic tryptamine derivatives. *Proceedings of the Fifth Collegium Internationale Neuropsychopharmacologium*, Washington, D.C., 1966.

106. Whitelaw, J. D. A. A case of fetishism treated with lysergic acid diethylamide. *Journal of Nervous and Mental Disease*, 1957, *129*, 573.

107. Yensen, R., DiLeo, F. B., Rhead, J. C., Richards, W. A., Soskin, R. A., Turek, I., & Kurland, A. A. MDA-assisted psychotherapy with neurotic outpatients—A pilot study. *Journal of Nervous and Mental Disease*, 1976, *163*, 233–245.

Author Index

Subject Index

a
b
c
d
7   e
8   f
9   g
0   h
1   i
8 2   j